A Glossary of
JOHN DRYDEN'S
CRITICAL TERMS

BY

H. James Jensen

UNIVERSITY OF MINNESOTA PRESS, MINNEAPOLIS

CONTENTS

Introduction

INTRODUCTION

NOT only is John Dryden the spokesman and greatest critic of his age, he is also what Dr. Johnson calls him, "The father of English criticism . . . the writer who first taught us to determine upon principles the merit of composition."[1] No critic before him can pretend to rival his accomplishment, and all who come after are his descendants. He established the basis for English criticism, complete with vocabulary, models of great works, and theories and principles of what is proper and great art. Dryden produced a constant stream of literary works and critical thoughts, over a period of thirty-seven years; moreover, he was vigorous in mind throughout his whole life. Early in his career, in 1668, Dryden wrote the "Essay of Dramatic Poesy," a beautifully executed Ciceronian dialogue, presenting different Restoration critical positions;[2] and he closed his career as a critic with the "Preface to Fables Ancient and Modern," a charming little masterpiece written just before his death in 1700. In his writing Dryden is everywhere delightfully fluent, everywhere confident, a man of the world interested in his world's reaction to what he writes. His principles never change. They are based on a balance between judgment and fancy, between "inventio" and "dispositio." But Dryden's stands on particular issues do change, depending on what he is interested in at the time he is writing, what critics he has just read, and at what stage of his growth we find him. In fact, Dryden spends less time establishing rules of criticism and writing than he does in justifying his own works and explaining what lessons the writers and critics of earlier times and of other countries have for his contemporaries. This gives Dryden's criticism its explanatory nature, its immediacy, its changing emphases and conclusions, its controversiality, and its perennial interest. As were T. S. Eliot, Samuel Taylor Coleridge, and Dr. Johnson, John Dryden was a professional man of letters to whom criticism was a natural occupation. He dominated English literature and criticism for the last half of the seventeenth century, and his influence was felt long after his death.

Dryden is the only Englishman of the seventeenth century who wrote extensively on critical matters. The others wrote only sporadically or translated criticism of other times or countries. Jonson's *Timber,* although valuable, is many times a translation of classical rhetoricians, especially Roman. Milton is precise and thoughtful, but is not much given to discussion of critical questions. Although Rymer is much more rigid in his views, Dryden respects him, and for us he is valuable as Dryden's complement. Highly regarded in his own time, Rymer introduced a number of critical terms into the English language and was quite conscious of the history of criticism. Earlier seventeenth-century critics, found in Spingarn's valuable edition, show the progress of English

[1] Samuel Johnson, *Works,* IX, 393.
[2] The "Essay of Dramatic Poesy" was Dryden's second published critical work. The first was his Preface to *The Rival Ladies,* published in 1664.

3

criticism and the importance of Dryden's achievements. The early critical language was inadequate. Henry Peachum, for example, uses circumlocution after circumlocution, clumsily trying to render into English the criticism of Horace, Quintilian, and Cicero. It is not until Hobbes and Davenant that a higher degree of critical subtlety is reached. From these meager beginnings, by borrowing eclectically from mainly classical, French, and Italian sources besides his own thoughts and experience, Dryden formulated an English criticism, with vocabulary, models, and ideas. Despite this magnificent achievement, Boileau is said to have forgotten Dryden's name. It was not until the eighteenth century that English criticism achieved international renown.

Dryden's criticism is difficult for twentieth-century readers to understand and appreciate. This is not because his style is hard to read, for it is perpetually entertaining, clear, and elegant, but because he continually digresses and because, although his words are still familiar, some of his intended meanings are not. His virtues as an entertaining stylist hide from us his excellence as a critic. He digresses continually because he writes as he thinks, capturing his thoughts as they occur to him in an open, familiar, charming style. He owes much of this style to Montaigne, and he says so.[3] Because of his rambling style, he never systematically develops a work or theory of criticism to any length, and his discussions of particular subjects, as well as many of his great critical statements, occur in isolated passages, many times in momentary digressions. One of his notable paraphrases from Bouhours' "Je ne sais quoi," for example, appears in his dedication of *Amboyna,* one of his less notable dedications.[4] "Beauty," in critical contexts, occurs eighty-six times in forty-three different works.[5]

One passage seldom represents Dryden's over-all views on a subject. He will cheerfully deny at one time what he confidently affirmed two years earlier. One can, for example, prove by quotations from several places that Dryden thought delight or pleasure the chief end of poetry. He says, "Delight is the chief if not the only end of poetry." Later he says, "The great end of the poem is to instruct." If one sees only one or two of these statements, he will accuse Dryden of pandering to the moment or occasion. Actually, Dryden thought about delight and instruction over a period of years, finally concluding reasonably that both are necessary, that to "instruct delightfully is the general end of all poetry." "All arts are made to profit," but pleasure must be the vehicle for instruction, not only to capture the audience but also to gain reputation and wealth for the author.[6] "Raillery" is another example. Before 1671, Dryden used "raillery" to mean rough, heavy-handed satire or jesting, connecting it to the older English verb "to rail." Later, he uses it to mean witty, refined abuse, relating it to the English verb "to rally" and the French verb *railler.* With only isolated quotations, Dryden's position on certain subjects and his definitions of specific words cannot be accurately ascertained.

While a critical concordance which locates Dryden's discussions of important words and concepts is useful, it is equally important to know Dryden's special critical vocabulary to understand what he is saying. In his criticism, Dryden noticeably avoids technical terms, such as those found in the jargon of rhetori-

[3] See p. 92.
[4] See Admiration.
[5] See Beauty.
[6] See Instruction.

4

cal textbooks. Instead, his terms are those in common, cultivated use, or critical words which came from the French, the polite language of precise and cultivated criticism. The French critics used most often are Corneille, Boileau, Rapin, and Bouhours.[7] Dryden wrote largely for ladies and gentlemen of wit and quality who, as he says, delighted in familiar, refined conversation.[8] Thus his style is free and familiar and his choice of words easy, but careful. Because Dryden's critical terms were in common use, they usually have both general and specific meanings. Many of Dryden's words are still current, giving his prose a superficial clarity. A modern reader thinks he understands Dryden, when in fact he does not. The words are the same, but the meanings have changed. Dryden was trying to create a critical vocabulary, which the English language did not provide, by expanding the meanings of the current English words, by using French meanings for English words with French critical equivalents (when the English meanings were sometimes quite different), and by introducing into English critical words, and their connotations, from other languages, such as French and Latin. The *OED* often does not record the meanings and connotations Dryden employed because it uses only a selected portion of his critical works.

"Humour" is an excellent example of a word with an expanded meaning, and although Dryden probably borrowed his meanings from earlier writers, one can trace its development as a critical term through his use. Dryden started by using "humour" to mean temperament, and then expanded it to mean an overriding whim, jest, mood, extravagant habit, etc. This is the common Restoration usage. In good satire, a "humour" and its depiction became more important than the character who displayed it. The character literally became a "humour." From this meaning it was an easy step to designate a kind of comedy, which represents "humours," as "comedy of humours" (sometimes called "mechanic comedy" [George Watson, ed., John Dryden, *Of Dramatic Poesy and Other Critical Essays*, I, 67]). "Kind" and "sweetness" also have expanded English meanings. Dryden so often used "kind" to mean a literary genre, and Barbara Strang corroborates this, that "kind" in Dryden finally means "genre." "Sweetness," which is usually associated with a vague, saccharine quality, becomes a relatively precise quality of smooth-running, pleasant verse. Dryden goes so far as to designate two different kinds of "sweetness": the one kind, found in good lyrical verse, is produced by using many vowels, avoiding open vowels side by side, and eliminating clashing consonants; the other, found in more dignified prose and verse, is produced by brevity, preciseness, and the exact placement of words for both meaning and sound.

Dryden's use of French meanings for English equivalents can sometimes be misleading (if either the French or the English meaning might apply) or puzzling (when an English meaning is quite different from the French). "Point," for example, cannot be understood without a knowledge of the meanings of the French *pointe*. Dryden's "point of wit" is, as Cayrou says, "Pensée qui surprend par quelque subtilité d'imagination, par quelque jeu de mots." A "point" thus must be regarded as rhetorical rather than emotional. Some of the meanings of "manage" come from the French *ménager*; others do not. A French meaning which Dryden uses extensively is "disposer avec art," "ména-

---

[7] Others he used are Chapelain, Dacier, Segrais, d'Aubignac, St. Évremond, du Fresnoy, Le Bossu, Perrault, Fontenelle, Balzac, La Mesnardière, and Goulu.

[8] See Easy and Language.

ger les termes, les expressions, parler avec une grande circonspection." Some English meanings he uses are "to regulate," "to carry out affairs," "to husband economically." "Delicacy" and "delicate" partake of French meanings, and always have French connotations. Neither "delicacy" as a term describing a painting or a sculpture, nor "delicate" meaning "overly sensitive in matters of taste" and "discreetly exquisite and refined" is listed in the *OED*. Dryden's description of certain figures of speech as "delicate" fits neither English nor common French usage. Only Littré gives an adequate secondary seventeenth-century definition: "Finement senti exprimé d'une matière ingénieuse et élégante. Expression délicat. Tour délicat." Dryden's use of "spirit" also cannot be understood without knowledge of the various meanings of *esprit*, and yet "spirit" is such a complicated word that in some areas neither the French nor the English meanings comprehend entirely Dryden's use. One of the meanings of "spirit" is similar to "genius," to the indefinable essence of a great work of art, and thus to the conception of Bouhours' "Je ne sais quoi," at least after 1671. Other English equivalents of French words are much simpler, such as "running," which becomes the synonym for *enjambement*. An example of a word that has both French and Latin connotations is "allusion," which is a similitude, a comparison made by a play on words. This meaning is not in the *OED*. It comes from the French meanings of *allusion* (or *badinerie*) and the verb "allude," which in turn comes from the Latin *alludere* (to play, to jest with).

"Turn" is a prime example of a word complicated by English and French meanings. Dryden uses it with traditional English meanings, with historical connotations, with French meanings of *tour* and *tournure*, and with his own expanded meanings. The use of "turn" to describe changes in direction of a plot in a play is traditional as it corresponds to "turn" of fortune, fate, etc. It also has historical connotations as it comes from Aristotle's "peripeteia" in the *Poetics*, Chapter XIII. Another meaning of "turn" is "a characteristic manner of expression," which comes mostly from the French. Dryden says, "[The poet's] particular turn of thoughts and expressions . . . are the characters that distinguish and as it were, individuate him from all other writers" (Watson, ed., John Dryden, *Of Dramatic Poesy*, I, 271). It is this "turn of thoughts and expression" which a good translator is supposed to capture. Littré says of *tour*: "Tournure, forme, mouvement de style, manière d'exprimer ses pensées, de construire ses phrases, d'arranger ses termes" (def. VI [1]). Dryden also uses "turn" to designate a kind of rhetorical figure he never defines. He uses only examples from Latin to show elegant turns on thoughts and words. An example of a turn from one of Dryden's translations illustrates the change of direction of thought caused by a play on the form and placement of the word "vain": "He laughs at all the vulgar cares and fears;/At their vain triumphs and their vainer tears" (Scott-Saintsbury, eds., John Dryden, *Works*, XIII, 187). Dryden is the only known person to apply the word "turn" to this kind of rhetorical figure. No dictionary defines "turn" in this way.

Another of Dryden's methods to improve the English critical vocabulary which is easier to recognize is his innovation of words. Many of these, such as "protagonist," are recorded in the *OED*. Others, such as "risibility" (from French *risibilité*) and "scenary" (*scenario*), the *OED* does not record. Some of Dryden's innovations are words which became immediately and widely used, such as "unity" (French *unité*) in the phrase "the unities of time, place, and

6

action" (which Dryden got from Corneille). Other examples of words which Dryden probably used first are "chromatic" (pertaining to color), and "protatic person" (from Corneille [a person who appears in the protasis of a play, who either hears or gives the narration]). Barbara Strang ably discusses Dryden's innovations in her article "Dryden's Innovations in Critical Vocabulary."[9]

Modern readers of Dryden also have difficulty with words which have obsolete English meanings and various historical connotations which have since disappeared from the language. By "actor," for example, half the time Dryden means a character or person in a play or poem, rather than a man who acts a part in a play. To "allege" in several instances means to cite (a passage or example) as evidence. To be "learned" or to have "learning" usually means that one is knowledgeable in ancient Greek and Roman literature, history, philosophy, etc., rather than in some modern subject. Besides the more obvious terms such as "beauty," "beautiful," and "ugliness," examples of other words with critical and aesthetic historical backgrounds are "pleasant" and "last perfection." If Dryden says that a work of art is "pleasant," he usually does not mean that it is amusing or merely delightful; he means that it appeals to one's sense of well-being, that it promotes serenity, and that each part is appropriate, fitting, and suitable to every other part. In other words, what is "pleasant" appeals to the viewer's judgment, his discriminating faculty. The "last perfection" of art is one of many of Dryden's terms that cause difficulty because of their reliance on classical, rhetorical backgrounds. The "last perfection" of poetry is elocution (which corresponds to coloring in painting). It comes from the classical rhetorical trivium (inventio, dispositio, and elocutio), and to Dryden consists of diction, eloquence of diction, and rhetorical ornamentation. It is the last both in importance and in the sequence of composition, and since it is the last consideration of a poet, Chaucer, Dryden says, is a better poet than Ovid, although Ovid's elocution is superior. Elocution by itself is less important than its appropriateness to the thoughts, manners, humours, etc., for which it serves as the vehicle of expression.

Some words which we expect to find in Dryden we do not. "Decorum" appears only seven times (replaced by "just," "proper," "propriety"). "Astonishment" appears only twice. Other words one meets in Dryden again and again appear to have definite meanings but do not. "Noble," for example, sounds as if it should be among such words as "sublime," "majestic," and "elevated"; yet Dryden uses it quite loosely. It is never synonymous with "sublime," and it inconsistently modifies over fifty different terms. It is merely an honorific descriptive term. Other words have meanings quite different from what a twentieth-century reader might expect.. They do not come from another language; they are merely odd meanings. In every case in Dryden, a "parody" is a serious passage from the work of a great poet which is inserted into a satire and made amusing by having its sense turned into something ridiculous. Another example is "caesura." To Dryden, a "caesura" is an elision (he uses it three times); for the twentieth-century meaning, he uses "breaking."

The problems arising from misunderstanding Dryden's words become more acute when one considers the combinations of words used in definitions. As an example, consider the first part of Dryden's well-known definition of a play, as delivered by Lisideius in the "Essay of Dramatic Poesy": "A just and lively image of human nature. . . ." Clear as this phrase may seem to us, it had,

[9] *Durham University Journal*, XX(no. 3):114–23 (June 1959).

nevertheless, important meanings for Neander, Crites, and Eugenius which we are likely to overlook or of which we are ignorant. "A just and lively image of human nature" we might read as "an accurate and entertaining reproduction of the way human beings think and act." However, this is not an accurate interpretation.

To understand Dryden's "just," a reader must always have in mind the French word *juste*. "Just" does not mean accurate, impartial, etc. in this use, but is the equivalent of *juste* which has meanings of appropriate, proportionate, and agreeable and pleasant. Therefore, "just" embodies several important critical considerations. The diction and general style of speech in a play should be appropriate or fitting to the quality of the characters, the subject, and the genre of the play. Also, the quality of the characters, the seriousness of the subject, and the importance of the genre should be in agreement with each other. A tragedy, for example, which is a part of an elevated genre, employs noble characters, a highly moral subject, and elevated words and expressions. The idea of appropriateness (or propriety) precludes rant and fustian, and cultivates the ideal of poetic wit. This meaning of "just" is akin to the modern French meaning of *juste* in the phrase "le mot juste." "Just" also connotes "proportionate," which leads to questions concerning the unities, "liaison des scènes," the bounds of the plot or fable, and the working up of the action. All should be regular. If a work of art is just, it is a product of the judgment, and appeals to it. If a play is just, therefore, it is agreeable and pleasant, qualities which appeal to the judgment.

"Lively" means entertaining or vivacious in the present day, but this is hardly what "lively" meant to Restoration readers. In Dryden's criticism, "lively" means lifelike, probable, truthful, and vivid (associated with *enargeia*), with only overtones of having energy (*energia*) or vivaciousness. But that a play is "lively" does not mean that it is a mirror image of nature. It is a reflection of what life should probably be, according to general rules of behavior. Because it is concerned with imitation of nature, "lively" also leads to implications of art as deception, and what constitutes its ends. Dryden, of course, says that an audience is never satisfied except with probability or verisimilitude. A play, then, has to be "lively" or probable to entertain or delight an audience.

By "image" Dryden does not usually mean a reproduction of nature, but an imitation of nature which can take several kinds of forms. An image is not nature itself. It is an idea formed in a poet's mind by his imagination. Tragedy, for example, shows men as better than they are; comedy shows them as they appear to their fellow men; farce, which Dryden calls grotesque, shows men as worse than they are. An image thus can improve, detract from, or reflect nature, even though it is probably derived from nature through the memory, by invention, or from sensory perception. The most important faculty in forming an image is the imagination or fancy. The concept of "image" thus leads to considerations of the psychology of the period, as it tried to explain the creative process or, more important, the effectiveness of outstanding works of art. A "just and lively image" thus emanates from both the judgment (from "just") and the imagination (from "lively"). The imagination invents the image, making it lively; the judgment controls the excesses of the imagination in making a play just.

"Human nature" does not mean, literally, "how human beings think and act," but how they probably think and act. Although human nature also is

8

probable, it is not a redundancy in Dryden's definition. "Lively image" refers to the work of art, the deception. "Human nature" refers to that nature which we would probably observe in the usual everyday actions and expressions of people. A "just and lively image of human nature," paraphrased, thus becomes, more accurately, a well-proportioned, appropriately expressed, and probable, lifelike representation, elevated or otherwise, of people as they would probably act, think, and talk under the circumstances given by the play.

Although Dryden's principles for writing and evaluating literature came mostly from the Ancients and the French, he applied them in a personal way, giving Restoration readers and audiences standards by which to judge art. His fundamental principle, which comes from the Ancients, is that art is imitation of nature. A record of his changing concepts of "wit" is a good barometer of the varying proportions of imagination and judgment Dryden demanded. In "wit writing" and "wit written," an excess of either imagination or judgment was an extreme; a balance of each carried to great heights, in the highest genres, manifests itself in a work of "sublime genius." Dryden's most characteristic personal stance appears to be his abhorrence of extremes, and therefore he constantly vacillates in attempting to find a balance, a golden mean, on every occasion, in judging all works of art and in debating all practical critical problems. The variations resulting from personal interpretations and common rather than technical usage make a glossary of Dryden's critical terms practical and valuable. It is the natural starting point for the study of the history and development of English criticism and its vocabulary.

This *Glossary of John Dryden's Critical Terms* has three purposes. The first is to help readers of Dryden, and in fact of all seventeenth-century critics, in understanding the special meanings of their terms, by themselves and as part of the English critical tradition. The second is to give students of neoclassical English criticism a much-needed general glossary. And the third is to provide a means of finding in his criticism Dryden's most important topics, concepts, and words, as well as the most important places these terms are found in the works of other seventeenth-century critics.

The texts from which I drew my critical terms and their definitions are George Watson's edition of Dryden's critical essays, which contains the bulk of Dryden's criticism;[10] the Scott-Saintsbury edition of Dryden's works, which contains some critical prose omitted by Watson[11] as well as the verse translation of Boileau's "L'art poétique," important because it shows how a seventeenth-century Englishman understood and translated certain French critical and aesthetic terms, and because, whether it is by Dryden or not, it sometimes echoes his spirit, style, and thoughts;[12] Ben Jonson's *Timber*; Spingarn's three-volume *Critical Essays of the Seventeenth Century*; the Columbia edition of Milton's works; and Curt Zimansky's *The Critical Works of Thomas Rymer*. The number of Dryden's works referred to in this glossary is more than one hundred; the number of pages covered is about nine hundred.

To discover which words were significant, and to establish a sound basis for

[10] See Watson under Key to Abbreviations.
[11] See SS under Key to Abbreviations.
[12] See Boileau and SS.XV.AP under Key to Abbreviations.

9

my work, I first compiled, recorded, and catalogued every word Dryden used in talking about critical matters, whether about literature, art, music, or different kinds of history. I then checked every citation of each word, verifying its accuracy and defining its meaning. After recording each meaning of a word, I checked it with the *OED* as well as with the French historical dictionaries by Littré, Cayrou, and Dubois-Lagane. When Dryden uses an English word with a meaning that is unrecorded by the *OED*, he is usually borrowing the meaning of a French equivalent.

If a word had a complicated history, if it had a complicated set of meanings, or if it seemed to be an important critical term to Dryden, I then wrote a short essay, trying to define as briefly as possible some of the background and nuances, as well as the meanings, of the term. The length of the essay depended on the importance and the complexity of the word's meanings. The limits of both the definitions and the essay were set at Dryden's usages, except where Latin, Greek, French, and older English meanings were necessary to understand what Dryden is trying to say. For further study of especially difficult words, I occasionally included references to applicable scholarly articles. I then deleted from the glossary words with meanings obvious to twentieth-century readers, words which needed no essays and which are at least adequately explained by either the *OED* or *Webster's New International Dictionary* (2nd ed., unabridged), and words with no consistent critical application, which Dryden merely happened to use in critical contexts. The words remaining constitute a highly selective glossary. After completing my work on Dryden's criticism, I took the words I had selected from Dryden and turned to Ben Jonson, John Milton, Thomas Rymer, as well as all the critics in Spingarn's *Critical Essays of the Seventeenth Century*, to see how they used these same words. In some cases, as for instance in the words "wit" and "genius," I found historical development and consequent changes in meaning. In others, I found illuminating quotations which helped clarify Dryden's usages.

The format is simple. A word is entered, its part of speech designated, and then it is defined and discussed. After each definition, the appropriate citations are listed. The volume in which each citation appears comes first: I. (Watson, Volume I); II. (Watson, Volume II); or SS.XXX. (Scott-Saintsbury, Volume XXX). The abbreviation of the preface, dedication, letter, or prologue in which each word is found comes next. The page number (of the appropriate volume) is third. By checking the Key to Abbreviations, one can find the name of the work corresponding to the abbreviation and the date the work was published. Thus "II.DCOPS 139" means that the word appears on page 139, in Watson's second volume, in "A Discourse Concerning the Original and Progress of Satire," published in 1693; "SS.VI.DKK 7" means that a word appears on page 7 of Volume VI of the Scott-Saintsbury edition, in the dedication to *Limberham: or The Kind Keeper*, published in 1678. "Davenant (Spingarn) II. 4," means that the word appears on page 4 of Spingarn's *Critical Essays of the Seventeenth Century*. The citations are complete and accurate to the best of my knowledge. Many words or meanings appear before the *OED* says they do. Because of its vast scope, the *OED* uses only selected, important texts by different authors, so that most of the earlier unrecorded usages occur in little known works. When such a word appears in this glossary, one cannot say with certainty that Dryden (or anyone else) used that particular word or meaning first. Someone as yet unknown could have used the word even earlier, or it could have occurred in conversation. I have therefore resorted to formulae such as "first recorded use" and "this could be an innovation."

This glossary is not intended to supersede but to complement John Aden's useful book, *The Critical Opinions of John Dryden*. Mr. Aden has constructed a classified arrangement of Dryden's most important critical passages. The *Glossary of John Dryden's Critical Terms* explains the meaning of Dryden's critical words through both a series of glosses and short quotations from Dryden and other critics of his time. A reader wishing to understand one of Dryden's important critical terms can find the word with its proper definition. A student of neoclassical criticism wishing to investigate Dryden's use of an important term can read the essay, which includes many of the notable quotations, and can look up the cross references to find related words and concepts. Anyone wishing to study more extensively a particular term or concept can read through the citations, the citations of related words, and the textual material surrounding the citations to comprehend fully Dryden's thoughts.

A Glossary of John Dryden's Critical Terms

KEY TO ABBREVIATIONS

I. WATSON, VOLUME I

AAHP (1677) "The Author's Apology for Heroic Poetry and Poetic Licence," prefixed to *The State of Innocence.*

DECG (1672) "Defence of the Epilogue" of the second part of *The Conquest of Grenada.*

DEDP (1668) "A Defence of An Essay of Dramatic Poesy."

EAZ (1676) Epilogue to *Aureng Zebe.*

ECG (1672) "Epilogue to the Second Part of the Conquest of Grenada."

EDP (1668) "Of Dramatic Poesy: An Essay."

EO (1679) Epilogue to *Oedipus.*

GCT (1679) "The Grounds of Criticism in Tragedy," and the Preface to *Troilus and Cressida.*

HAR (late 1677) "Heads of an Answer to Rymer."

LD (Sept. 1677) Letter to Charles, Earl of Dorset.

OHP (1672) "Of Heroic Plays," prefixed to *The Conquest of Grenada.*

PA (1673) "To My Most Honoured Friend, Sir Charles Sedley, Baronet," prefixed to *The Assignation.*

PAL (1678) Preface to *All for Love.*

PAM (1667) "An Account of the Ensuing Poem," prefixed to "Annus Mirabilus."

PAZ (1676) Preface to *Aureng Zebe.*

PEL (1671) Preface to *An Evening's Love.*

PWG (1669) Preface to *The Wild Gallant.*

PO (1679) Preface to *Oedipus.*

POE (1680) Preface to *Ovid's Epistles, Translated by Several Hands.*

PrAZ (1676) Prologue to *Aureng Zebe.*

PRL (1664) Preface to *The Rival Ladies.*

PrO (1679) Prologue to *Oedipus.*

PrSL1 (1668) Prologue to *Secret Love.*

PrSL2 (1668) Second Prologue to *Secret Love.*

PrT (1670) Prologue to *The Tempest.*

PrTL (1670) Prologue to *Tyrannic Love.*

PSF (1681) "To John, Lord Haughton," prefixed to *The Spanish Friar.*

PSL (1668) Preface to *Secret Love.*

PT (1670) Preface to *The Tempest.*

PTL (1670) Preface to *Tyrannic Love.*

II. WATSON, VOLUME II

CP (1693) "The Character of Polybius and His Writings," prefixed to *The History of Polybius, Translated by Sir H. S.*

CSE (1692) "The Character," prefixed to *Miscellaneous Essays by St. Evremond.*

DAV (1697) Dedication of the *Aeneid* in *The Works of Virgil, Translated.*

DCOPS (1693) "A Discourse Concerning the Original and Progress of Satire," prefixed to *The Satires of Juvenalis, Translated.*

ETV (1684) "To the Earl of Roscommon, on His Essay on Translated Verse," prefixed to "An Essay on Translated Verse."

LCM (Oct. 1699) Letter to Charles Montague.

LET (Nov. 1699) Letter to Elizabeth Thomas.

LJD (March 1694) Letter to John Dennis.

LL (c. 1696, pub. 1711) "The Life of Lucian: a Discourse of His Writings," prefixed to *The Works of Lucian, Translated by Several Hands.*

LP (1683) "The Life of Plutarch," prefixed to *Plutarch's Lives, Translated by Several Hands.*

LPe (14 July, 1699) Letter to Samuel Pepys.

LWW1 (1691) Letter to William Walsh.

LWW2 (12 Dec., 1693) Letter to William Walsh.

PAA (1685) Preface to *Albion and Albanius.*

PDS (1690) Preface to *Don Sebastian.*

PE (1692) "To the Earl of Abingdon," prefixed to "Eleanora."

15

PEP (1693) "To Lord Radcliffe," pre-fixed to *Examen Poeticum: Being the Third Part of Miscellany Poems.*

PF (1700) Preface to *Fables Ancient and Modern Translated into Verse.*

PPBPP (1695) "Preface of the Transla-tor, with A Parallel Betwixt Poetry and Painting," in *De Arte Graphica* by C. A. du Fresnoy.

PPV (1697) Preface to the "Pastorals" of Virgil in *The Works of Virgil, Trans-lated.*

PRAV (1697) "Postscript to the Reader," appended to the *Aeneid.*

PS (1685) Preface to *Sylvae: or the Sec-ond Part of Poetical Miscellanies.*

TCDD (1694) "To My Dear Friend Mr. Congreve, on His Comedy Called The Double-Dealer," prefixed to Congreve's *The Double-Dealer.*

SS. SCOTT-SAINTSBURY

AARHL (1684) The translation of "The Author's Advertisement to the Reader," prefixed to *The History of the League.*

AARLSFX (1688) "The Author's Adver-tisement to the Reader," prefixed to *The Life of St. Francis Xavier.*

ADFHL (1684) Translation called "The Author's Dedication to the French King," prefixed to *The History of the League.*

AP (1683) "The Art of Poetry" trans-lated from Boileau's "L'art poétique" by Sir William Soame and John Dry-den.

APa (1695) *The Art of Painting* trans-lated from *De Arte Graphica.*

CIE (1667) "Connection of the Indian Emperor to the Indian Queen."

CPd (1693) Watson's deletions from "The Character of Polybius."

DA (1673) Dedication of *Amboyna.*

DAL (1678) Dedication of *All for Love.*

DAM (1667) Dedication of "Annus Mi-rabilus."

DAm (1690) Dedication of *Amphitryon.*

DAVd (1697) Watson's deletions from Dedication of the *Aeneid.*

DC (1692) Dedication of *Cleomenes, the Spartan Hero.*

DCG (1672) Dedication of *The Con-quest of Grenada.*

DDG (1683) Dedication of *The Duke of Guise.*

DDS (1690) Dedication of *Don Sebas-tian.*

DEL (1671) Dedication of *An Eve-ning's Love.*

DF (1700) Dedication of *Fables Ancient and Modern, Translated into Verse.*

DG (1697) Dedication of Virgil's "Geor-gics" in *The Works of Virgil, Trans-lated.*

DHL (1684) Dedication of *The History of the League.*

DIE (1667) Dedication of *The Indian Emperor.*

DKA (1691) Dedication of *King Arthur.*

DKK (1678) Dedication of *Limberham: or The Kind Keeper.*

DLSFX (1688) Dedication of *The Life of St. Francis Xavier.*

DLT (1694) Dedication of *Love Trium-phant.*

DMLM (1673) Dedication of *Marriage à la Mode.*

DPL (1683) Dedication of *Plutarch's Lives.*

DPWDY (1686) "A Defence of the Pa-per Written by the Duchess of York."

DSI (1677) Dedication of *The State of Innocence.*

DTC (1679) Dedication of *Troilus and Cressida.*

DTL (1670) Dedication of *Tyrannic Love.*

EWTM (1682) "Epistle to the Whigs," prefixed to "The Medal."

LLd (1696) Watson's deletions from "The Life of Lucian."

LPd (1683) Watson's deletions from "The Life of Plutarch," prefixed to *Plutarch's Lives.*

LSFX (1688) *The Life of St. Francis Xavier.*

OAP (1695) "Observations on the Art of Painting" translated from du Fresnoy.

PAZd (1676) Watson's deletions from the Preface to *Aureng Zebe.*

PC (1692) Preface to *Cleomenes, the Spartan Hero.*

PDCW (1691) Preface to "A Dialogue Concerning Women, Being a Defence of the Sex." Dryden's Preface prefixed to Walsh's work.

PFAAP (1695) "The Preface of the French Author" of *De Arte Graphica.*

PHC (1696) Preface to *The Husband His Own Cuckold.*

PHP (1687) Preface to "The Hind and the Panther."

PNOEM (1674) Preface to "Notes and Observations on The Empress of Morocco."

PoHL (1684) Postscript to *The History of the League.*

PPBPPd (1695) Watson's deletions from the "Preface of the Translator, with a Parallel Betwixt Poetry and Painting."

PRLaici (1682) Preface to "Religio Laici."

SAVPMF (1697) "A Short Account of His Person, Manners, and Fortune" in *The Works of Virgil, Translated.*

TRAA (1681) To the Reader of *Absalom and Achitophel.*

VDG (1683) "The Vindication of the Duke of Guise."

Dictionaries, Texts, and Articles

Boileau: Nicholas Despréaux Boileau, "L'art poétique" and "Traité du sublime," *Oeuvres Complète de Boileau.*

Cayrou: Gaston Cayrou, *Le Français classique: lexique de la langue du dix-septième siècle.*

Dubois-Lagane: J. Dubois and R. Lagane, *Dictionnaire de la langue française classique.*

Horsman: E. A. Horsman, "Dryden's French Borrowings," *Review of English Studies.*

Jonson: Benjamin Jonson, *Timber or Discoveries.*

Ker: W. P. Ker, *Essays of John Dryden.*

Littré: Emile Littré, *Dictionnaire de la langue française.*

Milton: John Milton, *The Works of John Milton.*

OED: *Oxford English Dictionary.*

Simon: Irène Simon, "Critical Terms in Restoration Translations from the French," *Revue belge de philologie et d'histoire.*

Spingarn: J. E. Spingarn, *Critical Essays of the Seventeenth Century.*

Strang: Barbara Strang, "Dryden's Innovations in Critical Vocabulary," *Durham University Journal.*

Z: Curt A. Zimansky, ed., *The Critical Works of Thomas Rymer.*

THE GLOSSARY

A

ABSURD (adj.) (1) Ridiculous, indecorous, in bad taste; here, it comes from Corneille, *Discours de trois unités*, and is a direct translation of "mauvaise grâce": I.EDP 55. (2) Unnatural, silly: I.EDP 72, II.DAV 230. (3) Contrary to reason: I.DEDP 120, II.PS 26. (4) Ridiculous: I.OHP 165, DECG 172, SS.XV.PNOEM 405.

ABSURDITY (sb.) Something in a work of art (or imitation of nature) which is out of proportion to nature, or is distorted beyond reason. Thus, an unnatural or ridiculous statement, action, or custom. Particular incidents or actions, whether they are fact or not, are "absurd" when they break general rules of probability. An absurdity is not as extreme as a monstrosity. See also Nature, Monstrous, Probable. I.EDP 36, 64, DEDP 125, 127, 129, PTL 142, DECG 172, GCT 249, 261, II.PDS 50, DCOPS 123, PPBPP 201, LL 213, 214, SS. VII.VDG 181, VIII.DLT 375, 375, XV.PNOEM 398, 401; Rymer (Z) 154, 170.

ACCURACY (sb.) Preciseness. Accuracy, and things which are accurate, emanate ordinarily from the judgment, which regulates the vagaries of the imagination. However, I. 98 is irregular. It refers to the sharpness, lifelikeness, vividness, and appropriateness of idealized images as the poet imagines and then describes them (it is one of the "happinesses of imagination"). One other exception, SS.XVII. 293, "Art is more accurate than nature," also depends on the execution of the idealized images which emanate from the imagination: I.PAM 98, DECG 182, II.LP 10 (of judgment). Accurate: I.DEDP 123 (judgment), SS.XVII.PPBPPd 293.

ACT (sb.) (1) One of the three or five divisions of a play. There are three acts in each Spanish play, or *jornada*; French or English plays each have five (I. 34). Dryden, through Eugenius, implies that five acts are best. He says, however, that there should be a set number of acts (I. 34). In a regular play, each act should be in proportion to the others, each one comprehending the same amount of time, and each taking no more imaginary time than the time it takes to act it out on the stage. The intervals of extended time should occur between the acts (I. 28). "Act" twice implies that an act consists of an action (I. 28, 34). Otherwise, Dryden uses "act" merely to identify which section of a play he is talking about. Davenant (Spingarn II. 17–18) explains the functions of each act. Act I is preparative (Rymer says the same thing in Z 61). Act II introduces new "persons" and "some part of the promised 'design.'" Act III "makes a visible correspondence in the 'under-walks' . . . and ends with an ample 'turn' of the main 'design' and expectation of a new." Act IV, the longest act, "gives a notorious 'turn' to all the 'under-walks,' and a 'counter-turn' to that main 'design' which chang'd in the third [Act]." Act V "begins with an entire

18

diversion of the main and dependent plotts, then makes the general correspondence of the 'persons' more discernable, and ends with an easy 'untying of those particular knots' which make a 'contexture' of the whole." See Horace, *Ars Poetica*, ll. 189–90: I.EDP 28, 28, 28, 28, 29, 33, 33, 34, 34, 36, 36, 36, 37, 37, 37, 37, 37, 45, 54, 54, 58, 61, 62, 62, 64, 64, 64, 64, 71, 75, 76, DEDP 120, 126, 128, PrT 137, PEL 150, 155, OHP 159, 159 (see also Davenant; Spingarn II. 17), DECG 178, 180, PAL 222, 231, PO 234, GCT 240 ("[the play] is not divided into acts"), 241, 241, 241, 243, 243, 244, 257, II.PAA 41, 43, PDS 45, 50, PPBPP 198, 199, 201, SS.VII.VDG 203, PC 220, DLT 374, 375, PNOEM 401. (2) A deed or action in life (or in a play): I.PSL 106, PWG 131, II.PS 27, SS.XV.AP 237.

ACTION (sb.) (1) Deed or deeds: I.PRL 2 (world is on a stage; actions are in that world), EDP 29 (ambiguous, compares any action to the action of a play), 52, PAM 98, 99, PrSL 128 (in a play, here), PT 135, OHP 157, 159, 159, PAZ 190, AAHP 201, 203, GCT 243, POE 264, II.LP 5, 6, CP 66, 67, 68, 68, 69, 70, DCOPS 86, 140, PPBPP 188, LL 209, SS.IV.DCG 17, VII.VDG 153, 154, 201, 202, VIII.DKA 136, XVII.PPBPPd 297. (2) Military engagement, a battle: I.PAZ 191, II.DCOPS 86. (3) The unity of movement in a poem or play, a play's main plot or design. See Unity. I.PRL 3, EDP 28 (unity), 28, 28, 29 (unity), 29, 29, 30, 30, 30, 33, 33, 33, 35 (unity), 45 (unity), 45, 48, 48, 48, 49, 50, 50, 52, 52, 52, 59 (unity), 61, 63, 70, 71, 75, 75, PAM 95, 95 ("broken action"), PSL 107, PrSL 108 (unity), DEDP 119, 125, 125, PEL 151, 152, OHP 159, EAZ 193, HAR 216, PAL 222 (unity), 222, 223, GCT 243, 243, 243, 244, 244, 244, 244, 244, 244, 244, 244, 244, 245, 245, 247, 247 (unity), 248, 248, PSF 279, 279, II.LP 7, 8 (unity), PAA 41, 41, 41, PDS 44, 47, DCOPS 82 (unity), 82, 86, 95, 95, 96, 103, 103, 143, 143, 143, 143, 145, TCDD 171, PPBPP 188, 188, 189, 189, 189, 190, 193, 195, 196, 196, 199, 199, 202, 206, 206, DAV 224, 226, 226, 226, 226, 226, 227, 229, 233, PF 276, 276, 291, SS.II.DIE 288, VII.VDG 147, VIII.PC 220, 227, DLT 375, 375, XIV. DAVd 146, 183, 185, 187, 189, 192, 193, 193, 193, 194, 194, 194, 195, XV.AP 237, 237 (unity), 247, XVII.APa 351, 371. (4) Behavior or deeds of the characters in a poem or play: I.PRL 4, EDP 41, 51, 52, 53, 59, 61, 62, 62, 72, 87, 87, 87, PAM 95, PEL 155, OHP 165, 165, 166, 166, AAHP 199, HAR 213, 219, GCT 245, 248, 248, 249, 249, 250, II.DCOPS 83, 96, PPBPP 187, 188, 197, 197, 197, DAV 225, 228, SS.XIV.DAVd 191, XV.AP 243, XVII.PPBPPd 298, APa 355. (5) The acting or performing by players: I.PWG 131, PTL 139, HAR 214, GCT 244, PSF 275, 275, 278, 278, 278, II.PDS 45, 55; Rymer (Z) 19.

ACTOR (sb.) (1) Player, one who performs (in a play): I.EDP 51, 82, PEL 145, HAR 213, 213, GCT 240, 254, PSF 275, 278, II.PAA 41, PDS 45, 46, DCOPS 107, 107, 108, 109, PPBPP 199, 199, 199, 200, DAV 229, SS.VII.VDG 172, VIII.DAm 9, PC 220, 221, XV.AP 237, 238, 246. Shadwell (Spingarn) II. 152. (2) Character or person in a play or poem: I.EDP 35, 45, 51, 55, 55, 59, 60, 79, 88, PAM 95, HAR 213, 219, II.DCOPS 79, PEP 161, PPBPP 188, 196, DAV 229, SS.VIII.DLT 374, XVII.APa 357; Rymer (Z) 134.

ACTUAL (adj.) Real to the mind but nonexistent in nature. In this case, an "actual" image is the ideal or perfect image created by a poet or artist in his own mind. This ideal image the poet or artist derives from nature. A natural image (a reproduction of nature) is imperfect because nature itself is imperfect. The artist or poet thus improves upon nature to conceive his effigy, or actual image, in his mind: SS.XVII.PPBPPd 293.

ADMIRABLE (adj.) (1) Describing a work of art which moves or transports its viewers or auditors, which elicits admiration. See Admiration, def. (1). I.AAHP 199, GCT 240, 245, II.LP 10, PS 32, PE 62, DCOPS 80, 81, 86, 150, PEP 167, PPBPP 182, 204, SS.VIII.DC 215, XIV.DAVd 146, 176, 181, 185, XV.AP 249, PNOEM 406, XVII.PPBPPd 294, 297, APa 345, 365, 365. Admirably: II.PS 27, SS.XVII.APa 365. (2) Describing that which is worthy of esteem, which is excellent: I.EDP 49, 74, 75, PEL 154, DECG 170, 179, AAHP 201, HAR 220, PAL 224 (irony), POE 271, II.CSE 59, DCOPS 147, 148, PPBPP 186, SS. XIII.SAVPMF 315, XIV.DAVd 162, XVIII.CPd 25, LLd 78.

ADMIRATION (sb.) The highest esteem. The action of marveling at. The losing of oneself in the excellence of a work of art (II. 251), "a pleasure not to be expressed in words" (SS.V. 5, 5). (1) "Admiration" most often refers to the effect of tragedy, but applies as well to the effect of heroic poesy and painting. Dryden says, "The end of tragedies or serious plays, says Aristotle, is to beget admiration, compassion, or concernment." "Admiration" is a term not actually from Aristotle, but Renaissance writers, such as Scaliger in his "Poetics" and Sidney in his "Defence of Poesy," discuss the admiration which precedes consternation. Dryden means that the feelings of compassion (pity) and concernment (fear), as they are translated from Aristotle, can neither appear nor be purged in an audience, unless admiration is first elicited. Admiration comes from a high, appropriate style (I. 14), the greatness of the hero's rank and actions (SS.XVII. 345), and the elevation of all the characters and their actions above those of ordinary nature. Since admiration is the "delight of tragedy" (I. 119), and since purging is part of instruction (see Purge), delight is the first purpose of the tragic poet even though the final end is instruction: I.EDP 46, PAM 101, DEDP 114, 119, II.PEP 166, PPBPP 194, 199, 199, SS.V.DA 5, 5, XVII.PPBPPd 294, APa 345; Hobbes (Spingarn) II. 63 ("Novelty causes admiration, and admiration curiosity, which is the delightful appetite of knowledge"), 63, 64 ("The delight of an epic poem consisteth not in mirth but in admiration"), 68 ("The work of an heroick poem is to raise admiration"), 72, 72, 72; Rymer (Z) 51, 127. (2) "Admiration" also applies to art in general. In 1673, Dryden introduces admiration as "a pleasure not to be expressed by words" (rather than merely highest esteem). This concept (SS.V. 5) is a direct borrowing from Bouhours, "Le je ne sais quoi," *Entretiens d'Ariste et d'Eugene* (1671): I.PRL 5, EDP 26, 31, 39, 77, PEL 148, II.DCOPS 76, PEP 167, PPV 221, DAV 251 (a losing oneself in wonderment at a passage of Virgil), SS.V. DAm 5, DSI 103, 107, PAZd 190, XIV.DAVd 181, XVII.LPd 26.

ADMIRE (v.) (1) To be transported, to be lost in the pleasure of a work of art (especially tragedy) or the way a part of it is expressed (as by heightenings of nature, imagery, etc.). See Admiration, def. (1). I.PAM 101, PTL 139, AAHP 203, II.DAV 228, SS.IX.EWTM 422, XV.AP 230, 232, 243, PNOEM 400, XVII.PFAAP 337. Admiring: I.PrO 235. Admirer: I.PAM 99, PT 134, OHP 159, II.DCOPS 138, DAV 232, 243, 243, SS.XIV.DAVd 180, XV.AP 226. (2) To esteem highly: I.EDP 31, 40, 40, 70, 74, PT 134, PEL 145, 145, 148, 148, DECG 178, PA 188, AAHP 200, HAR 219, PO 233, II.PS 28, 32, DCOPS 83,

84, PPBPP 182, PF 279, SS.XIV.DAVd 181, XV.AP 226, 250, XVII.PPBPPd 297, XVII.CPd 31. Admirer: SS.XIII.SAVPMF 313.

AFFECTION (sb.) (1) A disposition (of the mind), a humour: I.EDP 73, SS. XVII.PPBPPd 297. (2) A feeling or emotion (of the mind): I.PAM 99, HAR 211, II.DCOPS 121, SS.XVII.APa 363. (3) Love, fondness: II.PPV 219. (4) Inclination (toward), a strong liking (for): SS.VIII.DC 215, XIV.DAVd 169, XVII.APa 289 (for the art).

AFTER-UNDERTAKER (sb.) A writer, composer, or artist who attempts an imitation of a previous work or follows an established genre: II.PAA 35.

AGGRAVATE (v.) (1) To exaggerate. See also Dryden's translation of the *Aeneid*, Book VII, l. 796, and Book XI, l. 341: I.HAR 215. Aggravating: SS.XVIII. PDCW 7. (2) To make more serious (as a charge): II.PS 27.

AGGRAVATION (sb.) Exaggeration (by use of bold figures, hyperbole, etc.). This is rhetorical aggravation (the *OED* first records use in 1743): I.AAHP 203, SS.VII.VDG 204.

AGREEABLE (adj.) Pleasant, describing that which gives satisfaction to the senses because of suitability, fitness, proper proportion, and congruence. That which is agreeable is formed by and appeals to the judgment. "Agreeable" is often used in conjunction with "natural" and "verisimilar" and is close to them. See Pleasant. II.LL 209, SS.VII.VDG 179, 179, 180, VIII.DLT 374, 376, XV. PNOEM 401, XVII.LPd 30, APa 357, 383. Agreeably: SS.XIII.SAVPMF 315, XIV.DAVd 182, XV.AP 238. Agreeableness: SS.VII.VDG 180.

AGREEABLENESS (sb.) Pleasantness arising from proper proportion or congruity. It is used in conjunction with beauty: II.DCOPS 140.

AIR (sb.) (1) Lightness of style, usually in conversation (as "gaeity, air and freedom" of conversation in *The Silent Woman*): I.EDP 74, PSL 105, DECG 182. (2) An appearance, a feeling or a quality (in writing or speech): II.LP 10 (air of goodness in writings), SS.XVII.PDCW 5 (air of gallantry in writings), CPd 38 (air of truth in writings).

AIRY (adj.) (1) Buoyant, as the French are of an "airy and gay temper": I.EDP 60. (2) Air-like, unsubstantial, as French painters draw their nymphs in "thin and airy habits": II.DAV 238.

ALEXANDRINE (sb.) Watson's Gloss: "A line of six feet, 'hexameter' (usually French), I.EDP 65 & n., PAM 96; II.PS 32 (defined), DAV 237; once applied to Spenser, II.DAV 238 ('which we call, though improperly, the Pindaric')."

ALLEGE (v.) (1) To cite (a passage or example) as evidence: I.PEL 151, HAR 212. (2) To plead as an excuse: I.POE 272, II.DCOPS 119. (3) To assert (something) as a reason: II.LP 7, SS.VIII.DLT 374. (4) To state positively (as if proof were readily available): SS.VII.VDG 209.

ALLEGORICAL (adj.) (1) Pertaining to allegory: II.PAA 41. (2) Figurative. This is the medieval meaning of "allegorical" which Dante mentions in his *Convivio* (Tractate II, part i) and which was used as the second step in Biblical exegesis (the historical, allegorical, and anagogical meaning of "The Song of Solomon," for example). Spenser, Ariosto, and Tasso wrote with this meaning of "allegory" in their minds. Dryden never indicates he is aware of it. In this citation Dryden has translated Segrais who obviously uses this meaning; Aeneas' armor, he says, might be an "allegorical defense," signifying that he was under the protection of the gods: SS.XIV.DAVd 166.

ALLEGORY (sb.) The substitution of one person or thing for another. This is Dryden's usual, simple definition. He never mentions allegory in connection with "The Hind and the Panther": I.PAZ 191 (for Maecaenas read Sheffield), II.PAA 41 (for Albion and Albanius read Charles II and James II), DAV 257 (for prayer read dedication). But he also uses allegory in two slightly different ways: SS.VIII.DC 214 (the swans stand for abstractions), XVII.DPL 13 (Adam and Eve are prototypes); Jonson (Jonson uses allegory in the same sense as Segrais, Spenser, etc.) 45, 45 (equated with translation and metaphor); Davenant (Spingarn) II. 6 (Spenser's allegory is a series of "moral visions"); Rymer (Z) 108, 108 (allegory consists of "mystery and tropological meaning"), 109.

ALLUSION (sb.) (1) A similitude, a reference or comparison made by a play of words. This meaning is not in *OED*, but comes from the verb "allude," which in turn is derived from the Latin *alludere* (to play, to jest with): SS. XIV.DAVd 191, XV.PNOEM 401, XVII.LPd 86; Jonson 100. (2) A play on words (*OED* says first used in 1731). Perhaps from the French meaning of *allusion* (or *badinerie*): I.PAM 99, SS.XV.PNOEM 399. (3) An implied reference: SS.VII.DAVd 171, XIII.SAVPMF 312.

ALTER (v.) To change. "Alter" actually means neither to improve nor make worse (see I. 170, 171, SS.XVII. 292), but is often used with the connotation of "to improve." See Correct (v.). (1) To change and to try to improve an already existing work of art or story (thus to claim it as one's own). This is common Restoration practice. Shakespeare was "altered" often. Dryden says, "'Tis the contrivance, the new terms, and new characters which make it [a play] ours" (II. 49). See II. 288 for reasons for altering Chaucer: I.EDP 69, DEDP 112, PWG 132, PEL 154, 155, GCT 239, 241, 243, II.PDS 49, CSE 57 (a character in a play), PF 288, 289, SS.II.DIE 288, VII.VDG 201, VIII. DAm 9, DKA 134 (Dryden's own work), XV.PNOEM 399. Altering: I.GCT 239. Alteration: I.PT 134, PTL 141, II.DCOPS 82, 100 (of a treatise), 144, 144, LSP 263. (2) To correct (an error): I.PTL 141, SS.VI.DKK 9. Alteration: II.PAA 43, CP 66. (3) To change: I.GCT 246, POE 268 (the sense of a translation), 272 (the substance of a translation), II.PS 23, PAA 42, LWW1 54, DCOPS 117, LWW2 175, 175, PPBPP 202, 204, PF 269, 279, 285, SS. II.CIE 322, VII.VDG 155, VIII.DLT 374, XIV.DAVd 170, 170, XVII.PPBPPd 292. Altering: II.DCOPS 149. Alteration: I.DECG 170, 170, 171, SS.XVII. PPBPPd 292. (4) To revise lines or passages (for better or for worse, but usually to improve): II.PS 24, LWW1 54, LWW2 175, PF 273, SS.V.PAZd 199, XV.AP 249, XVII.PFAAP 340. Alteration: SS.VIII.DC 217, PC 222.

ALTERATION (sb.) See also Alter. (1) The change of direction in the plot of a play: I.EDP 52. (2) Distortion owing to faulty revision: SS.XVII.APa 381.

AMBLE (sb.) An easy pace in poetry. Dryden says, "Horace is always on the amble." See also George Williamson, *The Senecan Amble*. II.DCOPS 130.

AMPLIFY (v.) (1) To expand or augment (rhetorically) by means of figures, etc. To transcend a literal imitation of nature by heightening of figures, etc. To "amplify" does not mean to "alter," only to expand (I. 268): I.GCT 254, POE 268, II.PF 277, SS.XI.DF 201, XVII.DPWDY 211. (2) To expand a story into a play or poem: II.DAV 226, 226, 226. (3) To add words to a language: II.PF 272.

ANCIENT (adj.) (1) Belonging to classic times (Greek or Roman): I.EDP 56, 67, 77, 77, 88, DEDP 111, 112, PEL 151, OHP 159, HAR 212, 217, 218, PO 234, 235, II.LP 7, 17, CP 69, DCOPS 88, 112, 113, 120, PEP 161, PPBPP 191, 191, 195, 204, DAV 232, PF 273, 278, 293, SS.VI.DKK 8, VIII.DAm 9, XIII.SAVPMF 312, XIV.DAVd 187, XV.AP 241, XVII.DPL 7, LPd 76, APa 351, 351, XVIII.PDCW 5, CPd 27. (2) Archaic, old, of olden times: II.DCOPS 96, 109, 113, 150, PF 288, SS.VI.DTC 250, XIV.DAVd 180, XV.AP 227, 234.

ANCIENTS (sb.) Classic writers, or men of Greece and Rome. There is one exception (I. 58), where the word means merely men of olden times: I.EDP 23, 23, 25, 25, 28, 29, 29, 30, 31, 32, 34, 38, 41, 43, 44, 46, 46, 49, 50, 53, 54, 58, 69, 77, 79, 83, 84, DEDP 115, 115, 121, 122, 122, 123, 124, 125, PEL 154, OHP 159, 159, 160, DECG 178, PA 186, HAR 212, 213, 216, 218, 218, 218, PAL 230, GCT 240, PSF 277, II.LP 7, 10, PAA 40 (not capped), DDS 48, PE 61, DCOPS 74, 75, 81, 81, 81, 85, 89, 90, 97, 141, 144, PEP 158, 161, LWW2 173, LJD 177, 178, 179, PPBPP 188, 201, 203, LL 212, 212, DAV 226, 246, PF 280, SS.IV.DMLM 253, VI.DTC 253, VIII.DLT 374, 375, 375, XIII. SAVPMF 311, 316, 316, XIV.DAVd 146, 192, XV.PNOEM 408, 408, XVII. PPBPPd 298, APa 347, 347, 359, 365, XVIII.LLd 78.

ANGLICISM (sb.) An English idiom (Watson's Gloss: "an unassimilated borrowing"): SS.VI.DTC 251.

ANTIQUE (adj.) Belonging to classic Greece and Rome: SS.XIV.DAVd 156, XV.AP 239 (hero).

ANTIQUITY (sb.) (1) The times of Greece and Rome: I.EDP 23, DECG 169, 170, PAL 224, PO 232, 234, GCT 247, II.CP 66, DCOPS 99, 99, 115, PF 271, SS.XVII.DPL 6, PPBPPd 295, 297, APa 349. (2) Ancient times, olden times: I.AAHP 198, II.LP 4, DCOPS 95, 96, PF 288, SS.XIV.DAVd 181, 182. (3) Customs of early times: II.DCOPS 104.

ANTITHESIS (sb.) The figure of contrast or opposition. Dryden refers only to inadequate "antitheses" which he calls "seeming" contradictions: I.EDP 22, PAM 98.

APPREHENSION (sb.) Understanding or capacity of the mind. The one exception is II. 213, which means fear owing to anticipation: I.EDP 40, DEDP 118, PAL 223, 224, GCT 253, POE 272, II.LL 213.

ARGUMENT (sb.) (1) A statement (of fact or otherwise) advanced to support or disprove something: I.EDP 80, 81, DEDP 124, 125, 125, 126, 127, 127, 129, 129, 130, PT 134, PTL 139, OHP 156, 157, 160, 161, 162, DECG 175, AAHP 200, HAR 214, 214, GCT 242, POE 271, 271, II.LP 5, 12, PS 26, DCOPS 88, 105, DAV 231, PF 283, 288, SS.V.PAZd 199, VII.VDG 161, 165, 188, IX.EWTM 427, 428, XIV.DAVd 151, 168, 170, 173, 194, XV.AP 248, XVII.

LPd 71, XVIII.LLd 66, 66, 68, 68, 69, 74, 78. (2) The main narrative element or subject of a play, poem, etc. Dryden says, "But by pursuing close one argument, which is not cloyed with many turns, the French have obtained more liberty for verse" (I. 48). He also says that the argument is the "principal action, the economy and disposition of it [a play, poem, etc.]" (SS.XIV. 185): I.PRL 9, EDP 48, PAM 103, PSL 105, DEDP 114, 115, AAHP 207, II. DCOPS 145, SS.VII.VDG 155, XIV.DAVd 185. (3) A summary of the subject matter of a book: II.PEP 165, 165, DAV 254. (4) A debate: I.EDP 43, II.PF 290. (5) A military battle: I.EDP 20. (6) Theme (of a poem, etc.): SS.V.DSI 106.

ARGUTENESS (sb.) Shrewdness, sharpness (of arguments): II.LP 12.

ART (sb.) The meaning is highly variable. Often, "art" is a vague, catchall word for all things which are man-made, or outside of nature. We can better understand the connotations of art by looking at Milton's use of the word "artful." "Artful" describes a product of human judgment and skill, which is not necessarily associated with either inspiration or elegance. It describes that which is well made, clever, or even cunning. Milton mentions "artful terms," and "wise and artful recitations sweetened with elegant and graceful enticements" (II. 471). He talks about "that elegant and artful symmetry of the promised temple in Ezekial" (II. 191). However, he also describes Comus as "artful" (I. 103). See also Milton III. 240. In the following classifications, there are many citations with debatable meanings. (1) An occupation in which conscious skill is used to gratify taste or to produce something which is beautiful (as poetry, painting, etc.): I.PRL 7, EDP 38, PAM 96, 100, PTL 139, PA 188, EAZ 193, 193, HAR 219, 219, PAL 225, 230, GCT 243, 245, 246, 246, 249, POE 271, PSF 279, II.ETV 15, 16, PS 31, PAA 35, 36, 40, DCOPS 73, 73, 73, 128, 135, PPBPP 182, 183, 183, 184, 187, 187, 191, 191, 191, 191, 191, 191, 191, 191, 192, 193, 193, 193, 194, 194, 194, 194, 196, 196, 199, 201, 201, 202, LL 214, 215, DAV 257, LET 267, SS.VII.VDG 163, XIII.SAVPMF 314, XIV.DAVd 152, 167, 181, 190, XV.AP 224, 224, 236, 248, 250, 252, PNOEM 405, PHC 410, XVII.PPBPPd 292, 298, 299, 299, 300, PFAAP 337, 338, 338, 338, 339, APa 343, 347, 347, 347, 347, 365, 389, XVIII.CPd 62, 63. (2) Liberal arts and sciences: I.EDP 26, 32, DEDP 111, DECG 169, AAHP 201, PAL 225, II.ETV 14, PS 30, PAA 36, DCOPS 74, 81, 81, 90, 139, PPBPP 191, 192, DAV 225, SS.VII.VDG 210, 210, VIII.DLT 375, XIV.DG 6, XV.AP 252, XVII.APa 345, 361, XVIII.CPd 64. (3) The conscious application of skill (rather than the skill itself) in the production of an object or work of art: I.EDP 34, 74, 79, 84, DEDP 121, PO 234, PSF 279, II.PDS 47, DCOPS 98, 98, LL 212, SS.VII.VDG 179, VIII.DLT 374, XV.AP 228, 233, 233, 234, 236, 237, 241, 243, 244, 247, 249, 249, 250, PNOEM 408, XVII.PPBPPd 297, APa 349, 349, 353. Artful: I.PRL 8, EDP 92, II.PDS 47, PF 291, SS.VIII.DKA 135, XV.AP 247, XVII.PPBPP 292. Artfully: I. AAHP 200, GCT 254, 254, II.DAV 226, 245, SS.XIV.DAVd 182, XV.AP 238. (4) Human skill (in artistic matters) as opposed to the workings of nature. Jonson (87) says that art perfects nature: I.EDP 54, 69, 82, 89, 89, PAM 98, PrSL 108, DEDP 124, PrT 136, PTL 140, PEL 154, OHP 157, 157, AAHP 203, GCT 254, II.ETV 15, PS 30, PAA 40, DCOPS 94, 97, 97, 98, 99, 106,

112, PEP 168, PPBPP 196, 201, DAV 235, PF 278, SS.II.DIE 288, VII.VDG 179, VIII.DKA 136, XV.AP 228, 228, 229, 233, 234, 236, 237, 238, 238, 238, 239, 241, 241, 246, 248, 250, 251, PNOEM 401, XVII.DPL 8, PPBPPd 293, 293, 296, APa 351, 355. Artless: SS.XV.AP 244. (5) Device, wile: I.DEDP 114, II.DCOPS 124, TCDD 169, PPV 221, SS.II.DIE 286, XIII.SAVPMF 311. (6) Art, as *objets d'art*: SS.XVII.APa 365.

ARTIFICIAL DAY A day designated as twelve hours. One of the neoclassical arguments over unity of time was whether a play should encompass a "natural" or "artificial" day: I.EDP 70, II.DAV 226.

ASTONISHMENT (sb.) Wonder, awe (of the beauty of a work of art; one step below adoration): SS.XVII.PPBPPd 294, 297.

AUDITOR (sb.) One who listens. This is not a playgoer. A playgoer, says Dryden, is a spectator: II.PEP 162; Flecknoe (Spingarn) II. 93; Rymer (Z) 87 (a spectator is one who watches a play rather than listens; a spectator is more important than an auditor).

AUTHORITY (sb.) (1) Weighty testimony or example (usually by a classic author) used to condone a practice or support an argument: I.EDP 38, 62, DEDP 124, PEL 151, OHP 162, AAHP 199, 200, PAL 228, GCT 255, 261, POE 273, II.PS 27, 28, PAA 36, DCOPS 105, 145, DAV 232, 248, PF 288, SS.VI.DTC 253, VIII.DLT 374, 375, XIV.DG 3, XV.PNOEM 405, 408, 408, XVI.AARLSFX 13, XVII.APa 345, XVIII.CPd 25. (2) Powerful position: I.EDP 71, GCT 246, II.PS 25, SS.VI.DKK 9, IX.TRAA 211, XVII.LPd 64.

B

BALD TRANSLATION Metaphrase. A word for word, or line for line translation which captures none of the poetic spirit of the original: II.PF 275.

BALLAD (sb.) (1) A popular song: (a) A libel: SS.VII.VDG 199; (b) A song which ridicules (something or someone): SS.XV.AP 227. (2) A ballade, in the technical sense. "A poem consisting of one or more triplets of . . . eight-lined stanzas each ending with the same line or refrain, and usually an envoy" (*OED*): SS.XV.AP 234.

BALLETTE (sb.) Ballet. A performance consisting of music, dancing, and pantomime (from the French; the *OED* says it is first recorded English use): I. EDP 62.

BARBARISM (sb.) (1) Ignorance of letters, music, etc.: I.DECG 181, II. DCOPS 112, PPBPP 192. (2) Rudeness of language. Dryden says that a "middling genius . . . is nice as to solecism or barbarism" (I. 197): I.AAHP 197, II.LP 11, PAA 37, DCOPS 86.

BARBAROUS (adj.) (1) Describing speech or language that is not Greek or Roman: II.PAA 37, LJD 178. (2) Rude and unpolished (speech or language): I.POE 272, II.DCOPS 106, 143, 152, 154, SS.XV.AP 229. Barbarously: I.EDP 83, II.PEP 166, SS.VI.DTC 251. (3) Uncultured, uncivilized (place or time): II.PEP 158, PPV 220, SS.XVII.APa 363. (4) Unpolished (lack of embellishments in a painting): II.PPBPP 202, SS.XVII.APa 379. (5) Harsh, savage (action): SS.VII.VDG 201. (6) Rude, uncultured (people): SS.VIII. PC 220.

BARD (sb.) Term of contempt for a poet: II.PF 292.

BEAUTIFUL (adj.) In Dryden's words, something perfect, great, noble, disentangled, without alteration, knit together, pure, having great and few parts, and comprised of bold and harmonious colors (SS.XVII. 381). In poetry there are three parts constituting the total effect of something beautiful: invention, disposition, and elocution. "Invention" in a work of art embodies the idealized, heightened images possible in an imitation of nature. The poet (or artist) conceives an image of perfection, what Nature originally intended. Nature can only produce something imperfect or faulty (SS.XVII. 347). Dryden says, "Chance could never produce anything so beautiful [as an artistically created object]" (I. 89), and that art is more perfect than nature (SS.XVII. 293). The perfect image or perfected imitation of nature, by means of the poet's imagination, is thus raised or heightened above nature, but only in proportion to that nature which is imitated (I. 114). Thus, tragedy, which is elevated by virtue of its almost perfect characters and high subject matter, is more beautiful than comedy (which reproduces nature) (I. 99, II. 192). "Disposition," the second part, includes harmony of order or of arrangement, in the total effect of the parts (II. 195), the manners, and the probability or naturalness of the contrivance or plot (II. 186). The "last perfection" is elocution. It includes the diction and all the tropes and figures. "Bold strokes" heighten the images. All tropes and figures should be harmonious and appropriate. By the beautiful arts (SS.XVII. 365), then, Dryden means those arts which raise in our minds perfect and ideal images and thoughts, satisfy our judgments by harmony and order, and please our senses by appropriate sounds, colors, etc. See Bold, Ugliness, Monstrous. I.EDP 50, 51, 63, 64, 89, PAM 99, DEDP 114, PEL 154, OHP 160, AAHP 196, 203, 204, GCT 242, POE 266, 272, II.PS 19, PAA 37, 43, CSE 57, PE 61, 61, DCOPS 90, 92, 149, 149, 149, PPBPP 186, 193, 193, 193, 195, 203, 206, PPV 219, DAV 229, 238, 252, PF 274, 275, SS.V.DSI 101, VIII.DC 215, XIII.SAVPMF 313, XIV. DAVd 181, 201, 204, XVII.PPBPPd 293, 295, 295, PFAAP 337, APa 345, 347, 347, 347, 349, 349, 359, 359, 365, 365, 381, 393. Beautifully: I.AAHP 205, HAR 215, II.PS 27. Beautify: I.EDP 55, PAM 101, DEDP 112, PEL 154, OHP 159, DECG 177, II.PAA 41, PPBPP 203, DAV 234, PF 277. Beautifying: I.PEL 155, SS.II.DIE 288, XV.PNOEM 408.

BEAUTY (sb.) See Beautiful for discussion of qualities which produce beauty, which make something beautiful. Beauty is not found in extremes (such as in stretched tropes and figures, piercing colors, shrill sounds, etc.). Dryden says, "The sight looks up with pain on craggy rocks and barren mountains, and continues not intent on any object which is wanting in shades and greens to entertain it" (SS.II. 286). Yet he continually says that the greatest beauties of poetry lie in judiciously bold tropes and figures. See Bold. (1) An ornament or a grace: I.EDP 27, 63, 64, HAR 212, POE 273, PSF 275, II.PS 19, DAV 236, 242, SS.VIII.DKA 135, XIV.DAVd 182, XVII.APa 347, 347; Rymer (Z) 18 ("Beauties" are "the proportions, the unities, and outward regularities, the mechanical parts of tragedies"). (2) Beauty personified: SS.V.DSI 101.

(3) A woman: I.EAZ 193, SS.V.DSI 104, XVII.PPBPP 296. (4) That which affords high pleasure to the senses: I.PAM 99, PrT 136, EAZ 193, II.PAA 35, DCOPS 88, DAV 228, 251, SS.II.DIE 286, 286, 286, 286, 287, 288, V.DSI 103, 103, XIII.SAVPMF 313, 313, XIV.DAVd 195, XV.AP 231, 238, XVII.PPBPP 292, 292, 292, 293, 294, 295, 296, 296, 296, 296, 296, 297, APa 345, 359, 361, 361. (5) That which gives high pleasure to the intellect: I.PRL 2, 8, EDP 52, 53, 55, 56, 56, 58, 61, 70, 77, 89, PSL 105, 106, 106, PrSL 108, 114, DEDP 128, OHP 158, 160, 161, DECG 177, 182, PA 188, HAR 212, 212, 215, 216, 219, 220, GCT 247, 247, 247, 248, 259, POE 266, PSF 278, 278, II.LP 3, 8, PS 20, 24, 29, PAA 40, PDS 46, 46, 49, 50, CP 65, DCOPS 94, 95, 96, 111, 113, 119, 140, 141, 143, 144, 148, 150, 151, 152, 152, 154, PEP 156, 157, TCDD 170, 170, PPBPP 184, 185, 186, 189, 194, 196, 196, 201, 205, 206, 207, LL 212, 214, PPV 220, 222, DAV 227, 230, 245, 246, 248, 251, 252, PRAV 258, LCM 266, PF 270, 270, 275, 275, 276, 279, 280, 288, 288, 288, 289, 291, SS.II.DIE 287, VIII.PC 221, DLT 374, XIII.SAVPMF 313, 313, 313, 315, XIV.DG 4, DAVd 168, 181, XV.AP 225, 244, PHC 410, XVII.LPd 30, DHL 83, AARHL 101, PPBPPd 293, 294, 295, 296, PFAAP 337, APa 349, 353, 357, 357, 365, 383, XVIII.LLd 73; Reynolds (Spingarn) I. 151; Sprat (Spingarn) II. 129 (The qualities of a "feminine kind [of poetry are] . . . smoothness and beauty. . . . Strength is the chief praise of the masculine.").

BELLES LETTRES The humanities, "books of humanity" (SS.XVII. 417). Some examples are the Bible, *The History of Josephus, The Roman History* of Coeffeteau, Livy, Homer, Virgil, Ovid's *Metamorphoses,* Plutarch's *Lives,* Horace's *Art of Poetry,* Spenser's *Faerie Queene,* Godwin's *Roman Antiquities,* etc., etc. According to Strang, the *OED* records Swift as first to use the word in 1710, but Rymer uses it in 1692 (Z 83): SS.XVII.OAP 416, 417, 493.

BIOGRAPHIA (sb.) "The lives of particular men" (II. 5). "The history of particular men's lives" (II. 7). "Histories of particular lives" (II. 8): II.LP 5, 7, 8.

BIOGRAPHY (sb.) See Donald A. Stauffer, *English Biography before 1700,* pp. 217–19, for uses earlier than Dryden, which are *Life of Dr. Fuller,* 1661, p. 105; and *Flagellum or the Life & Death of Cromwell,* 1663, epistle to the reader: II.LP 8, SS.XVII.LPd 63. Biographer: II.LL 209.

BLANK VERSE (1) Unrhymed iambic pentameter: I.EDP 55, 66, 79, 79, 80, 80, 81, 81, 81, 82, 83, 83, 84 (a poetic prose), 85, 87, 88, 90, DEDP 113, 115, 115, II.PS 22 (of Italian), PAA 41, DCOPS 84, DAV 240. (2) In French, "prose mesurée": I.PRL 6, 6, 7, 8, EDP 83, 83, 83.

BLOT (sb.) (1) Obliteration and correction (of something written): I.PAM 102. (2) Stain on someone's reputation: II.DAV 239 (in his escutcheon).

BOISTEROUS METAPHOR A violent metaphor, an "instrument of the sublime" (*OED* says this use of boisterous was introduced in 1695): II.DCOPS 121.

BOISTEROUS STYLE A crude style of writing: SS.XV.PNOEM 399.

BOISTEROUS WIT Crude, unrefined, but vigorous wit: II.TCDD 169.

BOLD (adj.) (1) Daring, vigorous, comprehensive, strong, original (referring usually to tropes, figures, colors, etc.). Without boldness, a poet can never reach sublimity, nor rise above mediocre performance. Without boldness a poet can at most achieve a dull, uninspired correctness. Dryden points out the difference between boldness and rashness in I. 199. What is bold or daring is good if it is not foolhardy. "Bold" is fundamentally a word of esteem. See Hyperbole, Sublime, Lofty, Majestic. I.TCDD 171, SS.XIV.DG 3, XVII.APa 381. Boldly: I.EDP 69. Boldness: I.PAM 100, AAHP 199, 203, 203, GCT 238, 253, PSF 278, II.LJD 179, PPV 218, DAV 234, SS.V.PAZd 187, DAL 318, X.PHP 112. Bold metaphor: II.PPBPP 204, SS.XIV.DG 3. Bold purity: II. PS 31. Bold satire: I.AAHP 199. Bold strokes: I.PAM 99. Boldest strokes (are most delightful): 1.AAHP 200. Bolder figure: I.AAHP 201. Bolder genius: II.DAV 247. Bolder ode: SS.XV.AP 232. Davenant (Spingarn) II. 3 (wit is displayed by "bold flights"); Hobbes (Spingarn) II. 61 (figures which not only "exceed the work, but also the possibility of nature"; then he mentions fantastic, magical images); Cowley (Spingarn) II. 86 ("The figures [in Pindaric odes] are unusual and bold, even to temeritie, and such as I durst not use in any other kind of poetry"); Sprat (Spingarn) II. 131 (there is "boldness of metaphors" in Cowley's "Pindaric Odes"); Wilmot (Spingarn) II. 283; Rymer (Z) 15 ("The boldest fancy" is sometimes fortunate in making a lucky hit. "The poet here truly represents the nature of man, whose first thoughts break out in bold and more general terms, which by the second thoughts are more correct and limited."). (2) Rash, foolhardy, audacious (always pejorative). The reference is usually to tropes, figures, etc. In every citation, Dryden means that something is "too bold." See Glowing Colours, Hyperbole. I.EDP 40, II.PF 280, SS.X.PRLaici 10, XVII.APa 347. Boldly: II.PS 19, SS.XV.AP 244. Boldness: II.DAV 256, SS.V.PAZd 200. Bold address: SS.XVII.LPd 90. Bold anger: SS.XV.AP 240. Bold attempt: II.LL 212. Bold expression: II.PS 24, DCOPS 93, PPBPP 207. Bolder expression: II.PPBPP 207. Bold figures: II.DCOPS 118. Bold metaphor: I.EDP 39. Bold strokes: II.PPBPP 204. Boldest part: I.DEDP 121. (3) Sweeping, vigorous, courageous (especially in some kind of action): I.PrTL 143, ECG 167, POE 270, II.DAV 248, SS.XIV. DG 3. "Bold" used as an adverb: II.PF 287. Boldness: II.DAV 237. Bold alteration: I.PTL 141.

BOMBAST (sb.) Inflated language; fustian: I.EDP 67, DECG 173 (speeches), AAHP 199, GCT 258, 259, PSF 278, SS.XV.AP 227, 229.

BORROW (v.) To take (something, such as a line, a scene, a character, a genre form, figures, words, etc.) from (someone or something). To borrow is not to invent (I. 267), but to employ the "common materials of poetry" used by someone else (SS.XIV. 185). To borrow is not the same as to copy; the borrower works up what he has borrowed for his own purposes. See Steal. I.PRL 5, PT 135, PTL 143, PEL 150, OHP 161, DECG 178, AAHP 196, GCT 241, 253, POE 267, II.PDS 48, DCOPS 81, 82, 97, 104, 119, PPBPP 204, DAV 229, 229, 252, PF 277, 290, 290, SS.XIV.DAVd 180, 185, 185, 186, 197, 201, XV.AP 225, XVII.LPd 71, XVIII.LLd 78. Borrowing: II.DCOPS 81.

BOYISMS (sb.) Trivialities or puerilities in thought and words (see Watson's note): II.PF 279.

BREAK (sb.) Caesura: I.EDP 84.

BREAKING (sb.) (1) Strang: caesura (or anacoluthon?): I.DEDP 118, II.PS 24. (2) Cessation: II.DAV 248. (3) The dividing line between one color and another: SS.XVII.APa 369, 373.

BURLESQUE (sb.) (1) A literary genre which ridicules by exaggerating and deforming nature: I.PAM 101, II.DCOPS 103 (Rymer uses "vers burlesque" in Z 89), 147, SS.XV.AP 226, 227, 248. Shadwell in Spingarn II. 150 says "burlesque" is "love and honor strained too high." See also Rymer (Z) 4, 84 (verb), 89, 89, 89, 170. (2) A kind of meter used in "vers burlesque" (octosyllabic couplets): II.DCOPS 147, 148.

BURLESQUE (v.) To ridicule by exaggeration: I.AAHP 205.

BY-CONCERNMENT (sb.) Secondary plot. See Concernment, Walk, Under-plot, By-walk. I.EDP 59.

BY-FEATURE (sb.) Secondary characteristic of a person (here, the Duke of Guise): SS.VII.VDG 154.

BY-WALK (sb.) Underplot or subplot: I.EDP 76, PO 234.

C

CAESURA (sb.) Elision. For modern application of "caesura," Dryden uses "breaking." See Breaking. II.DAV 235, 235, 236.

CATASTROPHE (sb.) The resolution of a play, the climax of the action. The place in a play where all things settle back to their "first foundation," where all the obstacles which hindered the action are removed; and the play "ends with that resemblance of truth and nature that the audience are satisfied with the conduct of it" (I. 33). See also Conclusion, Discovery, Unravelling, Untying. I.EDP 33, PEL 151, HAR 216, II.CP 68, SS.VIII.DLT 374. See also Rymer (Z) 48.

CATHARSIS (sb.) Watson's Gloss: "The term is never used by Dryden, though he twice borrows Aristotle's medical analogy of the purge in *Poetics,* ch. xiii, I.[GCT] 245, II.[DAV] 228. Reference to 'pity and terror' (sometimes 'admiration' as in [Sidney]'s apology (1595), sometimes 'compassion') are abundant. I.[EDP] 41, 46, +n., [HAR] 211, 212, 213, 216, 217, +n., 218, 219, [GCT] 243, 245, 245, 246, 247 (to distinguish Shakespeare and Fletcher) 250; II.[PEP] 167, [DAV] 227. Dryden commonly interprets Aristotle to mean that tragedy gives rise to pity and terror ('raise,' 'produce'), occasionally takes the medical analogy more literally, and occasionally attempts a compromise II.[DAV] 227 ('to expel arrogance, and to introduce compassion')."

CHAPTOR (v.) To reprove: SS.XVIII.CPd 41.

CHARACTER (sb.) (1) The personality of a person, or a personality or humor personified, usually in a play or poem: I.PRL 2, 9, EDP 33, 35, 42, 52, 61, 66, 71, 73, 74, 75, 76, 85, 87, 87, PSL 106, 106, 107, DEDP 124, PTL 139, 146, 148, 150, 150, 150, 150, 151, 151, 155, OHP 158, 158, 158, 159, 163, 163, DECG 178, 178, 179, 180, 180, 182, EAZ 193, AAHP 211, 213, 215, 216, 216, 217, 219, 220, PAL 222, 222, 223, 224, PO 233, GCT 240, 246, 246, 247, 248, 249, 249, 249, 249, 249 (definition), 249, 250, 250, 252, 252, 252, 252, 253,

253, 260, POE 272, II.PAA 35, PDS 45, 47, 50, 51, 51, CSE 57, 59, DCOPS 83, 103, PPBPP 184, 186, 186, 186, 190, 198, 202, 202, 203, 203, LL 211, DAV 228, 228, LPe 263, 264, PF 279, 282, 284, 284, 284, 284, 286, SS.IV. DCG 12, 15, V.PAZd 197, 197, VII.VDG 164, 170, 187, 187, 219, VIII.PC 226, 227, IX.TRAA 213, XIII.SAVPMF 311, 311, 311, XIV.DAVd 147, 161, 163, 172, 172, 174, XV.AP 246, PNOEM 399, 399, 400, PHC 410, XVII.LPd 71; Rymer (Z) 131 ("character" is the second of the four parts of tragedy [1. "fable," 3. "thoughts or scence," 4. "expression"], and is derived from "moral philosophy"), 134, 136. (2) Person in a play or poem (the distinction between (1) and (2) is sometimes rather tenuous): I.EDP 50, 56, 61, 61, 64, 65, 81, PSL 106, PTL 149, 149, 155, OHP 164, 165, AAHP 219, PO 234, GCT 246, 246, 246, 249, 250, 250, 250, 250, 250, 251, 251, 251, 252, 253, 255, 255, 257, 257, 260, II.PDS 50, DCOPS 145, LWW2 174, PPBPP 184, 199, 202, SS.II.CIE 321, VII.PC 226, XIV.DAVd 163, 189; Sprat (Spingarn) II. 130, Rymer (Z) 62. (3) A sketch of a person's qualities (as a "character" of Dorset): I.EDP 67, 69, PAM 102, PTL 151, OHP 164, DECG 169, II.PDS 51, DCOPS 75, 92, 115, 137, 138, PF 285, SS.VIII.DKA 137, X.PHP 117, XIII.SAVPMF 310, 310, 314, XV.PNOEM 398; Sprat (Spingarn) II. 146. (4) Specific traits (of poetry or tragedy, for example): I.DEDP 119, AAHP 205, II.DCOPS 102. (5) Definition of a concept by describing it (such as a character of wit): I.PTL 149. (6) Rhetorical figure of thought or expression: I.POE 271, SS.XVII.APa 363. (7) The personality of an author revealed through his writings. Thus, "character" means "style" (for an author to maintain his character is to maintain his style, or tone): II.PS 21, 21, 22, 23, 31, CSE 59, DCOPS 143, PEP 163, 166, PPBPP 184, 184, PPV 238; Sprat (Spingarn) II. 128 (he connects style and character: "In all the several shapes of his [Cowley's] style there is still very much of the likeness and impression of the same mind: the same unaffected modesty, and natural freedom, and easy vigour, and chearful passions, and innocent mirth, which appeared in all his manners"), 135 ("character of poetry and music"). (8) Reputation: I.PAM 104, II.DCOPS 77, 135, SS.VIII.DKA 132, PC 220, XIII.SAVPMF 310, XIV. DAVd 165, 178, XV.AP 239, XVIII.CPd 45. (9) A specific trait or virtue in a person: SS.XIV.DAVd 164, 165, 172, 173.

chorus (sb.) (1) Greek dramatic chorus: I.EDP 33, 36, PO 234, II.DCOPS 99, 101, 102, 102, 103, PPBPP 199, 200, 200, SS.XV.AP 238, 239. Rymer (Z) 84 ("the most important part of a tragedy"). (2) Group of singers or what they sing, in an opera: II.PAA 39, 43. (3) Jonson's version of the Greek dramatic chorus consisting of shepherds and shepherdesses: I.EDP 66.

chromatic (adj.) Pertaining to colors; the chromatic part of a painting is the coloring (first recorded use in English): II.PPBPP 203, SS.XVII.APa 365.

ciceronian (adj.) Modeled on Cicero's writing style: SS.XVII.PoHL 185.

classic (adj.) Describing a standard set by an ancient Greek or Latin writer (the classic authors are Greek and Latin): II.DAV 252, SS.XV.PNOEM 408.

clause (sb.) A part of a sentence, a phrase: II.DCOPS 143, 143.

clench (sb.) A pun: I.EDP 21, 67, DECG 179, II.DCOPS 139.

clench (v.) To pun: I.DECG 179.

CLEVELANDISM (sb.) A word "wrested" and "tortured" "into another meaning." Dryden is saying the poet John Cleveland used words in this way: I.EDP 21.

COLOUR (sb.) Because of Dryden's parallel between poetry and painting, definitions (1) and (2) are often interchangeable. See Horace, *Ars Poetica*, l. 86. Hobbes (Spingarn II. 63) uses "colour" in the sense of style or stylishness ("that which giveth a poem the true and natural colour . . ."). (1) A trope, a figure: II.PS 33, PPBPP 206, 207, DAV 243, PF 275, 275, SS.XIII.SAVPMF 313, XVII.PPBPPd 292, 299, APa 349, 351, 359. (2) A figure of speech in the most general sense: I.EDP 31, PAM 98, PrSL 108, DEDP 120, PSF 276, II.PEP 167, PPBPP 203, 205, SS.XV.AP 229, 244, 246. (3) Appearance, show (here, specious or false appearance): SS.VII.VDG 217, XV.AP 250, XVII.APa 367. (4) Show of reason, excuse: I.PEL 154.

COLOURING (sb.) The colors (in a painting), the diction (of a poem). Coloring, or elocutio, is the third most important consideration of an artist, poet, and reader or viewer (according to the classical classification of dispositio, inventio, elocutio). Dryden uses the term interchangeably with poesy and painting. Only in one place (SS.XVII. 365) does the word merely mean "hues and tints": II.LP 8, PS 19, DCOPS 80, PPBPP 186, 203, 203, 203, 203, 204, 204, 205, 206, 207, 207, 208, DAV 242, PF 275, SS.XIV.DAVd 188, XVII.APa 365, 365, 367.

COMEDY (sb.) (1) Branch of drama concerned with follies of man, amusing happenings, and laughable people. It is usually written in an informal style. It is the antithesis of tragedy: I.EDP 27, 30, 32, 34, 38, 44, 49, 56, 60, 60, 63, 66, 72, 73, 74, 78, 81, 86, PSL 105, DEDP 114, 114, 116, 116, 119, 119, 119, 119, 120, 120, 120, 128, 128, PWG 131, PEL 145, 146, 146, 147, 149, 149, 150, 150, 151, 152, 152, 152, 152, 152, 155, ECG 167, 167, DECG 172, PAZ 191, AAHP 199, 203, PAL 226, 244, II.PDS 45, 51, DCOPS 108, 109, 112, 112, 121, 135, LWW2 174, LJD 178, PPBPP 184, 185, 189, 193, LL 211, 212, SS.VIII.DAm 9, XIV.DAVd 190, XV.AP 245, 245; Rymer (Z) 175 ("And yet for modern comedy, doubtless our English are the best in the world"). (2) A play with a happy ending, dealing with the follies of man, amusing happenings, and laughable people: I.EDP 38, 38, 42, 56, 57, 65, 66, 69, 70, 71, 72, 73, 74, 75, 76, 84, PSL 107, DEDP 116, 120, 120, 120, 120, 128, PWG 131, PTL 141, PEL 146, 147, 147, 151, 153, 155, OHP 157, DECG 179, 181, 182, PA 184, GCT 244, 247, 250, 251, II.DCOPS 108, 109, 110, 111, PPBPP 198, SS.III. DEL 235, IV.DMLM 253, 256, VI.DKK 9, 10, VIII.DAm 8, DLT 375, 376, XV.PHC 409. (3) Amusing incidents in a play or poem (as the comedy in an epic): I.DECG 172, II.LL 212, SS.VIII.PC 220.

COMMEMORATION (sb.) A eulogistic mention or remembrance (of someone) by a writer: SS.XVII.LPd 76.

COMMONPLACE (sb.) (1) A stock theme for a writer (not derogatory): I.HAR 213, II.DCOPS 123, SS.X.PHP 118. (2) A heading under a major subject or topic: I.HAR 218, SS.VI.DKK 8. (3) A statement generally accepted as truth: I.GCT 248, II.DCOPS 132, PEP 162. (4) A miscellaneous collection of knowledge or jottings for one's own private use (two words, common place): SS. XVII.LPd 30.

COMPASSION (sb.) Pity. One of the ends of tragedy is to move compassion, for a tragic hero, in the audience. This is Dryden's term for what we call Aristotle's pity. It is the opposite of mirth, which is the product of comic relief in tragedy. See Admiration, Concernment, Fear, Pity. (1) Pity, as an end of tragedy: I.EDP 41, 41, 46, 46, 58, PAL 222, GCT 247, 250, 250, II.PPBPP 202, SS.VIII.PC 219. (2) Pity as moved, in a reader, by an epic: II.PEP 167, PPBPP 185, 185, 199. (3) A heroic quality in an epic hero: SS.XIV.DAVd 161, 169.

COMPLAINT (sb.) (1) Expression of grief: I.GCT 251. (2) A kind of poem where a speaker grieves about the beloved's indifference or cruelty: II.PS 30, DCOPS 151, PPV 219, 219, SS.XV.AP 238. (3) Statement of grievance: II.DCOPS 76, SS.V.DSI 106, PAZd 188, VII.VDG 218.

COMPOSE (v.) (1) To constitute, to make up: I.OHP 159, 160, II.DCOPS 112, 113. (2) To constitute (a part of a painting): SS.XVII.APa 355, 367, 381. (3) To invent in a musical form, to write music: II.PAA 42, 42, SS.VIII. DKA 135. (4) To write: II.DCOPS 113, 114, SS.III.DEL 235, X.PRLaici 15, 32, XV.AP 233, XVI.AARLSFX 11. (5) To make tranquil, to make serene: II.PE 60.

COMPOSITION (sb.) (1) The act of composing, invention; the construction and disposition of the parts of a work of art. Dryden says this form of "disposition" comes under the heading of invention (II. 195) and is a product of wit or the faculty of imagination (I. 97–98): I.PAM 96, 97, II.PAA 38, 41, DCOPS 114, PPBPP 195, SS.VIII.DAm 9. (2) The bringing together of parts to make a whole: I.DEDP 114, GCT 250, II.CSE 57 (of a hero), SS.VI.DTC 251, XVII.APa 379. (3) Orderly or artistic arrangement of the parts of a work: I.DEDP 123, II.PAA 37 (of words), 43, SS.XVII.APa 367. (4) A literary, artistic, or other intellectual production: II.DCOPS 76, 107 (of music), PPBPP 195, SS.VIII.DAm 10.

CONCEIT (sb.) (1) "Originally an imagined thing, hence thought, e.g. Chaucer, Troilus and Criseida, I. 269; Jonson, II. 279 and note" (Watson's Gloss). Hobbes calls conceits "strong lines" (Spingarn I. 22, 63). We think of "conceits" as characteristic of metaphysical poetry. Dryden usually means a poetic figure (or thought) which is farfetched, "thin," or obscure: I.EDP 20, 22, 65, 72, II.DCOPS 82, 122, 124, DAV 243, PF 279, 279, 279, 280, 286, SS.XV.AP 234, PNOEM 402, 405, XVII.LPd 63. See also Jonson 90. To an earlier generation "conceits" were admirable, but as time went on they lost prestige. Alexander (Spingarn I. 183 [1634]) says, "A witty conceit which doth harmoniously delight the spirits." Davenant, however (Spingarn II. 22), says that conceits are low. Cowley (Spingarn II. 88) mentions "the vulgar conceit of men that lying is essential to good poetry." And Phillips (Spingarn II. 266) says, "An epigram is . . . the fag end of poetry . . . [consisting] rather of conceit and acumen of wit than of poetical invention." (2) A well-stated product of (someone's) wit: I.PEL 148, DECG 178, 182, POE 269. (3) Epigrammatic wit (with overtones of def. 1): II.PS 22.

CONCERNMENT (sb.) (1) The emotional involvement (of an audience) effected by great art, especially high tragedy. "Concernment" is proportionate to the greatness of the tragic action. The more important the action, the greater is our anxiety. Dryden usually uses "concernment" as including both pity and fear, but several times he uses it to mean fear alone, as one of the emotions tragedy is supposed to induce in the audience. He says, "The end of tragedies or serious plays . . . is to beget admiration, compassion [pity], or concernment [fear]" (I. 46; see also I. 215). In an early quotation, he defines concernment as a specific kind of fear, the anxiety the audience feels while wondering what will happen next. Later, paraphrasing Rapin, Dryden says that concernment is an involvement, or agitation in the soul, produced by both pity and fear (I. 246). See Fear, Compassion, Pity, Admiration. I.EDP 21, 41, 41, 42, 45, 46, 46, 51, 54, 58, 60, 60, 81, PAM 99 (in Virgil), PEL 155, DECG 172, HAR 213, 213, 215, GCT 244, 246, 246, 250, 250, 257, II.DCOPS 130 (Juvenal), SS. VII.VDG 152, XIV.DAVd 189 (Virgil), 192, 192. (2) In a work of art, a character's involvement in and anxiety for another character and his problems: I.EDP 49, 74, II.CSE 59, PEP 166, SS.XIV.DAVd 203. (3) Anxiety, concern, involvement (in general): I.DEDP 111, PWG 131, PA 188, PAL 227. (4) That which causes anxiety, such as an underplot, a problem, business, etc. See By-concernment. I.EDP 42, 47, 74, 90, II.PPBPP 183, 199. (5) Importance: II.LP 6.

CONCLUSION (sb.) (1) Denouement of a play, ending of a play: I.PRL 2, EDP 54, PEL 150, II.PDS 47, LWW2 174, PPBPP 207, SS.II.CIE 321, V. PAZd 199, VIII.PC 227, DLT 374. (2) The climax of a poem: II.DCOPS 94, 94, SS.IX.TRAA 213, XIV.DAVd 176. (3) Ending (of anything): II.DAV 253, PRAV 258, SS.XVII. LPd 71. (4) Inference, deduction: I.DEDP 123, II.DCOPS 119.

CONDUCT (sb.) (1) The design, the structure, the unfolding of a play or poem. The management of parts to produce a whole: I.EDP 33, 50, AAHP 197, HAR 211, PO 234, POE 266, II.PDS 49, 51, PEP 161, DAV 224, SS.XIV. DAVd 187, 188. Conducting: I.EDP 74. (2) The plan, the design of a painting or sculpture. The whole as it is made up of parts: SS.XVII.APa 369. (3) Direction, guidance: II.PPV 218, SS.XVIII.LLd 63. (4) Action, behavior: I.PO 234, II.PAA 35, SS.V.PAZd 197.

CONDUCT (v.) (1) To plan, to carry out, to design (a play or poem): I.EDP 59, II.CP 66, DCOPS 90. (2) To lead, to carry, to direct: I.POE 266, II.PAA 41, DCOPS 141, SS.XVII.PPBPPd 297.

CONTEXTURE (sb.) The total effect (of an artistic composition) produced by the interweaving of all (its) parts, or inner workings (as opposed to frame, as differing from style): I.PSL 105 (of a play), POE 263, II.LP 10 (of the whole); Reynolds (Spingarn) I. 149, Alexander (Spingarn) I. 182, Davenant (Spingarn) II. 18, Hobbes (Spingarn) II. 69.

CONTINUITY OF SCENES Liaison des scènes. See also Unbroken Scenes. I.EDP 29, 37, 71.

CONTRIVANCE (sb.) (1) Artifice, plan, plot (many times "contrivance" has only to do with plot; sometimes it means "plot"). Rymer (Z) 20 says, "In the contrivance and oeconomy [see Economy] of a play, reason is always principally to be consulted": I.EDP 74, 74, PSL 105, PT 135, PTL 140, PEL 144,

HAR 217, PAL 222, GCT 241, II.PDS 49, LWW1 54, 54, PPBPP 186, SS. VII.VDG 202. (2) Scheme: SS.VII.VDG 220.

CONTRIVE (v.) (1) To plot out (a play or poem), to plan (a play or poem): I.EDP 30, 37, 47, 56, DEDP 141, HAR 211, POE 266, II.PPBPP 186, DAV 230, SS.V.DA 8, VIII.DLT 374. Contriving: I.EDP 68. (2) To devise with ingenuity: I.EDP 89, PEL 151, POE 270, II.PF 270. (3) To bring (a play) into a particular form, with ingenuity: I.DEDP 128.

CONVENIENT (adj.) Appropriate, suitable, and sometimes proportionate: I. DEDP 126, GCT 253, II.PPBPP 195, DAV 224, 224, SS.XIV.DG 4, DAVd 175.

COPIER (sb.) A transcriber, one who imitates (pejorative): I.EDP 27, GCT 253, POE 269, II.PPBPP 195, SS.XIV.DAVd 187.

COPIOUS (adj.) Full. Dryden uses "copious" as a general term, sometimes critically, sometimes not. His meaning varies. Horace's satires, for example, are more copious than Juvenal's because they contain more instruction (II. 127); Juvenal's satires are more copious than Persius' because "in Persius the diffi- culty is to find a meaning, in Juvenal to choose a meaning" (II. 139). Cicero, Homer, Juvenal, Horace, Plutarch, and Cowley for various reasons are copious, but Virgil, because he uses words sparingly, is not. In general, "co- pious" means florid, overflowing, full of variety, etc. Milton says, "And what if the author shall be one so copious of fancy, as to have many things well worth the adding, come into his mind after licensing" (IV. 325). Variety is often used as a synonym. Alexander (Spingarn) I. 182 says "copiousness" is "variety of invention": I.EDP 24 (Cowley), II.PS 23 (Virgil is not), DCOPS 127 (Horace more than Juvenal), 139 (Juvenal more than Persius), PEP 166 (English as a language), PF 274 (Homer's invention or Virgil's), SS.XI.DF 203 (the Duke of Ormond as a subject), XVII.PoHL 185 (Cicero's style). Copiously: II.DCOPS 84 (on Milton), PF 272 (on Rymer). Copious- ness: I.EDP 59 (of English plots over French), 65 (of Jonson's intrigues), DEDP 118, GCT 252, POE 265 (of English), II.LP 10 (of Plutarch's learn- ing), 10 (of Plutarch's words), PS 22 (of Homer), 32 (of Cowley), PAA 37 (of Italian), CP 69 (of Cicero); Jonson 100; Milton III. 351, IV. 325; Peachum (Spingarn) I. 123 ("variety"), Alexander (Spingarn) I. 182, 183, Hobbes (Spingarn) II. 60 ("copious imagery"), 65, Sprat (Spingarn) II. 112.

COPY (sb.) (1) A low kind of imitation, a reproduction, a duplication: I.DEDP 115, PT 134, OHP 163, AAHP 196, PO 233, GCT 241, II.PS 20, DCOPS 76, PPBPP 195, SS.XIV.DAVd 185, XVII.DG 8, XVIII.PDCW 6. (2) Printed version of a work: I.GCT 240, II.PS 21, DAV 253, PRAV 261, LET 268, SS.XVI.AARLSFX 10. (3) Manuscript: II.PS 24, SS.VII.VDG 146, VIII.PC 222, IX.EWTM 426, XV.PHC 411. (4) Written material, literary production: II.DCOPS 76, SS.XIV.DAVd 162.

COPY (v.) (1) To duplicate, to imitate, to reproduce exactly a writer's style or work, or nature itself. To transcribe, to plagiarize. For Dryden's discussion of differences between "copy" and "imitate" see SS.XIV. 187–88. I.PT 134, PrT 136, PAL 228, 231, GCT 248, 253, 260, II.ETV 15, PS 24, 25, 31, 33,

PAA 36, DCOPS 76, 84, 110, 110, 111, 150, PEP 159, 163, 164, PPBPP 195, 195, 204, LL 215, PPV 219, DAV 226, 228, 234, 247, 251, PF 277, SS.IV. DCG 17, DMLM 253, V.DAL 318, VII.VDG 161, 208, VIII.DLT 374, XIV. DAVd 166, 187, 187, 188, 188, 189, 197, 199, 204, XVI.DLSFX 6, AARLSFX 10, XVII.DPL 6, 6, PPBPPd 295, APa 393, XVIII.CPd 25, 31, 39. Copying: II.PF 275, SS.XIV.DAVd 189, 189. (2) To imitate another person's actions: II.PE 62, SS.IV.DCG 14, VII.VDG 202.

CORRECT (adj.) Describing that which conforms to standards of grammar, usage, genre form, decorum, the unities, and all the other so-called neoclassical rules. Correctness is obtained by using the judgment. Rymer says, "The poet here truly represents the nature of man, whose first thoughts break out in bold and more general terms, which by the second thoughts are more correct and limited" (Z 16). But to Dryden correctness is not the highest virtue. The French are more correct, but the English are better poets. Jonson is more correct than Shakespeare, but Shakespeare has more invention and is thus greater (I. 70): I.EDP 24, 70, 70, 83, DEDP 111, PTL 140, DECG 172, 173, 176, PrAZ 192, HAR 218, II.DCOPS 76, 114, PEP 163, DAV 253, SS. XIV.DAVd 175. Correctly: I.DECG 173, 176. Correctness: I.DECG 175, II.LWW1 53, PPBPP 207, LL 213, DAV 257.

CORRECT (v.) To revise, to criticize, to rectify. Correction is the function of the judgment rationally contemplating some object, idea, person, or writing. (1) To revise writing of some kind. Sometimes to criticize with the purpose of revising. Dryden says readers "owe . . . the correction to . . . judgment" (I. 103). To revise one employs cooler thoughts than those produced by the heat of invention (II. 42). That is why Dryden says one can over-revise, destroying the passion of invention, which need not be correct (see Correct, adj.): I.PT 135, 135, GCT 240, II.DAV 253, 258, SS.XIV.DAVd 200, XVIII.CPd 31. Correcting: I.EDP 68, II.PPBPP 183. Correction: I.PAM 94, 103, PT 135, 135, II.PAA 42, LCM 265, PF 287, SS.XV.PNOEM 403. (2) To rectify an error, such as a fact, solecism, spelling, etc.: I.PAM 97, II.CP 65, LWW2 174, SS.XVIII.CPd 39 (of history), 61 (in a text). Correcting: I.PAM 102, DECG 171, II.DCOPS 116. (3) To criticize faults in people or society by means of satire. The amending is done by the person who recognizes his own faults; satire itself, therefore, does not amend: II.DCOPS 78, 125, DAV 234. Correction: SS.IX.TRAA 214. (4) To rectify one's own vices (after satire has pointed them out): II.DCOPS 140, 141. (5) To improve (upon nature in a painting). Nature is faulty; art strives to embody perfection. Art corrects nature: SS.XVII.PPBPPd 292. Correcting: II.PPBPP 184. (6) To revise a painting: SS.XVII.APa 347.

COUNTERTURN (sb.) Catastasis. An unexpected development in the plot of a play which occurs at a critical juncture, after the turn and before the denouement or unraveling of the plot. See Crisis, Act, Turn. I.EDP 33, 65, HAR 216; Davenant (Spingarn) II. 18, Rymer (Z) 73.

CRABBED (adj.) (1) Unpalatable, unattractive: II.PS 25. (2) Perversely intricated and unidiomatic (style of writing): II.DCOPS 139. (3) Describing unidiomatic phrasing: SS.XVIII.LLd 81.

CREATURE (sb.) One who is actuated by the will of another. This word is used in connection with a skeptical, Hobbesian description of free will: I. PRL 4.

CRISIS (sb.) The high point, the crossing of the actions, the most critical point in the progress of the intrigues of a play. It follows a turn and counterturn, and precedes the denouement or unraveling: I.GCT 254.

CRITIC (sb.) (1) Faultfinder, many times "little critic" or "false critic." See also Hypercritic. I.PRL 2, PAM 100, PrSL2 108, 109, 109, DEDP 118, PTL 142, PrTL 143, PEL 154, OHP 166, ECG 167, DECG 173, PA 187, 188, AAHP 196, 202, 207, PAL 222, 224, 224, 224, 225, GCT 246, II.PS 19, PAA 40, DCOPS 120, 126, PEP 157, 157, LL 213, PPV 220, DAV 231, 239, 252, SS.VI.DKK 10, VII.VDG 162, X.PRLaici 32, XIV.DAVd 169, 182, 188, 191, 200, XV.AP 229, 237, 240, XVII.PoHL 185, PPBPPd 298, XVIII.LLd 80; Hobbes (Spingarn) II. 68 (censurer), 71, 71. (2) One skilled in literary theory, or one able to appreciate beauty when he sees it. See Judge. I.EDP 45, 71, 88, PSL 106, DEDP 112, 119, ECG 168, AAHP 197, 197, 199, 205, 207, PAL 225, 226, 228, PrO 235, GCT 245, 246, 247, 250, 252, 254, PSF 278, II.PS 20, 29, 30, PAA 38, PDS 49, 50, PE 61, DCOPS 81, 86, 88, 96, 96, 97, 97, 101, 101, 104, 104, 111, 116, 117, 136, 143, 153, PEP 158, 161, LJD 177, 178, PPBPP 186, 191, 191, 200, DAV 228, 232, 233, 240, 257, PRAV 261, PF 272, SS.IV.DMLM 257, V.PAZd 199, V.DTC 253, VII.VDG 159, 160, VIII.DLT 374, XIV.DG 3, 4, DAVd 148, 160, 162, 189, XV.AP 228, 249; Jonson 87, 89, 90; Milton III. 157 ("the greatest critics are Aristotle, Horace, Castelvetro, Tasso, Mazzoni, and others"), IV. 286 ("He may be the competent judge of a neat picture, or elegant poem, who cannot limn the like"), VI. 7.

CRITIC (v.) To find fault (with): SS.XIII.SAVPMF 315.

CRITICISM (sb.) (1) Judgment of qualities: I.EDP 31. (2) The art of estimating and judging the qualities of a literary work (Strang: Dryden may be the first to use this meaning). See Critique. I.AAHP 196, 196, LD 209, GCT 243, 243, 246, PSF 278, II.PS 28, 30, LWW1 55, CSE 59, DCOPS 74, LL 213, PPV 220, DAV 237, SS.VIII.DLT 376, XIV.DAVd 163, 197, XVII.LPd 70. (3) Faultfinding (in general): I.PEL 147, II.LWW1 53, DCOPS 116, SS.XVII LPd 25. (4) Unfavorable literary judgment: I.GCT 252, II.PEP 159, PF 292, SS.XIV.DAVd 192.

CRITICIZE (v.) (1) To perform the art of criticism, to estimate and judge a literary work: II.PAA 40, PRAV 261, SS.IX.TRAA 212. (2) To find fault: SS.VII.VDG 163.

CRITIQUE (sb.) A work of criticism which evaluates and judges a literary work: I.HAR 211 (Watson: earliest recorded use of word from French except for Wycherly to Mulgrave, 20 Aug. 1677 referring to same treatise by Rymer; word was no doubt current), 218, II.LWW1 52, 53, DCOPS 84, LWW2 174, 174, PF 292, SS.VI.DTC 253.

CURIOSA FELICITAS That curious or "secret happiness" in Horace's choice of words. He chose exactly the appropriate word according to style and meaning.

Dryden attributes words which fulfill this quality to chance, and says, "These hits of words a true poet often finds as I may say, without seeking; but he knows their value when he finds them" (II. 207). See Happy, Stroke. II.PS 31, PPBPP 206.

CURIOUS (adj.) (1) Irregular, odd (as a curious choice of words): I.PAM 99. (2) Artful, elaborate: I.PEL 153. Curiously: II.PPV 219. (3) Inquisitive: SS. VIII.PC 227, XVIII.LLd 65. (4) Accurate (and inquisitive): SS.XIII. SAVPMF 311. Curiously: II.PAA 36 (observed). (5) Discriminating, skillful (with overtones of mysterious): SS.XV.AP 229 (art), 236 (workman), 238 (art), 246 (art).

CURRENT ENGLISH The generally accepted speech of Dryden's upper-class England: I.PAM 96.

CUTTING (sb.) Lopping, "synalaepha": II.PEP 165, 165.

D

DECEIT (sb.) (1) The action of imitating nature (the basis of all art). Art deceives us with the appearance of truth, with what is probable (I. 47). The Puritanical argument that art is immoral (aside from subject matter) centers on the point that art is a lie because it deceives. Dryden admits art is a lie, but justifies it by saying that we willingly deceive ourselves, that "the fancy . . . contributes to its own deceit." A writer or artist only helps its operation (I. 163). The act of deceit takes place in the fancy while the judgment is willingly suspended or suppressed. Deceit as an imitation of nature produces pleasure, the first purpose of any work of art, which emanates from probability. The willingness to be deceived by art comes from the desire for this pleasure. Dryden says, "We know we are to be deceived and we desire to be so; but no man ever was deceived but with a probability of truth, for who will suffer a gross lie to be fastened on him" (I. 79). Rymer agrees (Z) 134, "Nothing is more odious in nature than an improbable lye" (Rymer is talking about the "improbabilities" in *Othello*): I.EDP 29, OHP 162, II.PPBPP 186, 193. (2) A technique or device of art which deceives: SS.XVII.APa 367 (coloring deceives the sight), 383 (the art which hides art). (3) A trick, act of deception: II.DAV 231, SS.XVIII.LLd 72.

DECEIVE (v.) To mislead, to cause (someone) to believe what is false. (1) To mislead the fancy by means of art. See Deceit, def. (1). I.EDP 47, 79, 79, PSF 275, SS.VII.VDG 179, 179, XVII.APa 365. (2) To mislead (in general): I.EDP 51, PSF 277, II.LP 5, DCOPS 80, PPBPP 191, 191, DAV 255, SS.V.PAZd 199, XVII.LPd 63, XVIII.LLd 72.

DECEIVING (adj.) Delusive. See Deceit, def. (1). SS.XVII.APa 365 ("The utmost perfection in painting is a deceiving beauty").

DECENCY (sb.) (1) A propriety (such as a correct case, proper usage, etc.) which makes writing acceptable: I.AAHP 197, PAL 223, 224. (2) Decorum (such as proper behavior or speech of a character in accordance to his rank, breeding, etc., or as a writing style appropriate to its subject). See Decorum. I.HAR 217, II.PDS 50, DCOPS 79 (of the stage), 82, 108 (of the theater),

127, SS.IV.DMLM 254 (of behavior), XV.AP 235; Cowley (Spingarn) II. 90; Rymer (Z) 65 ("Poetical decency will not suffer death to be dealt with each other by such persons, whom the laws of duel allow not to enter the lists together"), 110, 117.

DECENT (adj.) Decorous, fitting: II.PPBPP 196, SS.XVII.APa 347. Decently: I.PTL 139 (represented), SS.XV.AP 250 (expressed).

DECEPTION (sb.) See Deceit. (1) The act of being beguiled or misled by one's fancy: I.PSL 105. (2) A trick of art, a technique to beguile the viewer of a painting: SS.XVII.APa 381; Flecknoe (Spingarn) II. 96 ("Scenes [scenery] and machines make the most graceful deception of our sight").

DECORUM (sb.) Dryden does not use this term very often. See Decency, Proper, Propriety, Just. The important word is "just." (1) Propriety of the theater, or in plays. The fitness of all actions, speeches, and scenery to a play's characters and subject. Dryden is more moderate than Rymer, who says, for example, "In poetry no woman is to kill a man, except her quality give her the advantage above him, nor is a servant to kill the master, nor a private man, much less a subject, to kill a king" (Z. 65): I.EDP 56, 63, DECG 172, SS.XV.AP 240, 247; Flecknoe (Spingarn) I. 94; Hobbes (Spingarn) II. 54 ("maintenance of the characters of your persons"), 67 (discretion means decorum); Rymer (Z) 46. (2) Fitness (or appropriateness) of the parts of a literary work to the whole: II.PDS 50; Milton I. 333 (the models for decorum are Aeschylus, Sophocles, and Euripides), III. 239, 332 ("As ye bear any zeal to learning, to elegance, and to that which is called decorum in the writing of praise, especially on such a noble argument" [Parliament is a noble subject; therefore, use noble words when talking about it]), IV. 286 (after learning the genres of poetry [epic, dramatic, lyric], young scholars should learn about laws, decorums, and the proper masterpieces), V. 84, VII. 307. (3) Literary propriety (in a poem) of the parts to the whole and of actions and speeches to the persons: II.PPV 219; Alexander (Spingarn) I. 182, 188; Phillips (Spingarn) II. 267 ("Decorum is the well-management of invention"), 269 (decorum of words should be "of a majesty suitable to the grandeur of the subject"; but not too much so, "for fear of frightening the ladies"); Rymer (Z) 44 (he explains the proper behavior of a king).

DELICACY (sb.) (1) Sensitivity, lightness, refined grace of expression; or a passage which exhibits these qualities. See Delicate, def. (3). "Delicacy" is strongly influenced by French usage. Littré, def. (7), defines *délicatesse* as "Finesse et élégance dans le sentiment littéraire et l'expression." This meaning is not in *OED*: I.POE 263, II.LP 3, PS 20, 27, DCOPS 125, 149 (sublimity of expression is delicate), SS.IV.DMLM 254, VIII.DC 215, XVII.LPd 54, AARHL 101; Alexander (Spingarn) I. 186 ("delicacy of invention"). (2) A term of painting or sculpture. Light, graceful touches in painting, as opposed to strength and magnanimity. This definition is not in *OED*. Littré's def. (3) is "terme de peinture et de sculpture. Execution légère et soignée": SS.XVII.PPBPPd 296, APa 393.

DELICATE (adj.) (1) Overly sensitive in matters of taste. This meaning is not in *OED*, but Dubois-Lagane, in def. (1), defines *délicat* as "D'une sensibilité excessive en matière de goût, de plaisir." Dryden describes Crites (I. 19) as having "somewhat too delicate a taste in wit, which the world have [sic] mistaken in him for ill nature": I.EDP 19, SS.XVII.LPd 70. (2) Describing an acuteness of sensory perception: I.EDP 71. (3) Light, sensitive, finely expressed, refined, elegant, appropriate, and graceful (in literary expressions, turns, diction, raillery). Dryden extensively uses French connotations in this meaning of "delicate." He says, "*Délicat et bien tourné* are the highest commendations which they bestow on a masterpiece" (II. 151). He also says that the French "call [turns] delicate when they are introduced with judgment" (II. 279). Although Dryden's application of "delicate" was not an English usage, neither was it a common seventeenth-century French usage. The usual French definition (according to Cayrou) concerned people rather than literature ("de l'homme qui a le goût sensible aux moindres nuances, et la conscience sensible aux moindres scrupules"), and only Littré records, in def. (6), an applicable seventeenth-century definition ("Finement senti exprimé d'une manière ingénieuse et élégante. Expression délicat. Tour délicat."). Littré also differentiates *délicat* from *délié*, saying "Délicat implique un qualité, un art, un charme": II.DCOPS 136, 151, 153, PF 279; Rymer (Z) 94, 98 ("delicate turn of words"). Delicately: I.PAM 99, II.PS 30, 31. (4) Discreetly exquisite and refined. Not an English meaning. Dubois-Lagane: "raffiné, discret": SS.XIII.SAVPMF 312. (5) Subtle (in fineness of subject matter): SS.XVII. PFAAP 338.

DELIGHT (sb.) (1) Pleasure (as a purpose of art). Dryden postulates two purposes of art, delight and instruction. In his early works, Dryden says delight is more important: "Delight is the chief if not the only end of poesy. Instruction can be admitted but in the second place, for poetry only instructs as it delights" (I. 113). Later, he gives them equal importance in most genres. Profit or instruction becomes most honorable, delight most favorable (to readers and audience). Both become equally necessary. See Horace, *Ars Poetica*, l. 333. See also Pleasure, Instruction. I.EDP 25, 35, 38, 87, DEDP 113, 114, 120, PEL 152, 152, II.DCOPS 127, 132, LL 211, DAV 224, 230, SS.XV.AP 229, 250; Shadwell (Spingarn) II. 153 ("To delight is secondary to instruction"), 153. Delightful: II.LL 214. (2) Pleasure: I.PRL 3, EDP 62, PAM 98, 101, PrSL2 109, 109, DEDP 113, 114, 115, 119, PT 135, PEL 146, GCT 258, II.PS 21, PAA 35, DCOPS 75, 76, 130, 130, 147, 149, PPBPP 193, 194, LL 211, PPV 217, DAV 229, SS.V.PAZd 193, XV.AP 225, 232, 240, 243, 248, PNOEM 389, XVII.APa 389. Delightful: I.EDP 30 (suspense), 47, 71, PAM 98, DEDP 115, HAR 213 (representation), GCT 245, 245, II.LP 4, PS 22, PAA 36 (entertainment), 36, DCOPS 127, PPBPP 200, SS.XIV. DAVd 182, XVII.PPBPPd 299, PFAAP 337. Delightfully: I.PAM 98, GCT 245.

DELIGHT (v.) (1) To please (as one of the purposes of poetry): I.PAM 99, II.PS 26, SS.XVIII.CPd 25. (2) To please, to cause pleasure: I.DEDP 116, EAZ 193, AAHP 197, 200, GCT 245, II.DCOPS 131, PPBPP 194, PPV 218, DAV 233, SS.IV.DCG 12, XV.AP 236, PNOEM 408, XVII.DPL 13. Delighting: II.PEP 162.

DEPLORED (adj.) Hopeless, lamentable: SS.XV.PNOEM 399 (understanding).

DESIGN (sb.) Design as part of the rhetorical divisions of inventio, dispositio, and elocutio always falls under the heading of dispositio, whether Dryden uses it as a verb or a substantive. Hence, it assumes a corresponding position in theories of painting (invention, design, coloring). Literary use from French *dessein*. See Disposition, Invention. (1) A preconceived plan of action; a preconceived attack (in argumentation); intent: I.PRL 9, EDP 79, 89, DEDP 112, 125, 128, PEL 144, OHP 164, PA 184, 188, LD 208, PSF 278, 279, II.PS 29, PDS 45, 58, PE 63, CP 66, DCOPS 78, 89, 89, 91, 129, 150, PEP 159, 167, LL 211, DAV 234, 253, SS.II.DIE 288, VI.DTC 253, VII.VDG 165, 168, 202, VIII.PC 219, XIII.SAVPMF 316, XIV.DAVd 166, XVII. PFAAP 340. (2) The plan of the action of a literary work, especially a play or poem; a preconceived outline of what will happen in a literary work: I.EDP 33, 45, 47, 48, 50, 59, 61, 61, 61, 64, 65, 89, DEDP 128, 129, PT 134, 134, PTL 141, PEL 154, OHP 158, 158, 159, PAZ 191, 191, 191, AAHP 196, 197, HAR 211, 213, 215, 216, 216, 216, 219, PAL 222, PrO 235, GCT 241, 246, 247, 247, 249, POE 266, 271, II.PAA 36, 36, 36, 37, 43, PDS 50, 50, 51, 51, PE 62, 62, DCOPS 82, 82, 83, 83, 84, 86, 90, 92, 114, 122, 144, 145, 145, 145, 145, 146, 146, 147, PEP 161, 162, 166, LWW2 174, PPBPP 186, 186, 188, 195, 203, 204, 204, 204, 207, DAV 223, 242, 242, PF 275, 276, 280, 280, SS.VII.VDG 155, VIII.DKA 135, PC 220, IX.TRAA 209, X.PHP 117, XIII. SAVPMF 316, XIV.DAVd 163, 186, 187, 188, XV.AP 236, 239, 252, XVII. DPL 16, LPd 48, 68, XVIII.CPd 31; Davenant (Spingarn) II. 18, 18 (possible first usage), 19; Hobbes (Spingarn) II. 67 ("That every part of the poem be conducing, and in good order placed, to the end and design of the poet"); Rymer (Z) 48. (3) A part of the main plan of action in a play or poem (a person or an underplot, for example): I.EDP 52, 55, 59, 59, 59, 74, PAM 98, PEL 146, 155, GCT 244, II.PAA 41, DCOPS 92, DAV 224, SS.XV.AP 240; Shadwell (Spingarn) II. 148. (4) A model, a pattern: SS.XVII.DPL 17, AP 393. (5) The design or drawing, specifically as the second part of painting (invention, design, coloring): II.PPBPP 196, 203, 203, 208, DAV 252. (6) The plan or outline (a drawing) of a painting; the disposition of parts of a painting: II.DCOPS 80, PPBPP 182, 188, 197, 199, 203, 203, 203, 203, SS. XIV.DAVd 189, XVII.APa 383, 391, 393. (7) The plan of a part of a painting: II.PPBPP 185.

DESIGN (v.) See Draw. (1) To plan something in advance, to intend: I.EDP 74, 75, DECG 173, POE 262, II.LP 5, PS 29, PDS 46, DCOPS 78, DAV 232, 252, SS.XI.DF 203, XVIII.PDCW 7. Designing (pejorative): II.DCOPS 91. (2) To plan the action of a play or poem: I.PSL 106, PT 135, PEL 154, GCT 248, POE 266, PSF 274, II.PDS 44, 48, DCOPS 82, 82, PF 275, SS.V. PAZd 199, VIII.PC 219, IX.TRAA 213, XIV.DAVd 163, 187, XV.AP 237, 241. Designing: II.DCOPS 108, 145, SS.VIII.DLT 374. (3) To plan one part of a play or poem (where there are at least several): I.PSL 107, PTL 139, OHP 165, SS.VII.VDG 148, 153, VIII.DKA 135, X.PRLaici 32. (4) To plan and draw (as in a painting): II.PPBPP 187. Designing: SS.XVII.APa 353. (5) To plan a building or one of its parts (in architecture): SS.XV.AP 248.

DESIGNMENT (sb.) The action of planning a painting: I.EDP 80.

DETORT (v.) To pervert, to turn aside from a purpose. (Malone and Scott read "distorted." All subsequent texts have "detorted," which is in the original text.): SS.X.PRLaici 17.

DIALOGUE (sb.) (1) A literary form consisting of a conversation between two or more people (as Dryden's "Essay of Dramatic Poesy"): I.EDP 15, DEDP 123, 123, 128, DECG 171, II.LWW1 53, DCOPS 114, 115, 115, 115, LL 210, 211, 212, SS.XVII.PPBPPd 293, XVIII.LLd 62, 67, 70, 70, 71, 71, 72, 78, 81. (2) Conversation in a play or other literary work: I.EDP 78, 79, 86, 87, 87, PAM 99, DEDP 112, HAR 213, II.DCOPS 97, TCDD 170, LL 212, 212, 212, DAV 229, 233, SS.VIII.DAm 10, XIV.DAVd 190.

DICTION (sb.) Words and expressions. In poetry it can also refer to "harmony of numbers" (II. 275). Dryden introduces "diction" as if it were an innovation, although it is in Sidney's "Defence of Poesy." *OED* first records use as 1700. Dryden applies "diction" to both poetry and prose: II.PS 24, 31, DCOPS 118, 131, 153, LL 214 (prose), 214 (prose), DAV 248, PF 275, 278, 291. "Dictio" (words and discourses): I.HAR 219.

DISCOURSE (sb.) (1) A dialogue, or conversation (containing dispute or argument), such as the "Essay of Dramatic Poesy": I.PRL 9, EDP 13, 16, 17, 19, 58, 78, PAM 99, DEDP 112, 123, 124, 124, DECG 181, 182, PA 186, HAR 219, 220, GCT 249, 254, 256, II.LL 211, 212, PF 290, SS.XIV.DAVd 171, XVII.LPd 23, 23, XVIII.LLd 67. (2) An argument in the form of a speech (as part of a conversation): I.EDP 32, 42, 43, 44, 54, 60, 61, 62, 63, 81, 85, 91, 92, II.PF 284, SS.XVII.LPd 29, 30. (3) A set speech or disquisition presenting an idea or ideas from a particular point of view (in the form of an essay, satire, etc.) in either poetry or prose: I.PAM 100, DEDP 121, PEL 145, AAHP 205, GCT 248, II.LP 12, LWW1 55, DCOPS 95, 106, 106, 109, 110, 116, 125, 128, 139, 145, 155, PPBPP 193, 199, 207, LL 212, DAV 257, PF 271, 273, 274, SS.II.DIE 287, V.DA 8, VI.DTC 253, VII.VDG 169, 207, X.PRLaici 11, XIV.DAVd 177, 181, XV.AP 226, 228, 230, 232, 237, 246, 247, XVII.AARHL 100, DPWDY 210, 210, 211, PPBPPd 292, 299, APa 345. (4) Conversation: I.DECG 180, LD 208, PAL 226, GCT 255, II.LP 3, SS.IX.EWTM 424, XVII.LPd 63. (5) Expression of thoughts through words (in poetry and prose): I.AAHP 203, 203.

DISCOURSE (v.) (1) To speak or write (on a particular subject): SS.XIV.DG 4. (2) To present an idea (in a formal speech): Discoursing: I.PAZ 191. (3) To converse (with overtones of to argue and to dispute): Discoursing: SS.XVII.LPd 25.

DISCOURSIVE (adj.) Conversational, in the form of dialogue: I.PRL 8 (scenes), EDP 87 (scenes).

DISCOVERY (sb.) (1) Strang: Connected with denouement. *OED* first recorded use is Chambers' *Cyclopedia* 1727–51. See Unravelling, Untying, Catastrophe. The uncovering or revealing of the plot (a particular point in a play): I.EDP 33, 76, II.PDS 51, PPBPP 207, SS.XIV.DAVd 200. (2) The action of uncovering or exposing something (either to the eyes or to the mind) in a play or elsewhere: I.EDP 74, II.LWW2 174, PPBPP 194, SS.VIII.DLT 374, 375.

DISPOSITION (sb.) (1) From "dispositio," the second of Quintilian's five parts of oratory, from *Institutio Oratorio* (III, iii). The "connection of [the] parts" of a work of art to make a harmonious whole, the arrangement of the ideas which come from invention, the ordering of ideas to make them clear to a reader or audience. To design is to arrive at disposition; and "design" is usually synonymous with "disposition." Where "design" and "disposition" differ (as on II. 8 and 242), "design" has more to do with a poet's or writer's purpose, with the accomplished and harmonious whole; whereas "disposition" pertains to the actual arrangement of the invented ideas, with the action of ordering or arranging. See also Judgment. I.HAR 219 (design is the same as disposition), II.LP 5, 8, 10, LWWl 52, PPBPP 195, DAV 242, PF 275, 280, 291, SS.XIV.DAVd 185, 186, XVII.APa 393; Jonson 38; Hobbes (Spingarn) II.54 (the first part of a work of art), 54. (2) Personality or inclination of a person (with overtones of astrological influence): I.HAR 214, SS.XIII.SAVPMF 312, 315, 315, XIV.DAVd 188, XVII.APa 349.

DIVERSIFY (v.) To differentiate, to show difference (as an author diversifies "the recitative, the lyrical part, and the chorus" of an opera): II.DAV 226, SS.XVII.PPBPPd 296, APa 359. Diversifying: II.PAA 39.

DIVINE FURY "Furor poeticus," godlike, poetic inspiration: II.PPBPP 205, SS. XV.AP 251.

DIVISION (sb.) "Variations on a musical theme" (Watson's Gloss). Dryden is describing Cowley's odes: I.POE 268 (on the groundwork).

DOUBLE ACTION of a play. Two plots appearing side by side in the same play. One of the actions is usually subservient to the other. Dryden speaks as if "double action" can also be thought of as two lines of argument in satire. See Double Tale. I.GCT 243, 243, SS.VIII.DLT 375, 375.

DOUBLE RHYME What Dryden calls "female rhyme" (II. 40). An example might be "pother" and "bother" when they each end adjoining lines, to form a couplet. See Female Rhyme. II.PAA 40, 40, DCOPS 147.

DOUBLE TALE See Double Action. The "doppia favola" of Mascardi in *Prose Vulgari* (1630): II.DCOPS 145.

DRAMA (sb.) (1) The branch of literature which comprises works to be performed on the stage or to be read as if they were to appear on a stage; the dramatic art: I.EDP 24, 27, 41, 66, 69, 79, PAM 99, OHP 159, 159 (stage poetry), 162, II.PDS 47, PEP 161, 168, PPBPP 195, DAV 226, 226, 228, 229, 230, SS.VII.VDG 162, VIII.PC 227. (2) A play: I.EDP 37, 45, 61, PSL 107, DEDP 125, 126, PEL 150, OHP 158, DECG 179, II.PAA 35, 37, 41, DCOPS 96, 101, 109, 110, 145, PPBPP 207, SS.VII.VDG 209, VIII.DLT 374. (3) A kind of play, such as a tragicomedy, a tragedy, a comedy: I.EDP 45 (tragicomedy), II.PPBPP 199, DAV 228, 229, 231, 233.

DRAPERY (sb.) (1) The clothing of a human figure in a painting or sculpture: II.PPBPP 196, SS.XVII.APa 355, 359, 361, 361, 361. (2) Figures or colors of rhetoric: Davenant (Spingarn) II. 17.

DRAW (v.) To design, to image. To draw is closely associated with design. See Design and Drawing. See also SS.XVII. 297 for connection of draw and dispositio. Drawing follows invention in the process of constructing a work of art. (1) To write, to compose, to arrange: I.EDP 32, DEDP 129, SS.VII.VDG 203 (Dryden "drew the scenery of the whole play"). Drawing: II.DCOPS 73. (2) To depict, to image, to describe (in either writing or painting): I.PAM 101 (a pun, using the meaning "to pull"), PrT 136, AAHP 204, PAL 222, PO 233, GCT 249, 252, II.PE 61, PEP 159, 167, PPBPP 184, 185, 190, 197, 202, DAV 228, 238, LCM 266, SS.IV.DCG 17, V.PAZd 197, VII.VDG 154, 203, 203, IX.TRAA 213, EWTM 422, X.PHP 109, XVII.DPL 16, PPBPPd 296, XVIII.LLd 73. Drawing: I.PAZ 190, POE 267, II.PS 19, PDS 47, SS.II. DIE 287, XVII.PPBPPd 294 (in either writing or painting). (3) To contract, to pull together (and thus focus on something more exactly): I.DEDP 128, II.DCOPS 91 (something "drawn into example"), SS.VIII.DKA 134. (4) To withdraw, to cease an attack (in argumentation): I.PEL 150 ("to draw home"; to prepare to defend oneself). (5) To persuade (people), to entrance an audience by an argument, or its presentation: I.PrO 235, GCT 256, II.DCOPS 113. (6) To extract (from): II.LP 12 ("arguments . . . drawn from reason"), 12 ("arguments . . . drawn from wit"), PDS 51 (to draw specific characteristics from particular people for literary entertainment), DCOPS 149 ("comparisons drawn from empires, and from monarchs"), PPBPP 185 (to draw ideas from the mind), DAV 226 ("rules of imitating nature which Aristotle drew from Homer's *Iliad* and *Odyssey*"), SS.VI.DKK 10, VIII.DLT 374 ("manners are . . . drawn from nature"), XVII.PPBPPd 292. (7) To sketch, to outline (as a term in painting): I.POE 272, II.DCOPS 78, 94, 137 ("to draw a full face," with no shadowing), DAV 248 ("to draw a battle"), PF 278, SS.XVII.PPBPPd 294, 297, APa 353. Drawing: SS.XVII.PPBPPd 294, APa 263. (8) To pull, to bring into line: I.GCT 241 ("I have drawn his English nearer our time"). Drawing: II.DAV 253. (9) To extend, to lengthen (to draw out): II.DAV 257. (10) To debase, to lower (to draw down a style): II.PPV 220.

DRAWING (sb.) (1) Design, the second part of painting (the first being invention; the third being coloring): II.PPBPP 196, 203. (2) The original sketch of a painting, before the colors are laid on: SS.XVII.APa 377.

DRIVE (v.) (1) To propel, to carry on, to push: I.EDP 29 (an action of a play is driven on by a writer), II.LP 7 (to focus material in a book on one thing), II.DCOPS 131 (Juvenal drives his reader along with him by his rhetoric), 145. (2) To mold, to work over (a thought) (not in *OED*): Driving: I.PAM 98.

E

EASY (adj.) (1) Without difficulty, free from difficulties: I.PRL 6, EDP 74, OHP 159, GCT 244, II.LP 8, DCOPS 154, 155, SS.XV.AP 251. Easiest: I. PO 234. Easiness: I.PRL 8, EDP 90, II.PS 32. (2) Describing a witty, sophisticated, graceful style of verse or prose, free from harsh and complicated words, cacophonous sounds, and complex thoughts. An easy style approximates the cultivated, well-bred language of polite society's conversation. Ideally, an easy style lacks effort, ostentation, obscurity, pedanticism, ardent passion, or any other extremes of behavior, thought, and expression. It is a familiar style. Good examples of easy prose are Dorimant's speeches in "easy" George Etherege's *Sir Fopling Flutter*; an example of easy verse is Waller's "Go Lovely Rose." The style is identified with the court and is in part a reaction against the hard lines of poets like Donne and Cleveland: II.LP 5, 12, 12, LWW1 53, DCOPS 94, TCDD 170, PF 290, SS.XIV.DG 4, DAVd 162. Easy words: I.EDP 25, SS.XV.AP 228. Easy language: I.EDP 40. Easy rhyme: I.EDP 82, SS.XV.AP 233. Easy verse: I.PAM 95, SS.XV.AP 227. Easy conversation: I.DECG 182. Easy thoughts: SS.XV.AP 240. Easier: SS.XV.AP 244. Easiness: I.DECG 182, PA 187, II.PEP 162, 164, DAV 247, SS.XVII.LPd 30; Suckling (Spingarn) I. 191; Sprat (Spingarn) II. 128 ("easy vigour" of Cowley's poetry); Rymer (Z) 12, 127.

ECLOGUE (sb.) A pastoral dialogue (in the genre of the pastoral). Dryden usually means a pastoral dialogue by Virgil. Only in SS.XV. 231, 232 does he not refer to Virgil: I.EDP 39, AAHP 201, II.PS 30, DCOPS 131, PPV 218, 218, 219, 219, SS.XV.AP 231, 232; Hobbes (Spingarn) II. 55 ("Eclogues . . . are but essayes and parts of an entire poem" [of a heroic poem]).

ECONOMY (sb.) Management, organization (especially of the fable or action in a work of art). It is concerned with disposition and is therefore a product of the judgment. See Judgment, Disposition, Design, Draw. II.DAV 225, SS. XIV.DAVd 185; Jonson 38; Milton I. 333, XVIII. 232; Rymer (Z) 20 ("In the contrivance and oeconomy of the play, reason is always principally to be consulted").

EFFEMINACY (sb.) See Masculine. (1) Unmanly weakness: I.GCT 260. Effeminate: I.GCT 252. (2) Kind of pronunciation. Effeminacy occurs when consonants are not enunciated clearly and hard enough, and the vowels are not given full quantities. Dryden says, "The effeminacy of our pronunciation (a defect common to us, and to the Danes) and our scarcity of female rhymes, have left the advantage of musical composition for songs, though not for recitative, to our neighbours" (II. 38, see also SS.VI. 252): II.PAA 38. Effeminate: SS.VI.DTC 252. (3) Describing Seneca's style as opposed to Plutarch's. A style relying more on flights of fancy than the discrimination of judgment: SS.XVII.LPd 75.

ELEGANCE (sb.) A quality contained in that which is tastefully correct, smooth, delicate, simple, well-bred, and gracefully refined or ornamental. "Elegance" usually refers to words. Elegance of words is the opposite of vulgarity and expresses an author's good breeding. Elegance is primarily a quality of elocutio in writing, and coloring in painting. It is an ornamental quality. (1) Of words: II.PS 31, PPBPP 206, DAV 235, 246, SS.XIV.DAVd 204. (2) Of expression: II.PPBPP 201, DAV 242; Milton III. 31 (a "virtuoso" is "a lover of elegance"), 223, 303 (in "what judgment, wit, or elegance was my share" [elegance is a kind of eloquence]), 332, 342; Wilmot (Spingarn) II. 283 ("for elegance sake, sometimes allay the force of epithets; 'twill soften the discourse"). (3) Of language: II.DAV 248, SS.VI.DTC 251, XVII.LPd 75; Sprat (Spingarn) II. 112, 132. (4) Of poetry and music: II.PAA 38, DCOPS 136. (5) Of design (of a painting): SS.XVII.APa 349.

ELEGANCY (sb.) See Elegance. An elegancy is any particular trait or well-used stylistic device which helps give a style elegance. (1) Of words: I.EDP 31, 39. (2) Of expression: II.PAA 40, PEP 164, PPBPP 203. Jonson 34, 34, 35, 47, 87, 88, 89; Phillips (Spingarn) II. 271 (an elegancy is artificial). (3) Of language: II.PDS 46, DCOPS 84. (4) Of numbers (verse): II. DCOPS 130.

ELEGANT (adj.) Describing a person, a style, an object, etc., which has within him or it the quality of elegance. See Elegance. See also Art. "Artful" can describe something rough, and refers more to rhetoric. "Elegant" is more a term of aesthetics. (1) Describing a writer's style (i.e., Petronius, Sir Charles Sedley, Virgil, Horace): I.AAHP 160, PA 185, II.CP 70, DCOPS 154, DAV 234, 246. Elegantly: SS.XVI.AARLSFX 11; Milton III. 157, 191, 234, 328 (describing "a just cadence which scans easily"), IV. 214, 286, 295, 300, X. 251, XVIII. 308, 316; Phillips (Spingarn) II. 257, 266. (2) Describing words: I.AAHP 206, II.DAV 250, 252. Elegantly: I.AAHP 207, SS.VIII.PC 222. (3) Describing expressions and forms of expression: II.LWW1 53, DCOPS 150 (turns), PPBPP 203, DAV 243, SS.VIII.DC 215; Peachum (Spingarn) I. 125, 128; Rymer (Z) 127. (4) Describing an ornamented, imitative translation of the original which de-emphasizes metaphrastic qualities Dryden describes as "familiar, clear, and instructive": II.PPBPP 183; Wolsely (Spingarn) III. 23 ("elegantly adapted" means "lively" [lifelike]). (5) Describing poems: II. DCOPS 114, 115. (6) Perfect as opposed to natural (in regard to ideas used in painting): SS.XVII.PPBPPd 293, 297. (7) To Milton, "elegant" sometimes has prurient connotations of seductive smoothness: Milton II. 296 (after Adam and Eve have eaten the apple, Adam sees Eve as "elegant"), III. 329 ("those . . . of soft and delicious temper . . . will not so much look upon truth herself, unless they see her elegantly drest").

ELEGIAC POETRY One of the lesser poetic genres. Elegiac poetry is poetry of lamentation, many times funeral poetry. See Elegy. II.DCOPS 81.

ELEGY (sb.) A poem of lamentation on death or love's vicissitudes. It is one of the lesser genres. Dryden says only that it is far below heroic poetry (see order of genres on II. 81 and 238 where the "light and trifling" French language is "more proper for sonnets, madrigals, and elegies, than heroic poetry"). See also Elegiac Poetry. I.EDP 20, PA 185, POE 263, 263, 264, 266, II.PE 61, DAV 238, SS.XIV.DAVd 176, XV.AP 232, 232, 234.

ELEVATE (v.) (1) To raise an audience in mind and feeling, to exalt minds to great, important, and noble thoughts: I.PTL 139 (by harmony of words), GCT 243. (2) To heighten an author's style. An elevated style is one raised to a high, lofty, exalted, refined pitch by the significancy and the sound of the words used. See Sublime. I.EDP 24, PSF 278, II.PS 31, SS.IX.EWTM 431 (his style), X.PRLaici 33.

ELEVATED (ppl. adj.) (1) Describing the thought or ideas of an author, or character in a play, as profoundly serious and important or as improving upon nature: I.EDP 74, 78, 89, DEDP 118, II.DCOPS 84, 130, PPBPP 194. (2) Describing the mind of a writer as unconfined in genius, and exalted, great, and comprehensive in a high, noble way. See Sublime. I.POE 271 (elevated genius), II.DCOPS 74.

ELEVATION (sb.) (1) A high flight of style: II.PS 32. (2) The act of exalting or raising the thought and style of writing: II.PAA 40 (of fancy). (3) The lofty, detached, Olympian stance of an objective writer: II.DCOPS 124. (4) In general, a high, exalted style, using sounding and significant words, combined with profound thought. See Sublime. II.DAV 240, 247. (5) High level of intensity, as an emotion pitched at an uncommonly high intensity (an indication of mental illness): SS.XV.PNOEM 406 (of fancy).

ELOCUTION (sb.) The art and act of manipulating and adorning thoughts with words and expressions (in writing). It comes from elocutio which is the third of Quintilian's five parts of rhetoric. In Dryden, elocution pertains to writing, not to the modern ideas of speech and delivery. As embodied in a work of art, it is one of the three happinesses of the imagination (I. 98), and is the last perfection of art or beauty. See Beautiful, Expression, Ornament, Last Perfection, Last Rank of Beauties. I.EDP 39, PAM 97, 98, 99, PEL 154, AAHP 203, II.LP 10, DCOPS 153, SS.XIII.SAVPMF 310, XV.PNOEM 399; Hobbes (Spingarn) II. 54 ("expression" means "elocution"); Cowley (Spingarn) II. 90.

ELOQUENCE (sb.) (1) Effective, forceful, fluent style or manner of expression (in conjunction with sound thoughts). "Eloquence" concerns primarily the way words are arranged. Polybius has great thought without force of expression and therefore lacks eloquence, but Seneca, whom Dryden says is witty without soundness of thought, has a "false eloquence": I.DECG 179, II.LP 11, PAA 37, CP 69, LL 214, PF 276, SS.II.DIE 288, V.PAZd 190, VIII.DKA 134 (in argument), XVII.LPd 76, PPBPPd 293, 297, XVIII.CPd 29, 31, 32, LLd 64, 80, 81. (2) Style, manner of expression (in general): I.PT 133, II.LP 10, 10, PF 281; Milton III. 186; Cowley (Spingarn) II. 80 ("Wit and eloquence are employed by the divine science [poetry] basely in flattery of great persons"); Sprat (Spingarn) II. 115 (eloquence should be used only by good men); Glanville (Spingarn) II. 276 ("A bastard kind of eloquence consists in affectations of wit and finery, flourishes, metaphors, and cadencies").

ELOQUENTLY (adv.) Appropriately, expressively, fluently, clearly, effectively: II.DCOPS 102.

EMBLEM (sb.) (1) A symbol, a parallel, a type: SS.IX.DAM 88 (London, after the fire and plague is "a great emblem of the Deity"). (2) A personification or a symbolic representation of an abstraction in a literary work: SS. XIII.SAVPMF 311 (Iris, in the *Aeneid*, is "the emblem of inconstancy").

ENGINE (sb.) (1) A dramatic cause (in a play) which moves the emotions of the audience: I.EP 236 (pity and terror). (2) Mechanical contrivance, as a lever: I.GCT 247. (3) Epic "machine": II.DCOPS 89 ("would have made the ministry of angels as strong an 'engine' for the working up of heroic poetry").

ENGLISH HEROIC A line of iambic pentameter in English. See Heroic. II.PS 32.

ENTHUSIASM (sb.) (1) True poetic inspiration or possession by a supernatural power which reveals itself in what a poet describes: I.AAHP 203, II.DAV 249. (2) False inspiration, fancied poetic fervor: SS.XVII.DPL 16; Rymer (Z) 10.

ENTHUSIASTIC (adj.) Describing parts of poetry which a poet composed while being inspired by the divine furor which elevates poetry. Dryden seldom uses "enthusiasm," and "enthusiastic" (or "zeal") in his criticism. The more widely used seventeenth-century meaning of "enthusiasm" applies to the fanaticism of extreme religious sects, their "inner lights" which they thought were divinely inspired (Dryden regarded this as false inspiration). See Meric Casaubon's *Of Enthusiasm* (1655), and Dryden's comment on Shaftesbury's allies in *Absalom and Achitophel* (l. 530). See Inspiration, Fury. I.OHP 160 (parts).

ENTRANCE (sb.) (1) Protasis, the first part of a play, the explanatory section of a play. See Act, Preparation. I.EDP 33. (2) The action of an actor coming on stage: I.EDP 34, 36, 55, 55, 84, PO 233, GCT 240, II.PPBPP 185.

EPIC (adj.) See also Heroic. (1) Describing a poem, such as the *Iliad* or *Aeneid*, written in a grave, majestical, sublime style, inculcating a moral, and displaying a primarily virtuous hero, who is depicted as having one prime virtue, such as magnanimity, constancy, patience, and pity. An epic poem must elicit admiration; it employs supernatural machinery; it is written for the good of all men; it has great scope. To Dryden it is the most important kind of poem, a poem in the highest ranked genre of poetry. Most of the time, "epic poem" is the same as "heroic poem." See Heroic, Epopee. I.EDP 87, PAM 95 (here, Dryden differentiates an "epic" from a "historical poem" in terms of "unity of action"), OHP 160, AAHP 199, II.DCOPS 84, 85, 86, 90, PEP 166, PPBPP 186, 187, 188, 188, 188, 193, 199, DAV 224, 225, 226, 226, 227, 228, 228, 228, 229, 230, 231, 238, 247, PF 275, 293, SS.IV.DCG 16, VI.DTC 250, XIV.DAVd 200; Hobbes (Spingarn) II. 55, 64 ("The delight of an epic poem consisteth not in mirth, but in admiration"). (2) Describing a genre of poetry of which an epic poem is a part. It is related to historic and panegyric genres of poetry. It is sometimes supplanted by heroic: I.PAM 101, II.DAV 224, PF 290 (Chaucer's "Palamon and Arcite" is epic). (3) Describing verse which partakes of the qualities of an epic poem and is able to carry the magnificence of an epic poem. It is elevated and majestic. It need not be found in epic poetry, but may merely designate a kind of verse or poetry different from lyric or dramatic: I.PRL 7 (*Cooper's Hill* is "epic poesy"), EDP 17, 24, 41, 86, 87, OHP 162, GCT 245 (differentiated from "dramatic poetry"), II.PAA 35, DCOPS 82, 87, PPBPP 185, 199, 202, 203, DAV 230, 233, 238, SS.XV.AP 252. (4) Describing a poet, such as Homer or Virgil, who has written an epic poem celebrating a great hero of history or tradition: I.EDP 34, II.DCOPS 96, PPBPP 185, 204, PF 275. (5) Describing drama. This is a unique use, since Dryden usually uses "heroic poesy" for heroic or epic drama: I.PTL 142.

EPIC (sb.) "Epic" is usually an adjective. Here it means an epic poem or epic poetry: II.DCOPS 96, 96, PPBPP 195, SS.XV.AP 241 (Here the heading may or may not be Dryden's. He is talking about a genre called "epic").

EPISODE (sb.) (1) A secondary or minor plot in a play (see Under-plot and By-concernment): I.HAR 215, 216, PAL 222, PO 233, 234, II.PDS 51, DCOPS 95, PEP 161. (2) An "underaction" or minor plot in an epic: II.PS 23, DCOPS 82, 92, 96, PPBPP 188, 199, 199, DAV 224, 226, 242, PF 275, SS.XIII.SAVPMF 314, XIV.DAVd 186, 199. (3) An "underaction" in a narrative poem: SS.X.PHP 117. (4) A series of events in an epic which is part of the main action (as Dido and Aeneas in the *Aeneid*): SS.XIV.DAVd 176, 181, 182, 182, 188.

EPOPEE (sb.) Epic poetry as a genre. "Epopee" is a substantive form of "epic." See Epic. II.DAV 229, 232, 233.

EQUALITY OF NUMBERS The condition of having the same number of syllables or the same meter in each line of verse in a poem: I.PTL 141, II.PF 281.

EQUIPAGE (sb.) The social situation, condition, station (of a character in a play): I.PO 233.

ESSAY (sb.) (1) A general prose disquisition or inquiry (on or into any subject). See Preface. I.EDP 10 ("Of Dramatic Poesy: An Essay"), DEDP 123, 127, 130, OHP 156, 162, DECG 169, 169, II.LWW1 52, DCOPS 74, PPBPP 194, 207, SS.XVII.LPd 76. (2) An attempt, an endeavor, a trial: I.OHP 160, II.PS 33, LWW2 175, PPV 218, PF 270, SS.VI.DTC 253, VII.VDG 146, XV.PHC 409. (3) A poem of inquiry (modestly called an "essay"). Roscommon and Mulgrave, for example, call their poems, on translation and poetry, "essays": II.ETV 14, 15, PS 19, DAV 230, 257.

EXACT (adj.) (1) Perfect, as a work of art resembles ideal nature rather than nature itself. See Nature. I.POE 272, II.DCOPS 141, SS.VII.VDG 162, XV.AP 240. Exactly: I.EDP 87, II.LP 8, SS.XIV.DAVd 176. Exactness: I.EDP 80, PSL 105, OHP 158. (2) Precise, as something which exists in its entirety or fullness, with clearly defined boundaries: II.DCOPS 152 (sense), PPBPP 193 (rules), 204 (words), DAV 234, PF 269, SS.VIII.DKA 132, XIV.DAVd 163 (method), 171 (judgment), XV.PNOEM 402, XVII.APa 357. Exactly: II.DCOPS 96, 140, SS.X.PHP 109. Exactest: I.PrSL 107, SS. XV.AP 229 (sense), 233. Exactness (of writing): I.EDP 43 (according to the rules), 56, DEDP 119, OHP 160, II.LP 2, PS 31, LWW1 55, PEP 156, DAV 237, LCM 266, SS.VI.DTC 247, VII.VDG 159, XVII.LPd 40 (of method), DHL 83, HL 103, XVIII.CPd 24.

EXACTLY (adv.) (See Exact for other citations.) In a precise way; to write in precise imitation of another author; to write according to neoclassical rules; or to write according to the practice of the Ancients: I.EDP 66 (formed), 86, 92, II.PDS 48, PPV 221, DAV 256, SS.XVI.AARLSF 11.

EXAMEN (sb.) "A critical analysis [of a play]" (Watson's Gloss). The term comes from Corneille's *Théâtre* (1660), although H. Holland first used it in English in 1606: I.EDP 66, 70, PT 133.

EXAMINE (v.) (1) To edit a literary work; to correct the outlines of a painting: I.PRL 9, SS.XVII.APa 383. (2) To conduct a critique, to analyze a work of art (either formally or informally): I.EDP 66, OHP 157, II.PF 286, SS. XVII.PFAAP 338, APa 359, 381, 391. Examining: II.DCOPS 83. (3) To criticize a fault in writing: I.DEDP 118. (4) To criticize or conduct a critique on only part of a literary work: I.DEDP 122. (5) To investigate (in general): II.DCOPS 112, SS.VII.VDG 218, XVII.AARHL 95, APa 349. Examining: II. DCOPS 140, SS.XVII.AARHL 100.

FABLE

EXEMPLAR OF THE MIND Idea of perfection as it exists in the mind, not in nature; perfect nature as it exists in one's mind, as opposed to actual nature. See Nature. SS.XVII.PPBPPd 297.

EXPLODE (v.) (1) To reject, to exclude with some vehemence: I.GCT 257. (2) To hoot, to disparage vehemently: II.PDS 44 (an entertainment). (3) To discredit (a belief): II.CP 67, DCOPS 109. Exploding: SS.VII.VDG 146; Davenant (Spingarn) II. 6 ("Exploded words" are out of date, as are many of Spenser's words).

EXPRESSION (sb.) (1) Manner and means of clothing ideas with words as accurately and as admirably as possible. It is identical to elocution, the third of Quintilian's rhetorical categories. In II. 10, Dryden uses "elocution," "style," and "expression" interchangeably: I.EDP 21, 25, PAM 98, 102, DEDP 121, DECG 177, 178, AAHP 201, 203, 203, PO 233, GCT 257, 258, 259, 259, PO 263, 272, 272, PSF 276, 278, II.LP 3, 5, 9, 10, PS 24, 27, 32, PAA 35, 40, PE 61, DCOPS 75, 131, 144, 148, 149, PPBPP 201, 203, 203, 203, 204, LL 215, DAV 234, 242, 243, 251, LET 268, PF 276, 290, SS.IV.DMLM 254, V.DAL 318, XIII.SAVPMF 315, XV.AP 229, 230, 230, 235, XVIII.CPd 24; Milton IV. 157, V. 81, X. 101; Hobbes (Spingarn) II. 54, 62; Rymer (Z) 127, 131 (the fourth part of tragedy [the first three are "fable," "characters," and "thoughts or sence"]), 136 (expression cannot be discussed where there is no "sense or meaning"). (2) A word or a phrase. "Diction" can substitute for "expression" when "expression" is plural. Dryden defines "diction" and "expression" in II. 31: I.EDP 39, PAM 100, DEDP 118, PTL 142, DECG 171, 178, AAHP 199, 207, PAL 223, GCT 239, 248, 260, POE 269, 272, II.PS 19, 20, 23, 25, 30, 31, PAA 34, DCOPS 107, 121, PEP 163, PPBPP 183, 203, 203, 206, 207, 207, PPV 220, PF 273, 274, 279, 293, SS.VI.DKK 7, XI.DF 201, XIV.DAVd 162, 204, XV.AP 228, 240, 250, XVI.DLSFX 6, XVII.PPBPPd 297; Milton VI. 121 (a *bon mot*); Hobbes (Spingarn) II. 63 ("strong lines"). (3) A written or verbal statement (usually in words, but also in painting, gestures, facial characteristics) of description, of idea, or of an emotion. It is usually of an emotion (as "an expression of tenderness"): I.PSL 106, AAHP 197, 198, POE 267, 269, II.LP 5, PS 21, 30, PAA 35, CSE 57, CP 69, DCOPS 81, 93, 130, 153, LJD 179, PPBPP 187, 187, 205, SS.III.DTL 374, VII.VDG 171, 184, 213, VIII.DC 215, PC 221, X.PRLaici 32, XVII.PPBPPd 299, APa 351, 385, XVIII.LLd 71; Jonson 52; Rymer (Z) 39.

EXTRAVAGANCE (sb.) See Absurd, Fustian, Probable, Decorum, Just. (1) Unrestrained excess in a literary work exceeding limits of decorum: I.EDP 72, GCT 239, PSF 276, II.LWW2 174, SS.XV.PNOEM 405. (2) An incident or line in a literary work which exceeds limits of decorum: I.PEL 146, II.DAV 229, SS.XV.PNOEM 408. (3) Actions (in general) which exceed limits of decorum, which exhibit unrestrained excess: I.PEL 150, PA 186. Extravagancy: I.GCT 247, II.DCOPS 137, SS.VII.VDG 167.

F

FABLE (sb.) (1) The plot, the story, the action (of a play). In his discussions of drama, Dryden consistently equates "fable" and "action." (See I. 28,

215, 248. He mentions Aristotle's beginning, middle, and end of a "fable" [I. 217], and elsewhere, while discussing the same allusion to Aristotle, substitutes "action" for "fable" [II. 41].) Dryden, however, makes a distinction between "fable" and "design" in drama. "Design" is the outlines of the "fable" (II. 203); the "fable" is the full story, consisting of all the "episodes," "retrospective glances," etc. See Design, Action. I.EDP 28, HAR 211, 211, 211, 215, 217, 217, GCT 248, 248, II.PAA 41, 42, DCOPS 109, 142, PPBPP 203, SS.VIII.DKA 137, DTL 374, 374; Rymer (Z) 18, 41, 131. (2) Action or story of an epic. Here, since the epic consists of a long story, "design" becomes synonymous with "fable" and "action" (II. 186): I.AAHP 207, II.PPBPP 186, PRAV 262, SS.XIV.DAVd 180, 181, 185, XV.AP 241, 243. (3) Story (in general): II.PDS 41, 42, DCOPS 87, 89, 102, 109, LPe 263, PF 269, 273, 277, 290, SS.VII.VDG 203, XV.PNOEM 408, XVII.AARHL 96, XVIII.LLd 65; Jonson 92, 93, 94.

FABRIC (sb.) The framework, the structure, the body (of a play or other work of art) as it appears from the outside. It is the opposite of "contexture." "Fabric" is often used in conjunction with metaphors of building or raising a structure, a house. God is the architect of the fabric of the universe within which one can analyze the contexture (SS.XVII. 292). The fabric of a work of art emanates from the judgment: I.EDP 74, PSL 105, AAHP 200, HAR 215, PAL 222, GCT 248, II.PAA 43, SS.III.DLT 375, XIV.DAVd 149, XVII. PPBPPd 292.

FACETIOUSNESS (sb.) Urbane pleasantry: II.DCOPS 114.

FACULTY (sb.) A section of the mind which has the power to accomplish certain tasks (such as the imagination, memory, judgment, fancy): I.PRL 8, PAM 98, II.PF 272.

FAIRY KIND OF WRITING The kind of writing that "depends only upon the force of imagination." A kind of writing describing an imaginative world created by the mind, or the fancy: SS.VIII.DKA 136.

FANCIFUL (adj.) See Fancy. (1) Describing someone disposed to indulge himself in the unrestrained exercise of his fancy: I.PRL 2, GCT 254, SS.XV. PNOEM 406. (2) Describing poetry which appeals to the fancy and which is a product of it. That which is "fanciful" lacks contact with nature or reality. Thus it may be whimsical, fantastical, overly romantic, etc.: SS.XV.PNOEM 406.

FANCY (sb.) (1) The faculty which envisions those images and ideas which emanate from invention, which have their origin in the mind as opposed to nature. "Fancy" in this sense is the same as "imagination" (see Imagination, def. 1). The two terms, "imagination" and "fancy," would be always interchangeable except that "fancy" frequently has connotations of being included within "imagination" as that part of the mind which produces whims, idiosyncrasies, and superficial characteristics of style (see def. 2 and 3). "Fancy" or "imagination" in an audience or reader is stimulated by what it reads or by what it hears and sees on a stage. "Fancy" is a lawless faculty which the judgment controls by bringing it in line with nature and common sense, the realities of the world. Uncontrolled fancy is madness. Dryden tries to balance judgment and fancy. Some critics are more extreme. See Judgment, Reason, Imagination, Wit, Invention. I.PRL 2 ("When the 'fancy' was yet in its first work, moving the sleeping images of things towards the light, there to be distinguished, and then either chosen or rejected by the judgment"), 3, 8 ("fancy" and "imagination" are used interchangeably on this page), 8, 9, EDP 22 (and "antithesis" is the product of fancy), 66, 74, 78, 80, 80, 80, 90, 91, 91, 92, 92, PSL 105, 105, PrSL2 109, DEDP 126, 126, PEL 146, 146, 146, 155, 155, 155, OHP 159, 161, 162, DECG 173, 178, 178, 181, 181, 182, PA 187, EAZ 193, PAL 226, GCT 255, 257, 261, 261, POE 265, 272, PSD 275, II.PS 25, 31, PE 61, CP 68, SS.VII.VDG 168, 168, 203, XIV.DG 2, 3, XV.PNOEM 405, 405 ("Men given over to 'fancy' only are little better than madmen . . . but [fancy] when cooled . . . by the 'judgment' produces admirable effects"), 406, 406, 406, XVII.PPBPPd 294, 295, 297; Jonson 52 (Shakespeare "had an excellent fancy"); Milton I. 24, 32, 39 ("Shakespeare is fancy's child"; "fancy" is "invention" of a high, but not the highest, order [divine inspiration is highest]), 105, 110, 358, 365, II. 135 (fancy at its worst produces bad dreams removed from reality), 145, 147 ("fancy forms imaginations, aerie shapes,/Which reason joyning or disjoyning, frames"), 148, 161, 242, 246, 252 ("fancy" is Milton's "internal sight"), III. 93, 168, 323, 328 ("fancy" brings memories to view in the mind), IV. 261, 316 (unconstrained fancy is unhealthy and perverse), 325, V. 40 (the whimsical faculty), 138, 147, 228, 272, VI. 76, X. 117, 321; Reynolds (Spingarn) I. 141 ("the art of painting [is] a frute of the fancy"), 146, 154, 165; Hobbes (Spingarn) II. 54 ("fancy" is the third part of the mind; the first is memory and the second is judgment), 59, 59 ("Fancy begets the ornaments of a poem"), 59, 60 ("Fancy consisteth not so much in motion as in copious imagery discreetly ordered and perfectly registered in the memory"), 60 ("Fancy guided by the precepts of true philosophy has produced all that is beautiful or defensible in building or marvellous in engines and instruments of motion"), 67, 70, 70 ("Men more admire fancy than they do either judgment, or reason, or memory"), 70 ("Elevation of fancy [is] . . . wit"), 70 ("The sublimity of a poet" is in his fancy), 72; Sprat (Spingarn) II. 121, 130 (opposed to judgment; but "invention" is separate), 125 ("[Cowley's] book of poetry . . . ought rather to be esteemed as a probleme of his fancy and invention than as a real image of his judgment"); Shadwell (Spingarn) II. 159 ("Fancy rough-draws, but judgment smooths and finishes"), 159 ("In fancy madmen equal if not excel all others"); Sheffield (Spingarn) II. 287 ("Without judgment, fancy is but mad"); Rymer (Z) 3 (unbridled "fancy" gives "conceptions" which are "monstrous and have nothing of exactness, nothing of resemblance or proportion"; "fancy" must be controlled by "judgment"), 15, 20, 62. (2) The second happiness of the imagination as embodied in a work of art, coming from the faculty which plays with ideas and images. Dryden says that the first happiness is invention, the second fancy, the third elocution. "Invention" is the finding of a thought, "fancy" the variation and molding of the thought, and "elocution" "the art of clothing that thought . . . in apt, significant and sounding words" (I. 98). An audience, or a person in an audience, will perceive a vigorous fancy in a work of art by the way it stimulates his fancy or imagination: 1.PAM 98, 98, 101, 102, DEDP 121, 121, PT 135,

135, PrT 137, PrL 143, AAHP 205, PAL 229, II.PS 32, PAA 4υ, PEP 163, DAV 251, SS.XIV.DG 4, XV.AP 228, 230, 244, PNOEM 399, 405, 406; Milton I. 6, 20; Davenant (Spingarn) II. 3 (exhibited in a poem by "quickness" and "activity"), 22; Shadwell (Spingarn) II. 153; Phillips (Spingarn) II. 266; Rymer (Z) 5. (3) An author's thought, caprice, or whim as exhibited in little idiosyncrasies of his style or in his general style: I.DEDP 118, II.PAA 34 ("Propriety of thought is that 'fancy' which arises naturally from the subject, or which the poet adapts to it"), DCOPS 110, 117, SS.XV.AP 236; Milton III. 450 (a fantasy, a lie), 475, IV. 170 (imaginary scene), 330 (whim), V. 284.

FANCY (v.) To imagine, to invent: Milton II. 296.

FARCE (sb.) (1) A laughable interlude in a serious play: I.EDP 45, 48, GCT 247. (2) A kind of drama, lower than comedy, given completely over to laughter, and whose sole purpose is, by whatever means possible, to make people laugh. It consists of unnatural events and appeals to the fancy alone: I.EDP 78, DEDP 119, 119, 119, PEL 145 ("Farce . . . consists principally of grimaces"), 146 ("Farce . . . consists of forced humours and unnatural events"), 146, 146, 146, II.DCOPS 102, 102, 108, 109, 111, SS.VIII.PC 219, XV.AP 246. (3) A play given over completely to eliciting laughter: I.PT 133, PEL 145, 146, GCT 244 (a farce is not really a play), II.DCOPS 78, 103, 106, 108, 109, 110, 142, PPBPP 190 ("farce is to poetry as a grotesque picture is to painting"), SS.VII.VDG 152, 162, XV.PHC 410.

FEAR (sb.) An emotion or passion having to do with the apprehension of evil threatening one's safety or physical well-being. See Concernment, Terror. (1) An emotion or passion induced in an audience through an example of misfortune presented in the form of a tragedy: I.GCT 243, 245, 245, 245, 246. (2) The emotion felt for a character who is endangered in a tragedy or epic: I.GCT 246, SS.XV.AP 241.

FEMALE RHYME (or "double rhyme," as Dryden also calls it). A rhyme on an accented penultimate and unaccented last syllable, as commonly found in Italian poetry: I.PAM 96, 96, II.PAA 38, 40.

FESCINNINE (adj.) "A gross and rustic kind of raillery in ancient satire" (Watson's Gloss). It is the same as "Saturnian": II.DCOPS 106, 107.

FIGURE (sb.) (1) Any rhetorical turn of expression or thought which is not to be taken literally. In a more restricted sense, "figure" usually means "figure of thought" and it is different from "trope" which is a "figure of speech," and has to do with the arrangement of words. (a) A figure of speech or thought, any nonliteral turn of speech: I.AAHP 203, PSF 278, II.LP 3, 5, PDS 46, DCOPS 144, DAV 242, SS.XV.AP 241, PNOEM 408 ("a new figure of rhetoric"); Cowley (Spingarn) II. 86 ("The figures [in a Pindaric ode] are unusual and bold"); Sprat (Spingarn) II. 130; Phillips (Spingarn) II. 257. (b) A figure of thought: I.DEDP 118, AAHP 200, 201, 201, 202, 202, 203 (figure differentiated from trope, versification, cadence, and turns of thought), 206 (tropes are in the words, figures are in sentences and propositions), GCT 239 (figures go beyond words), II.PE 61 ("the magnificence of words and the force of 'figures' "), DCOPS 118 ("figures" are separate from diction),

118 (a metaphor is a "trope"; a "figure" is something else), 141 (a "figure" is a sentence or parenthesis), PPBPP 204, LL 211 ("irony" is a figure), DAV 235 (a "figure" of thought goes from language to language), PF 275 (words are used to "clothe" figures), SS.VII.VDG 204, X.PHP 112 (an example of a "figure of thought"), XIV.DG 3, DAVd 185, XV.AP 244 ("figures" [thoughts] are "clothed" in "colours" [words]). (2) "Grammatical figure," which has to do with grammatical inflections: I.PAM 95. (3) The evolution of dancers in a movement of a dance: I.EDP 89. (4) Shape, form, outline, characteristics, descriptions (of objects or persons in a poem, play, or painting): I.PAM 99, PAZ 190, II.LP 8, 8, PEP 159, PPBPP 184, 190, 196, 196, 196, 196, 197, 199, 202, 203, 208, PF 278, SS.XIII.SAVPMF 312, XIV.DAVd 188, XV.AP 240, 246, 250, XVII.PPBPPd 293, 298, APa 353, 355, 355, 355, 355, 355, 355, 357, 357, 357, 357, 359, 361, 367, 371; Hobbes (Spingarn) II. 55 ("The figure therefore of an epic poem and of a tragedy ought to be the same"). (5) A geometrical design in a painting: SS.XVII.APa 357. (6) Posture (of an actor on a stage): I.PEL 146.

FIGURE (v.) To image, to depict (an idea in human form): Figuring: I.OHP 159, SS.XVII.PPBPP 294.

FINE RAILLERY Delicate, refined, rapier-like raillery which contains "the nicest most delicate touches of satire" (II. 136). It is "not obscene, not gross, not rude, but facetious, well-mannered, and well-bred" (SS.XVIII. 75). See Raillery, Rally. II.DCOPS 110, 136, LL 215, SS.XVIII.LLd 75.

FLIGHT (sb.) A heightening of thought in poetry, an excursion into noble imaginings, thoughts, ambitions, etc. "Flight" is connected with the sublime and with the fancy, but bombast and fustian occur when the flight outstrips judgment, when the images outstrip the sense of what is being said, or when a brilliant image means nothing. "Flight" refers to the sublimity or heightening of thought rather than of words: I.EDP 22 (flight of fancy), AAHP 199 ("flight of heroic poetry"), GCT 258 ("flight" is used ironically; here is Dryden's great example of bombast), II.PS 31 (sublimity and Pindar's flights), DCOPS 149, SS.XV.AP 229, 232, 232, 234, 237, 243; Rymer (Z) 136 ("The tragical flights of Shakespeare." Rymer uses flights as fustian.).

FLOWERS (sb.) Tropes and figures: SS.XV.AP 241 (of rhetoric).

FLOWING (adj.) (1) Describing poetry or prose which is unmarked by roughness of thought and word order and extremes of false passions. Each word runs into the next with no hiatus between either open vowels or closed consonants: I.EDP 24 (describes Waller's poetry), DEDP 121, II.LP 12, DAV 234, SS.XIV.DAVd 162. (2) Describing something gracefully drawn in a painting. Dryden says, "The parts must be drawn with flowing, gliding outlines, large and smooth, rising gradually, not swelling suddenly": SS.XVII. APa 353.

FOND (sb.) Source of supply, storehouse, (one's own) mind: II.PS 30, PAA 40 (of ideas on criticism).

FRAME (sb.) The structure of a work of art as seen in its totality, from the outside. See also Fabric, Contexture. I.PSL 105, DEDP 123, SS.IX.TRAA 213;

Jonson 57; Milton III. 238 ("Some others [are] in their frame judicious, in their manner most . . . faulty").

FREEDOM (sb.) A quality of conversation, painting, and poetry which is fluent, spontaneous, and yet artful. It is without constraint because it is free from too much ceremony, too many rules, fear of reprisals, and awkward stilted style. See Rules. I.EDP 74, AAHP 206, SS.XV.AP 235, 235, XVII.APa 379.

FURY (sb.) Inspired rage, poetic frenzy (also prophetic inspiration), exemplified by fierce passion or beautiful, inspired lines. Dryden directly connects "fury" with "fancy." To write inspired poetry which is good poetry, one must control fury with judgment. See also Enthusiasm, Madman. I.OHP 160 (of a prophet), GCT 254, 257, II.PE 61, PPBPP 205, SS.XV.AP 229, XVII.APa 349 (of the fancy).

FUSTIAN (sb.) The false sublime. Extravagantly figurative writing which, owing to its excess, degenerates into gibberish, nonsense, or meaningless sound. Thoughts and words are ill-sorted, out of proportion to each other, and sometimes completely unrelated: I.AAHP 199, 203, PSF 277, II.PPBPP 183, DAV 229, 232, 243, SS.XV.PNOEM 398, 401, 402.

FUSTIAN (adj.) Describing someone or something with the qualities of fustian (sb.). See Extravagance. II.PPBPP 204, SS.XV.AP 229, 244. Fustianist: Milton III. 347.

G

GENIUS (sb.) Natural ability, talent, intellectual strength and robustness, inclination, aptitude (of a person, country, people, age, etc.). "Genius" is an innate force or power, emanating from the imagination and revealing itself in creations of the mind. St. Francis Xavier, for example, had a "sublime genius," "capable of the greatest designs" (SS.XVI. 17). Dryden also says, "Genius must be born; and never can be taught" (II. 171). A "genius" originally was a kind of guardian angel, a force or being which causes men to act in certain ways. In the seventeenth century, "genius" was in transition from the earlier meaning to the eighteenth-century meaning (which approximates our own), where "genius" is the power of invention or imagination (see meanings 3 and 4). The English use of "genius" in this period parallels the French use of *génie*. (1) Pertaining to and what is distinctive in an age, a generation, a people, or a country: I.EDP 26 ("Every age has a kind of universal genius which inclines those who live in it to some particular studies"), 85, HAR 214, 215, PAL 224, II.PAA 38, PDS 49, DCOPS 110, 132, DAV 238, 239, PF 277, SS.VI.DTC 253, VIII.PC 220, XVII.PPBPPd 298, APa 351, 351, XVIII.LLd 75; Sprat (Spingarn) II. 112. (2) Pertaining to a person, an artist, a poet, etc.: I.EDP 38, 41 ("He . . . who had genius most proper for the stage was Ovid"), 69, 73, ECG 167, DECG 181, AAHP 197, HAR 216, 217, POE 271, 272, PSF 279, II.PS 21, 25, 25, DCOPS 83, 85, 91, 136, 136, 138, PEP 161, 163, PPBPP 204, 210, LL 214, DAV 250, PRAV 258, LCM 266, PF 272, 274, 289, SS.XIV.DAVd 182, XV.AP 224, PHC 411, XVII.PPBPPd 298, APa 347, 359, 359, XVIII.CPd 24, LLd 62, 63, 75; Jonson 58; Rymer (Z) 5 (Spenser had "a genius for heroic poesie"), 21. (3) Imagination and invention of the highest sort (in the artistic creation of something sublime). This usage of "genius" is always qualified or modified (by sublime, lofty, transcendent, etc.), and is employed when discussing great poetic power, force of imagination, great inspiration, force of spirit, etc. "Sublime genius" is genius raised to greater heights and expanded. It is inborn (I. 254); it can be improved by study (II. 240); it must not be stifled by rules (SS.XVII. 345). In praising Shakespeare, Dryden says, "Genius alone is a greater virtue (if I may so call it) than all other qualifications put together" (II. 178). After becoming acquainted with "the sublime," subsequent to Boileau's "Traité du Sublime" (which appeared in 1674), Dryden published his "Author's Apology for Heroic Poetry" in 1677. In it, Dryden not only first uses the term "sublime" but also "sublime genius" (I. 197). After the middle part of his life, Dryden relates genius to sublimity less and less often. Finally, in PF, "genius" is entirely the "genius" of defs. (1) and (2). See Happy, def. (2), Sublime, def. (2). I.AAHP 197, 197, PAL 225 (Aristotle), 231 (Shakespeare), GCT 240 (Shakespeare), 243, 246, 247 (Shakespeare), 254, 255, POE 271 (Pindar), 271 (Cowley), II. PS 32, 33, PAA 39, PE 62 (Donne), DCOPS 74 (Dorset), 81, 90 ("genius" contains the "natural endowments of a large invention, a ripe judgment, and a strong memory"), 96, 96, 150 (Milton), TCDD 170, 171, LJD 178 (Shakespeare), 178 (Shakespeare), PPBPP 192 (Raphael), 194, 198 (Lee), LL 215, PPV 218 (Virgil), DAV 237, 240 (Spenser), PRAV 258, SS.III.DEL 233, V. DAL 320, VI.DTC 250, VIII.DAm 9 (Plautus and Molière), DKA 135 (Purcell), 136, IX.TRAA 211, XIII.SAVPMF 315, XIV.DG 3, DAVd 202 (Milton), XV.AP 224, 228 (Waller), 238 (Sophocles), XVI.AARLSFX 17 (St. Francis Xavier), XVII.APa 345, 345, 345, 349, 363, 385, 385, 385, 385, 387, XVIII. LLd 63 (Lucian), 73 (Lucian and Juvenal). (4) The inanimate spirit which moves men to action. This meaning is close to the idea that one's "genius" is a guardian angel: Milton XII. 251 ("My fate or my genius did not wish me to depart from my early love of the muses"); Rymer (Z) 44.

GLOWING COLOURS Strong, sound, excellent tropes, figures, and diction (which fit the sense). "Glowing colours" are sound, "glaring colours" are not: II.PPBPP 204, 207.

GOLDEN VERSE "Two substantives and two adjectives with a verb betwixt them." Watson (from Strang) says that the term is unrecorded, that it might be Restoration jargon: I.POE 266, II.PS 22.

GOOD LETTERS "Les belles lettres": II.DAV 257, PRAV 261, SS.XVIII.CPd 25.

GOOD SENSE Soundness of judgment (as the French bon sens). See Sense, Judgment. I.PA 187, GCT 260, II.PAA 39, DCOPS 74, 80, 102, 127, 147, 153, PEP 161, PF 274, 280, 286, 288, SS.VII.VDG 160, DDS 299, VIII.DAm 7, DKA 132, XIV.DG 4, 10, DAVd 151, XV.PNOEM 402, XVIII.CPd 25; Jonson 40.

GOTHIC (adj.) Unrefined, crude, undisciplined, deformed, grotesque: II.PPBPP 202, SS.XVII.APa 363.

GRACE (sb.) See Curiosa Felicitas. See also Bouhours, "Le je ne sais quoi," Entretiens d'Ariste et d'Eugene (1671); Quintilian, Institutio Oratorio, IX, iv, 117; Boileau, "L'art poétique," IV, 78; Pope, "Essay on Criticism," I. 144;

S. H. Monk, "A Grace beyond the Reach of Art," *Journal of the History of Ideas*, V (1944), 131–50. (1) An indefinable excellence in art. It is related to effortlessness, ease of displaying wit, sweetness, easy liveliness of imagination, smoothness of movement in verse, lightness (as opposed to heaviness of touch): I.PRL 8, EDP 60, 80, DECG 177, HAR 214, PSF 275 (of action), II.PS 24, DCOPS 122, TCDD 170, DAV 246, PF 288, SS.II.DIE 286, IV. DMLM 255 ("of . . . behaviour"), XV.AP 226, 229, 230, 232, 233, 241, XVII. LPd 63, APa 357, 363, 391. Graceful: I.AAHP 203, POE 272, II.PS 20, 21 (pictures), CSE 57 (speaking), DCOPS 111 (turn), 111 (turn), PEP 165, PPBPP 197, PF 276, SS.XIV.DAVd 188. Gracefully: I.EDP 69, II.PAA 37, DAV 226. Gracefulness: I.POE 266, 269 (of motion), 269 (of motion), PSF 278 (of action), SS.XVII.PPBPPd 296, APa 345, 353; Drayton (Spingarn) I. 138 ("grace of Ovid"); Hobbes (Spingarn) II. 56 ("grace of style"). (2) A touch, an ornament, a flourish skillfully employed and partaking of def. (1). It arises from consummate skill, genius, or chance: I.EDP 34, 57, 60, PAM 99, PEL 149, 154, 155, PSF 278, II.LP 8, 10, ETV 15, PE 62, DCOPS 76, 80, 113, LL 212, DAV 244, 246, SS.XVII.APa 349; Jonson 34, Davenant (Spingarn) II. 17. (3) Creditable behavior under adverse circumstances: I. PAL 227, II.DCOPS 139, PF 292. (4) One of three sister Goddesses (according to Hesiod) who are the three graces (Aglaia, Thalia, Euphrosyne): II.PEP 162, 162, TCDD 172. (5) Favor: SS.V.PAZd 199.

GREAT (adj.) Sublime, lofty, elevated. (1) Pertaining to surpassing excellence and genius: I.EDP 67, DEDP 119 (ironic), 121. Great genius: II.PS 33. Great poet: I.EDP 55. Great wit (a man of surpassing perception and cleverness): I.PrSL2 108, II.PF 289, SS.XVII.LPd 76. Greater: I.EDP 67, PAM 102, PSL 105, DEDP 127, II.DCOPS 96, PPBPP 193, PF 286 (moment), SS.X.PRLaici 33. Greatest: I.EDP 71, 80 (thoughts), 85, 87, AAHP 196, II.DCOPS 96, DAV 223 (of man is the heroic poem), SS.XVII.PPBPPd 295 ("Rafaelle," the greatest of the modern masters). (2) Describing a style of writing or speaking which rises to elevated heights, is noble, and inspires wonder: I.EDP 81, PAM 100, DEDP 115, 128, PEL 151, PAZ 191, GCT 244, 245 (equated with wonderful), II.PPBPP 188, 191, 197, SS.XV.AP 227, XVII.PPBPPd 294, APa 353.

GREATNESS (sb.) (1) Nobility, stature, loftiness of character or characteristics in persons in a heroic poem or play, in men in public office, in certain things in nature: I.EDP 61, 61, 65, PAM 97, 97, PAL 223, II.PDS 51, SS.V.DCI 101, 103, 103, 107, XVII.APa 381. (2) The scope, nobility, comprehensiveness, loftiness of a work of art, especially an epic or heroic poem. In two places (I. 277, II. 243) greatness is equated directly with sublimity: I.EDP 59, PSF 277, II.DCOPS 92, 96, DAV 229, 232, 243.

GROTESQUE (adj.) Describing something unnatural, false mannered, the distorted product of a "wild imagination" (as farce): II.PEP 159, PPBPP 190, 190 (painting), DAV 229 (painting); Jonson 35.

GROTESQUE (sb.) That which is unnatural, which distorts nature. See Nature. SS.XVII.DPL 16.

GUSTO (sb.) "Taste," aesthetic perception, standards of aesthetic perception (which give pleasure): SS.XVII.PFAAP 337, 341.

H

HABITUDE (sb.) Familiarity: II.PS 20 (or informality in conversation), PPBPP 193, SS.XVII.APa 389, 391.

HALF LINE The last half of a line of verse. See Half Verse. II.DAV 249, 249.

HALF RHYME "Pain" rhymed with "man." The included vowel sounds vary in quantity: II.LWW1 54.

HALF VERSE An incomplete line of poetry. "Half verse" or "hemistich" refers to an incomplete line; "half line" refers to the last half of a complete line of poetry: II.DAV 248, 248.

HAPPY (adj.) (1) Describing a work of art or a part of a work which is beautiful because of a poet's or artist's felicitous, lucky, and appropriate inventiveness, rather than his skill (II. 137). Felicitous invention depends on a certain amount of luck. A poet, for example, has to "hit" on the proper expression ("wit written . . . is the happy result of thought" [I. 98]). "Happiness" or a "happy" quality is always found embodied in a work of art; the success, the inventiveness, etc., of a poet's imagination can be seen in the happinesses of the invention, fancy, and elocution (I. 98), or simply, as in Horace, the happiness of "curiosa felicitas" (II. 31): I.PAM 98, PF 135 (thoughts), II. PAA 43 (design), PE 63, DCOPS 82, LL 212 (invention), SS.VIII.DAm 9 (performances). Happiness: I.EDP 79, PAM 98, 100, II.PS 31, PAA 39 (of imagination), PE 61, LL 215 (of expression). Happily: I.EDP 30, II.PS 28, DCOPS 131, 137, 138, 152, LL 211, PRAV 258, SS.VIII.DTL 374; Peachum (Spingarn) I. 128 (Claudian's "happy invention"), 128; Davenant (Spingarn) II. 17 ("happy strokes"). Felicity: Jonson 25 (ability to produce happy hits of style); Rymer (Z) 110 ("felicity of invention"). (2) Describing an imagination or genius which is inventive, lucky, and successful. All citations are to "happy genius" unless otherwise indicated. "Happy genius" and "happy imagination" Dryden specifically defines as "invention" (II. 94, SS.XVII. 349). He also says, "A happy genius is a gift of nature; it depends on the influence of the stars, say the astrologers, on the organs of the body, say the naturalists; it is the particular gift of heaven, say the divines, both Christian and heathen. How to improve it, many books can teach us, how to obtain it, none; that nothing can be done without it, all agree": II.PS 32, DCOPS 74, PPBPP 194 (chemistry), 194, SS.XV.AP 228, XVII.APa 349 (imagination). Happily: II. DCOPS 73 (describing the way Shakespeare's mind worked). (3) Joyful, fortunate: II.PAA 37. Happy event (describing the happy ending of a play): II.DCOPS 102, 103.

HARD (adj.) (1) Describing poetic diction, tropes, metaphors, etc. which are farfetched or overly bold. They are the excesses of metaphysical poetry. "Hard discord" (metaphysical poetry) is what Waller improved to "soft harmony" (SS.XV. 228). Cleveland's poetry is Dryden's example: "To express a thing hard and unnaturally is his [Cleveland's] new way of elocution" (I. 39). "We cannot read a verse of Cleveland's without making a face at it. . . . He gives us common thoughts in abstruse words" (I. 40). Persius, whose tropes are "fit for nothing but to puzzle the understanding" is also criticized as "hard." "Hard" is a pejorative term used where the words do not fit the sense: II.

DCOPS 118, 121, 121, SS.XV.AP 228. Hard (adv.): I.EDP 39. Hardness: II. DCOPS 125; Hobbes (Spingarn) II. 63 (Hobbes uses the term "strong lines" to describe "metaphysical poetry." He says, "Strong lines are no better than riddles"), 63. (2) Describing bold expressions, metaphors, etc., which are not excessive (I. 201). "Hard" metaphors, expressions, etc., are beauties rather than faults when they are used artfully (I. 201), when they are "produced from the occasion" rather than "for the sake of the description" (I. 202): Hardest: I.AAHP 200. Hardness: I.AAHP 201. (3) Harsh, overly critical: II.PD 292. Hardly: SS.IX.TRAA 213. (4) Inflexible and full of effort: Hard (adv.): II.PS 29.

HARMONIOUS (adj.) Agreeable, smooth, flowing, musical; antonyms are "cacophonous" and "jarring": II.DAV 251. Harmonious composition (of lights and shadows in painting). See Harmony. SS.XVII.APa 379. Harmonious numbers: II.PAA 40, DAV 251, SS.XIV.DAVd 162. Harmonious sound (of language): II.PEP 166. Harmonious strains (of Orpheus): SS.XV.AP 251. Harmonious sweetness: II.PAA 35. Harmonious tongue (Italian): II.PAA 37. Harmonious verse: II.DCOPS 84, PF 281, SS.VIII.DKA 135. Harmonious version (of an epic): II.PEP 167. Harmoniously: II.PAA 38, DAV 245, SS.XVIII.LLd 75.

HARMONY (sb.) A quality produced by the agreeable combination of parts forming an aesthetically pleasing whole, which is elegant, easy, tuneful, flowing, soft, etc. (in poetry, music, painting, and prose): II.PAA 38, DCOPS 99, 204, DAV 234, SS.XV.AP 228, XVII.PPBPPd 299, APa 377 (of consent). Of words: I.PTL 139. Of lights and shadows (in painting): SS.XVII.APa 351. Of numbers: II.PS 21, DAV 242, PRAV 258, PF 271, 275, SS.XIV.DAVd 204. Of order: SS.XVII.LPd 30. Of prose: II.PF 272. Of verse (depends on metrics and words): II.PS 32, DCOPS 106. Of the tints: SS.XVII.APa 393.

HEIGHTENING (sb.) (1) Catachresis, hyperbole (in poetry). "The strength and vehemence [the heightening] should be suited to the occasion, the subject, and the persons": I.PSF 278. (2) A lightened area which causes an object or figure to stand out (in a painting), the opposite of "shadow" (heightenings are to art as catachreses and hyperboles are to poetry): I.AAHP 201.

HERO (sb.) (1) Any person, historical or fictional, of great stature, of heroic virtue. See Heroic. (a) Fictional: I.PRL 4, EDP 60, PO 233, GCT 255, POE 267, II.PAA 35, 37, PDS 50, CSE 57, DCOPS 144, PEP 167, PPBPP 185, 188, 188, 197, 199, 202, DAV 224, 228, SS.IV.DCG 17, VI.DTC 250, VII. VDG 179, 179, XIV.DAVd 158, XV.AP 232, 234, 237, 238, 239, 239, 240, 242, XVII.PPBPP 299. (b) Historical: I.EDP 76, PAM 101, DEDP 121, OHP 166, PrAZ 192, GCT 241, 241, 242, II.LP 4, 9, CP 68, 68, DAV 250, SS.III. DEL 234, DTL 375, IV.DCG 11, 12, 17, VII.VDG 159, 212, VIII.PC 221, 226, IX.EWTM 422, XIV.DAVd 188, XV.AP 224, 233, 239, 243, 251, XVII. LPd 20, 63, PPBPPd 294, XVIII.PDCW 7, CPd 40. (2) Chief male character in an epic or tragedy who is of heroic stature: I.OHP 163 (Achilles is Homer's hero), 164 (Rinaldo is Tasso's hero and "chief character"), GCT 252, II.PDS 47, CSE 57, 58, DCOPS 83, 92, 96, LL 211, DAV 228, PF 275, 276, SS.VIII. PC 227, XIV.DAVd 146, 156, 157, 160, 161, 163, 163, 165, 165, 168, 168, 168, 172, 175, 176, 177, 178, 179, 186, 187, 188, 189, 194, 199, 200, XV.AP 252. (3) Protagonist. Any chief male character of tragedy, epic, or painting, not necessarily of heroic virtue. Watson and Strang both say this is the first recorded use of "hero" as strictly a literary term: I.PAZ 191, PAL 222, 224, 224, PO 233, GCT 246, 250, 251, 251, 252, II.LWW1 174, PPBPP 186, 199, 199, DAV 228, 228, 228, 230, 233, SS.VIII.PC 221, XIII.SAVPMF 311, XIV. DAVd 157, 163, 168, 168, XV.AP 238, 239, 239, 240, 243, PNOEM 400.

HEROIC (sb.) (1) A line of iambic pentameter: II.PS 23, 32, DCOPS 147, 149. (2) The epic (an epic poem). See Epic (sb.). SS.XV.AP 241.

HEROIC (adj.) (1) Describing anything that is solidly elevated, impressive, of high seriousness, etc. "Heroic" describes an active rather than a passive virtue or quality. A heroic man, for example, is so because of significant deeds: SS. XV.PNOEM 400 (Settle's *Empress of Morocco* is falsely heroic because it is fustian). Action: I.PAM 95, II.DCOPS 86, SS.IV.DCG 12, 15, 17, VIII.DKA 136. Actor (a character in a play): I.PAM 95. Enterprise: II.DCOPS 85–86 (requires strength and vigor of body, duty, capacity, and prudence). Imagination (a thought): I.GCT 238 (Aeschylus produced many). Measures: SS. XV.AP 253. Passion: I.HAR 212 (love fit for men of heroic stature). Subject: I.PAM 94. Virtue: I.OHP 163, II.DAV 224, SS.III.DEL 230, IV.DCG 15, IX.TRAA 213. Heroical: SS.VIII.DAm 7, XIV.DAVd 164. Heroically: I.PRL 6. Milton III. 237 (*Paradise Lost* is more heroic than the *Iliad*); Sprat (Spingarn) II. 130 ("Heroic characters of charity and religion"). (2) Describing verse written in rhymed iambic pentameter couplets: Rhyme: I.EDP 87. Verse: I.OHP 156, II.PE 61, DCOPS 153, DAV 245, 247, PF 281; Milton II. 6 (The verse of *Paradise Lost* is "heroic verse without rhyme"). (3) Describing one who writes epics (as Homer, Virgil, etc.): Heroic poet: I.OHP 161, II.PAA 36, DCOPS 82, 85, DAV 232, PF 271, SS.XIV.DAVd 190.

HEROIC PLAY A play modeled on a heroic or epic poem, a play which imitates qualities of a heroic poem (see Heroic Poem). It glorifies a central superhero, whose actions and passions are heroic as they surpass those of ordinary men. Dryden says, "An heroic play ought to be an imitation, in little, of an heroic poem; and consequently that Love and Valour ought to be the subject of it" (I. 158). Some examples Dryden gives are his own *Conquest of Grenada* and *Indian Emperor*, as well as Davenant's *Siege of Rhodes*: I.PEL 144, OHP 156, 157, 158, 162, 162, 163, SS.II.DIE 285, III.DTL 375.

HEROIC POEM An epic poem such as Homer's *Iliad*, Virgil's *Aeneid*, Cowley's *Davideis*. It is dignified in its hero and in its verse. It is "the greatest work of human nature" (II. 96), "the greatest work of man" (II. 223). It is a part of a literary genre higher than that of tragedy. Sometimes Dryden uses "heroic poem" to describe a play different from and above tragedy: I.PAM 98, OHP 158, 159, 159, 159, 159, 159, 160, 162, PAZ 191, HAR 217, GCT 248, II. DCOPS 84, 84, 86, 96, 96, 96, 150, DAV 223, 227, 228, 232, 233, 248, SS. III.DTL 375, V.PAZd 197, DAL 324, XIV.DAVd 175, 185, 189, 198; Hobbes (Spingarn) II. 60 ("A heroic poem is a venerable and amiable image of heroic virtue"), 60, 68 ("The work of an heroick poem is to raise admiration, principally for the three virtues, valor, beauty and love").

HEROIC POESY Poetry which is epic poetry or heroic plays: I.PAM 101, SS.IV.

DCG 11, X.PHP 117, 117; Rymer (Z) 5 (Spenser had "a genius for heroick poesy").

HEROIC POETRY (1) The genre which includes the epic (the highest genre). It can also be poetry (from an epic) which is elevated and dignified in style, subject, and content, sublime in its conception and execution: I.OHP 161, 161, AAHP 198, 199, 207, II.DCOPS 81, 81, 85, 86, 89, 149 (needs turns on words for dignity of expression), LJD 178, DAV 229, 229, 232, 237, 238, 239, 247, PF 274, SS.IV.DCG 12, X.PRLaici 32, XIV.DAVd 190.

HEROINE (sb.) "Chief female character"; the earliest recorded use is Rymer in 1678 (Z 58): I.GCT 252, POE 266, 267, II.LWW2 174, PPBPP 188, SS.XIV. DAVd 180, XVIII.PDCW 7.

HIDDEN BEAUTIES Those beauties in a play or poem not evident at first sight or reading. "Propriety of thoughts and words": I.PSF 278, II.DCOPS 144 (in a design of a poem).

HISTORIC POESY A branch of epic poesy; for its characteristics, see Historical Poem. I.PAM 101.

HISTORICAL PLAY A play which records actual events (as found in annals). It has more than a single action and therefore is not a tragedy (like one of Shakespeare's chronicle plays): I.EDP 47, DECG 172, GCT 243.

HISTORICAL POEM A poem which, though both actions and persons may be heroic, is nevertheless not an epic poem because it lacks unity of action and is "tied too severely to the laws of history" (I. 95). Dryden refers specifically to *Annus Mirabilus*. Davenant (Spingarn II. 19) calls *Gondibert* a "historical poem" without actually making the distinction between "historical" and "epic": I.PAM 93, 95, 98.

HISTORY-PIECE A work of art recording the events of the past. It may be heroic but it lacks unity of action. See Historical Poem. II.LP 8.

HUDDLE (v.) To put together in slapdash fashion (as a play): II.PDS 50 (up).

HUMAN (adj.) Describing what is natural to man and thus imperfect, or what is within the realm of his imperfect capabilities: Action: SS.XVII.PPBPPd 297. Beauty: SS.XVII.PPBPPd 292. Body: II.DAV 228. Figure: II.PPBPP 190. Frailty: I.OHP 164, AAHP 198, II.PF 273, 283. Imperfection: II.PPBPP 185. Impossibility: II.PAA 35. Life: I.PRL 2, OHP 159, 159, HAR 213, II.DCOPS 127, PPBPP 189, DAV 226, PF 275. Miseries: II.DAV 227. Nature: I.EDP 87, 88, DEDP 122, PEL 146, 152, AAHP 198, 200, HAR 215, II.PAA 35, DCOPS 96, 106, 119, SS.II.DIE 287, VII.VDG 199, XVII.PPBPPd 298. Passions: I.OHP 164. Performance: SS.XVII.PPBPPd 297. Person: II.DCOPS 84, DAV 233. Understanding: II.DCOPS 129, SS.XIV.DG 4. Vices: II.DCOPS 143. Way: II.CP 68. Wit: II.DAV 232.

HUMEUR (sb.) (Dryden uses the French word in EDP.) Temperament, not yet some extravagant habit, passion, or affectation: I.EDP 73.

HUMOUR (sb.) The old meaning of "humour" is temperament, as it is controlled by one of the four chief bodily fluids (or humours). The literary meaning (def. 1) easily comes from the old meaning. Def. (2) is the most important, general,

Restoration meaning of "humour," and Dryden defines "humour" in this way on I. 71–73. The prevalence of def. (2) shows Restoration playwrights' obsession with whims, affectations, extravagant habits, or states of mind. In good general satire, the "humour" itself (as in def. 2) becomes more important than the identity of a single character in which it is embodied (def. 3). The technique of "writing a humour" leads Dryden into using "humour" as a literary genre (def. 4), as a kind of comedy. Comedy of this kind is lower than comedy of wit but higher than farce. Dryden tends to give up the older meaning of "humour" (def. 1) during the middle part of his career (the 1670's and 1680's), but in the 1690's attempts to revive its use. Most consistently, Dryden uses def. (2). (1) Temperament, as it is ruled by one of the four chief bodily fluids, of a person in real life or in a poem or play. The ruling fluid causes him to act in a certain way: I.PRL 2, 4, EDP 25, 69, 71, 71, DEDP 116, PEL 145, II.LP 12, PPBPP 198, PF 278, 284, SS.XV.AP 239, 246; Davenant (Spingarn) II. 12 (the "humour" or temperament of a nation). (2) Overriding fancy, whim, jest, state of mind, mood, extravagant habit (passion or affection), quirks of behavior or manners: I.EDP 49, 71, 73, 73, 74, 75, 75, 85, DEDP 116, 116, 120, PEL 146, 146, 147, AAHP 203, 205, PSF 279, II.PS 18, DCOPS 123, DAV 243, PF 284, SS.VI.DKK 10, VIII.PC 219, XIII.SAVPMF 311, 312, XV.PNOEM 406, XVII.PFAAP 340, XVIII.LLd 70; Shadwell (Spingarn) II. 162 ("A humour is a bias of the mind,/ By which, with violence, 'tis one way inclin'd;/ It makes our actions lean on one side still,/ And in all changes, that way bends the will"). (3) A whim, fancy, etc., personified by a character in a comedy. The character becomes, literally, a "humour," or the representation of an amusing whim, etc. Sometimes called a "person of humour" as opposed to a person of wit: I.EDP 56, 56, 57, 72, 72, PEL 150, 150, GCT 250, II.PDS 45; Shadwell (Spingarn) II. 150 (a character with a consistent foible). (4) Comedy based on characters, in a play, being dominated by a single whim, fancy, state of mind, etc., sometimes called "mechanic comedy" because of the "mechanic" people in it (I. 69). A kind of comedy (thus a genre) lower than comedy of wit: I.EDP 57, 58, 69, 69, 69, 71, 72, PrSL 108, DEDP 115, PEL 144, 147, 149, 149, 149, 150, 152, 155, ECG 167, DECG 182, 182, 182, AAHP 199, II.DCOPS 79, SS.XVIII.LLd 73; Sprat (Spingarn) II. 112 ("Humour and wit and variety and elegance of language come from the city"; Sprat is moving in the direction of the modern meaning of "humour"); Shadwell (Spingarn) II. 149 ("A play of humour" is different from a play of plot).

HUMOUROUS (adj.) (1) Whimsical, capricious: SS.XV.AP 233 (the "humourous god," Apollo), 234 ("humourous rhyme"), 246. (2) Whimsical, with overtones of comical, droll, amusing: SS.XV.AP 248 ("our humourous tale").

HYPERBATA (sb.) The plural of hyperbaton. The rhetorical figure of transposition, which is used to achieve a natural sounding, strong, and violent passion. Dryden calls it "disordered connection of discourse." Watson says Puttenham (II. 111) calls it the "trespasser figure" or "disorder." See Longinus, ch. XII; see also Boileau, "Traité du sublime," ch. XVIII: I.AAHP 203.

HYPERBOLE (sb.) "The rhetorical figure of exaggeration. See Longinus, xxviii; Puttenham (III. xviii) calls it 'the lying figure' or 'overreacher'" (Watson's Gloss). Dryden is careful to distinguish between proper or natural hyperbole

and unnatural or strained hyperbole: I.AAHP 200, 201, 201, 202, 202, SS.VI.
DTC 247, XV.AP 235, PNOEM 398.

HYPERCRITIC (sb.) A "malicious and unmanly" man who "snarl[s] at the little
lapses of a pen from which Virgil himself stands not exempted." Scaliger is one
of Dryden's examples. A man who condemns human frailties: I.AAHP 198,
II.PEP 158.

I

IDEA (sb.) An image in the mind. See also Image. Since Dryden is interested
in how an artist creates, he has much to say about the origin of ideas and what
they are. There are three ways to conceive an idea: one is to recall it from
the memory, where an image or idea is stored; the second is to invent it by using
the imagination or fancy to combine disparate elements (see Invention, Imagination, Second Notion, and Fancy [sb.]); the third, from the point of view of
the audience, is to read or hear and then conceive an idea expressed by someone else. "Idea" is derived from both Greek and Latin. Peachum, for example,
shows its Latin derivation: "idea or form [Latin *forma*] of things" (Spingarn
I. 122). Cowley in his spelling indicates his awareness of its Greek origin:
"Idoea" (Spingarn II. 81). (1) An image of something seen, known, or conceived as it exists in the memory and can be recalled to the conscious, active
mind: I.PAM 98, PSL 105, GCT 242 (a beautiful work of art to be imitated
takes the place of the image in the memory), PSF 275, II.PEP 157 (men are
born with "notions of morality"), 164, SS.IV.DCG 12, XIV.DAVd 187, XVII.
PPBPPd 293, 294, 295, 296, 297, 297, 297, APa 359; Peachum (Spingarn)
I. 122. (2) An image or pattern of perfection as conceived or invented by the
imagination or fancy: II.PPBPP 185, 185, 194, DAV 228, SS.XVII.PPBPPd
291, 292, 292, 292, 294, 295, 295, 295 (perfect ugliness), 297, 297, 298, APa
383; Cowley (Spingarn) II. 81, 90; Rymer (Z) 5 (Spenser in his "heroick
poesie" lacked "a true idea"), 9. (3) The image received from a work of art
(as it appears in the mind of an audience or reader): I.GCT 250, II.LP 5, 8,
DCOPS 111, 140, DAV 251, SS.XV.AP 229, XVIII.LLd 70. (4) A thought:
II.CSE 59.

IDIOTISM (sb.) An idiom: SS.XVII.LPd 63.

IMAGE (sb.) In all the arts the artist conceives his work before he executes it.
This idea of perfection is an image. In works of literature, the image exists as
a description to be conceived by the mind of the reader or auditor. A literary
description is a verbal painting, and therefore in the plastic arts the image is
the physical object seen by the viewer. Aesthetically, a work of art imitates
(images) nature, or is a reflection (image) of nature. "Nature" can mean
physical nature or idealized nature as it is interpreted by an artist. Def. (1)
is the most important meaning of "image." The other definitions are related to
it, except for def. (5) which is different because it concerns the plastic arts.
In the plastic arts, the image is the physical object which is seen as the work,
as the image. An image is primarily visual, although the other senses can also
provide images. Auditory images, for example, are found in Dryden's 1687 "Song
for St. Cecilia's Day." Even abstractions, such as "revenge" or "nature" tend
to be personified, as we see in the paintings of the period (see Jean Hagstrum,

The Sister Arts). See Imitation, def. (1), Idea. (1) An idea, a picture of something as it is conceived in the mind or as it was imprinted on the mind by an external sensation: I.PRL 2, 4, EDP 47, 67, PAM 100, OHP 163, 191, AAHP 205, POE 272, II.PDS 46, PPBPP 205, SS.VII.VDG 211, XIV.DAVd 156, XVII.PPBPPd 293. Hobbes (Spingarn) II. 63, 71; Sprat (Spingarn) II. 125. (2) A reproduction or mirror image of something in actual nature. Theoretically, this kind of image is an accurate reflection of nature, but practically it is always either improved nature or objects selected from nature which fit into or improve a work of art (this meaning usually applies to a larger work of art, such as an epic, play, etc.): I.EDP 25, 42, 72, 87, 87, DEDP 122, POE 267, II.PPBPP 197, LL 210, SS.XIV.DG 10; Milton III. 238 ("The Apocalypse of St. John is the majestic image of a high and stately tragedy"); Hobbes (Spingarn) II. 60; Sprat (Spingarn) II. 120. (3) A model, an ideal, a perfect idea of what something should be like, what something would be without natural defects and distortions: I.EDP 32, 33, 38 ("image of revenge"), PTL 139, OHP 157, 159, DECG 174, AAHP 202, 203, 204, II.LP 7, PEP 167, PPBPP 183, 190, 194, PPV 221, SS.V.PAZd 197, XV.AP 240, XVII.PPBPPd 293, 294, 294. (4) A description, a picture, an illustration as it appears in a play or a poem, a rhetorical analogy. (See Hobbes: "An image is always a part, or rather the ground, of a poetical comparison" [Spingarn II. 71]): I.PAM 99, 99, 100, 101, 101, 101, PSL 106, PEL 150, AAHP 205, GCT 257, 257, SS.XIV. DAVd 190; Hobbes (Spingarn) II. 73; Rymer (Z) 39. (5) A painting, an engraving, a sculpture. Here, the conception in the artist's mind is an idea; the image is the visible, finished product of that idea in stone, on canvas, on cloth, etc.: SS.IX.EWTM 422, XVII.PPBPPd 292, 297.

IMAGE (v.) To describe, to depict, to illustrate (see Image [sb.]). I.EDP 87, 99, AAHP 204. Imaging: I.EDP 42, PAM 98, AAHP 203, 203, 204.

IMAGERY (sb.) Images. See Image (sb.). Hobbes (Spingarn) II. 60 ("copious imagery"); Rymer (Z) 81.

IMAGINATION (sb.) The creative faculty in a poet; the creative faculty of a poet as seen in a work of art; the faculty in an audience which makes it receptive to art. Dryden uses "imagination" interchangeably with "fancy" except in defs. (5) and (6). "Imagination" is a more comprehensive term, however, because it can include "fancy." (1) The faculty in a poet (sometimes wild and lawless) which invents and plays with ideas, images, etc., but does not order them: I.PRL 2, 8, EDP 64, 80, 91, 92, PT 134, OHP 161, AAHP 201, II.DCOPS 147, PEP 159, PPBPP 190, SS.V.DSI 100, VIII.DKA 136, XIII.SAVPMF 315, XIV.DG 3, XVII.APa 387, 391, XVIII.LLd 78. (2) The faculty which clothes images and ideas with words. Characters, figures, antitheses, conceits, and jests are a product of it. This function of imagination is a part of elocution. It puts images into effective words (or colors, lights, and shadows) which adorn the plot, characters, wit, passions: I.EDP 22, 87, PEL 150, II.DCOPS 148, SS.XVII.PPBPPd 292, 299. (3) The faculty which orders images and ideas. The imagination not only recalls images from the memory, or invents them, but it can also combine these images to produce more complex ideas and images. This function of the imagination, as it is expressed in a work of art, reveals the quickness and copiousness of an artist's wit or genius: I.EDP 98,

98 (the mind of the poet), AAHP 205, GCT 253, II.PS 32, PAA 43, DCOPS 91, SS.XVII.PPBPPd 295, 297, APa 349 (this is invention). (4) The faculty (in a member of an audience or in a reader) which receives images and forms ideas and images corresponding to the quality of what is seen or heard. The imagination works with these received images and, overpowering the judgment, leads an auditor or reader to the land of the poet's or artist's creation. Although the imagination here is receptive, it is not passive: I.EDP 51, 62, 80, DEDP 125, 125, 125, 126, 126, 126, OHP 162, II.LP 12, PPBPP 206, 208, DAV 242, SS.IX.EWTM 422, XIV.DG 4, XVII.LPd 68. (5) A quality in a work of art which comprehends invention, fancy, and elocution. Dryden says that the three happinesses of the imagination are invention (finding the thought), fancy (molding of the thought), and elocution (the clothing and adorning of the thought in "apt, significant and sounding words"). See Fancy, def. (2), Happiness, Invention, Elocution, Genius. I.PAM 98, 98. (6) An image, a thought: I.PS 135, GCT 238, SS.VIII.DKA 136, XIV.DAVd 157.

IMITATE (v.) To copy. There are many variations in meaning and usage, and the following definitions are merely a rough classification of them. See also Imitation, Copy (sb.). (1) To reproduce (a style, or someone's style); to mimic; to counterfeit; to reproduce the model of a genre perfected by others (both style and genre as imitated are parts of translation): (a) Reproduction in translation: I.POE 270, II.PS 31, DCOPS 153, PPV 220. (b) All others: I.EDP 17, DEDP 123, PAL 231, 231, II.PS 20, 24, 25, 30, PAA 36, DCOPS 84, 104, 108, 109, 110, 111, 111, 112, 113, 114, 114, 115, 136, 142, 150, PPBPP 196, PPV 221, 229, 236, 249, 251, PF 275, SS.X.PRLaici 32, XIV. DAVd 179, 186, 187, 189, 197. Imitating: I.EDP 57, OHP 159, II.PS 32, DCOPS 115, DAV 242, SS.XVII.PPBPPd 298; Jonson 86, 87. (2) To emulate; to follow an example (of someone): (a) Someone, anyone: I.GCT 242, II.PS 20, PPV 228, 228, SS.XIV.DAVd 185, XV.AP 249. Imitating: I.DECG 181, SS.XVII.PPBPPd 292 (poet imitates or emulates God). (b) The French: I.EDP 65. (c) Jonson: I.PEL 148, DECG 182. (d) Shakespeare: I.PrT 136, PAL 231, GCT 241, 243, 246, 260. Imitating: I.PAL 231. (e) Fletcher: I. DECG 182, PAL 231, GCT 243, 246, 253. (f) The Ancients: I.EDP 25, 46, OHP 163 (and Tasso), HAR 219, POE 267, II.PS 22, CP 69, DCOPS 82, 84, 136, PPBPP 186, LL 211, 211, DAV 224, SS.XIV.DAVd 180, 189, XV. PNOEM 408. Imitating: SS.XVII.APa 391. (g) An admirable character (which we should emulate): I.PTL 140. (3) To copy, reproduce, or represent either literal or ideal nature (or a selected part of it). See Imitation. I.EDP 35, 47, 51, 51, 68, 72, 86, DEDP 114, 114, 122, 122, OHP 157, ECG 167, DECG 182, PA 186, II.DCOPS 98, 99, PPBPP 182, 191, 193, 193, 195, 195, DAV 229, 239, SS.IV.DCG 11, DMLM 253, XIV.DAVd 187, 187, 189, XV.AP 243, XVII.DPWDY 210, APa 347, 351, 355, 359, 371. Imitating: I.DEDP 114 (conversation), 122, 122, II.DAV 226 (nature), SS.XVII.PPBPPd 294, APa 379.

IMITATION (sb.) There are three kinds of artistic imitation: the first is the representation of nature; the second, the emulation of artistic models; the third, a loose form of translation. (1) The representation of nature. (a) Representation of things in general in an artificial likeness, a reproduction, or a copy (literary or otherwise): I.PRL 4, EDP 72, 73, 73, 80, 87, DEDP 114, PT 134, PEL 148, OHP 157, 158, 162, DECG 178, 182, 182, AAHP 203, GCT 241, 242, 242, 243, 246, POE 267, II.DCOPS 107, PPBPP 193, 193, 194, 194, 194, 194, SS.XVII.ADFHL 93; Davenant (Spingarn) II. 7. (b) The representation of probable human life, human passions, etc., expressed through art in the phrase "imitation of nature." "Imitation of nature," Dryden says, is the basis of all art (I. 122): I.EDP 35, 56, 56, 78, 79, 89, DEDP 122, 122, 124, PTL 140, AAHP 200, 203, POE 265, 265, II.PPBPP 193, 193, 194, PF 275, SS.XVII.DPL 16. (c) A representation of idealized nature first seen as an image in the mind and then expressed through art. Thus "perfect nature" is nature beautified or, as Dryden says, "raised to a higher pitch." This meaning pervades def. (1a) and influences (1b) as "imitations of nature" overlook blemishes in nature: I.AAHP 204 (fairies, pygmies, magic), II.PPBPP 194, SS.XVII.PPBPPd 293, 293, 294, 294. (2) The emulation of the example of models. To imitate the *Iliad*, for example, was common procedure, but Dryden, being a Modern, claims that imitation of models produces only second-rate literature when invention is missing. He also feels, however, that the model which establishes a genre must be imitated by all subsequent works in that genre: I.AAHP 200, 201, GCT 242, 242, 243, II.PS 32, DCOPS 109, 109, 115, 136, 136, 148, DAV 228, SS.IV.DCG 11, VI.DKK 7, XIV.DAVd 187, XVII. PDCW 6, CPd 40; Jonson 86, 86, 93. There are also specific models: (a) The Ancients: I.EDP 32, 53, PAM 100, PAL 228, II.DCOPS 144, 148, LWW2 173, SS.III.DEL 233, XVII.APa 353 (Greek sculpture). (b) Shakespeare: I.GCT 253. (c) The French: I.EDP 66 (a servile act). (d) Jonson: I.DECG 182. (3) Translation which varies, and occasionally departs from the words and sense of the original. Cowley's "Pindaric Odes" are examples. Dryden says, "The translator (if he has not lost that name) assumes the liberty not only to vary from the words and sense, but to forsake them both as he sees occasion" (I. 268). It is "an endeavor of a later poet to write like one who has written before him on the same subject; that is, not to translate his words, or to be confined to his sense, but only to set him as a pattern, and to write, as he supposes that author would have done, had he lived in our age, and in our country" (I. 270). See also Metaphrase, Paraphrase. I.POE 268, 270, 270, 271, 271, 271, 273, II.PS 31, DCOPS 119, 152, PRAV 262, SS.VIII.DAm 9.

IMITATOR (sb.) One who copies or imitates. There are two kinds of imitators, servile and inventive. "The copier is a servile imitator" (SS.XIV. 187) who merely reproduces literally either nature or a model. Dryden quotes Horace: "Imitators are a servile kind of cattle, says the poet, or at best the keepers of cattle for other men" (II. 195). An inventive imitator adds something from his imagination or invention. Dryden says, "Rafael imitated nature. . . . There is a kind of invention in the imitation of Rafael; for, though the thing was in nature, yet the idea of it was his own" (SS.XIV. 187). (1) One who reproduces nature too closely or translates another work of art: II.PPBPP 185 (Homer imitated nature in Achilles), 195, SS.XIV.DAVd 187. (2) One who emulates or imitates a model: I.EDP 31 (Jonson imitates Horace), II.LP 9 (Montaigne imitates Plutarch), SS.XVII.LP 75 (some imitate Seneca's style).

IMPERFECT (adj.) Describing that which falls short of its idealized image. See

Perfect. (1) Faulty, flawed, incomplete: I.GCT 247 (plot), 250 (idea), II. DCOPS 79 (sense), PF 275, 275, SS.XV.PNOEM 405 (thoughts). Imperfectly: II.PRAV 260, PF 288. (2) Unfinished, rude, undeveloped: I.EDP 47 (images), II.DCOPS 90 (system), DAV 224, 235, 249 (sense), 249, 249, SS.XIII.SAVPMF 316 (verses), XIV.DAVd 156 (poem), 156 (work), 161 (poem), 161 (work), XVII.APa 351 (the art of painting). (3) Natural, too close to nature, unelevated: II.DAV 228 (character), SS.VIII.DKA 137 (character).

IMPROPER (adj.) See Proper, Decorum, Just. (1) Unnatural, indecorous, lacking in propriety: I.EDP 82, PAM 101, DEDP 125, DECG 171, II.PS 20, PF 272, 284, SS.XV.AP 230 (terms), XVII.APa 351. Improperly: I.HAR 217, II.PPBPP 183, DAV 238, PF 279. (2) Incorrect, ungrammatical: II.PEL 167, SS.XV.PNOEM 298.

INCLINATION (sb.) (1) Taste, the way (someone's) taste or liking tends: I.EDP 78, II.PPBPP 182, SS.XIII.SAVPMF 313, XVIII.LLd 71. (2) The state of someone's mind as it leans or tends toward a way of thinking or a way of action: I.PTL 138, GCT 246, 248, 249, SS.II.DIE 287. (3) A "humour" or way of acting. A character in a play can be portrayed as an "inclination." See Humour. I.GCT 249, 250, 250, 251, II.LP 12, PF 274, 276, 284.

INGENIOUS (Ingenius) (adj.) (1) Talented, having good taste. When used to describe a person it is a highly flattering word, ascribed to one who has a great deal of ability and a refined appreciation of what is well performed. "Ingenious" is usually found combined with "learned" (as the "ingenious and learned" Mr. Congreve), and it implies being endowed with genius. See Genius. I.EDP 49 (Thomas Sprat), DEDP 111, 115, PEL 148, 150, II.PS 29, DCOPS 115, PPBPP 187, 194, LL 211, PRAV 261, PF 270, 283, SS.VIII.DLT 375, X.PRLaici 31, XV.AP 239, XVII.DPL 7, LPd 74, PPBPPd 291, XVIII. PDCW 5, LLd 67; Milton IV. 282; Chapman (Spingarn) I. 68, 73 ("My own earnest and ingenious love of Homer"). (2) Superficially clever (a term of opprobrium): II.PS 20, SS.VII.VDG 167; Reynolds (Spingarn) I. 154 ("ingenious nothings" come from "ungrounded fancy"); Phillips (Spingarn) II. 256 ("ingenuity" is associated with "brute animals"). (3) Cleverly constructed, or clever (as "ingenious flattery"): I.DEDP 114, II.DCOPS 83, 151, PPBPP 184, SS.XVII.APa 349. Ingeniously: I.DEDP 121. Reynolds (Spingarn) I. 147, 159 ("The ingenius Ovid").

INSPIRATION (sb.) That sudden animation or insight which moves a poet to write; the "furor poeticus" found in "priests of Apollo" (poets) when they feel the god within them. That which moves a poet to prophecy or to see relationships in nature that ordinarily one overlooks. Inspiration takes place in the imagination with such force that the judgment is paralyzed. The poet thus becomes an instrument which merely records an idea. See Enthusiasm. II.PE 61, PEP 162, SS.V.DSI 103, PAZd 192, XV.PNOEM 407 (used in ridicule).

INSTRUCTION (sb.) (1) Enlightenment, art of teaching, admonition, information: I.DEDP 118, GCT 254, II.LP 4, DCOPS 96, 146, PPBPP 185, 186, SS.X.PRLaici 33, XVII.LPd 25, 51, PFAAP 338. (2) A piece of advice or information: I.PO 234, II.DCOPS 127, 128, 128, PPBPP 182, 193, SS.XVII.

INVENTION

DPL 7. (3) An end of art. Dryden changes from delight (or pleasure) to instruction (or profit) as the "great end" of art, but always they are both important. At first, "delight is the chief if not the only end of poetry; instruction can be admitted but in second place, for poesy only instructs as it delights" (I. 113). In PEL he says, "The first end of comedy is delight, instruction only the second" (I. 152), although he does not mention tragedy. In HAR he first gives his most often repeated view: "The chief end of the poet is to please, for his immediate reputation depends upon it. The great end of the poem is to instruct, which is performed by making pleasure the vehicle for that instruction: for poetry is an art, and all arts are made to profit" (I. 219. See also II. 132, II. 186). Delight is important, however, for "without the means of pleasure, the instruction is but a base and dry philosophy; a crude preparation of morals which we may have from Aristotle and Epictetus, with more profit than from any poet" (II. 153). Dryden tries to balance both ends, for "to instruct delightfully is the general end of all poetry" (I. 245): I.EDP 25, DEDP 113, PTL 138, PEL 152, HAR 219, 219, GCT 245, II.LP 7, DCOPS 132, 153, 153, PPBPP 186, DAV 230, SS.X.PRLaici 32, XIV.DAVd 204, XV.AP 250, PNOEM 408, XVIII.CPd 31.

INTEGRITY OF SCENES Where the action in a scene is unbroken. See Liaison des Scènes. I.EDP 64.

INVENT (v.) To make something up, to imagine, to think something up, to devise, to originate, to discover (something) in one's own mind. See Invention. I.EDP 25, 58, PT 133, OHP 158, AAHP 201, GCT 245, 246, 246, 257, POE 271, II.PAA 36, 37, 37, 41, 43, PDS 51, DCOPS 96, 97, 100, 101, 106, 109, 111, 143, PPBPP 193, DAV 251, PF 271, SS.VII.VDG 153, VIII.DLT 374, XIV.DG 4, DAVd 178, 180, 182, 184, 197, XV.AP 236, 242, PNOEM 408. Inventing: SS.XV.PNOEM 408. Jonson 57, 58, 60, 97.

INVENTION (sb.) A faculty of the mind; the artist's creative power as expressed in a work of art; the act of artistic creation; a work of art. Invention comes from the traditional classical rhetorical trivium: inventio, dispositio, and elocutio. See T. S. Eliot, *The Use of Poetry and the Use of Criticism* (London, 1964), pp. 55–58 (Eliot comments on the provocative passage on I.PAM 98). See also Murray Bundy, "Invention and Imagination in the Renaissance," *JEGP*, XXIX (1930), 535–45. (1) The faculty of the mind which "makes" ideas, which thinks up things. The artist's creative power is contained within this faculty. Sometimes it is equated with or is a part of imagination and is set in opposition to judgment. Where invention is differentiated from wit or fancy, it has absorbed the word-producing function of elocutio: I.EDP 45, PEL 154, II.PAA 41, PDS 48, DCOPS 76, 90 (and judgment), 90 (the three parts of the mind are invention, judgment, and memory in 1693. Note the comparison with the traditional classical rhetorical trivium. "Elocutio" has disappeared to become a part of both judgment and invention), 92, 110, 115, PEP 167 (invention and judgment), DAV 229, 229, PF 275, 291, SS.VIII.DLT 374, X.PHP 118, XIV.DAVd 180, 182, 184 (a poet "makes or invents"), XV. PNOEM 405, XVII.APa 391; Jonson 39, 55, 59, 75; Peachum (Spingarn) I. 127 (Horace's is "sweet and pleasant"), 128 (invention has more to do with rhetoric than does wit), 130, 130 (the ability to think up ideas), 130, 132,

132 (the ability to write and to think up ideas); Alexander (Spingarn) I. 184 (the imaging faculty); Davenant (Spingarn) II. 5; Hobbes (Spingarn) II. 56; Cowley (Spingarn) II. 90; Sprat (Spingarn) II. 125 (differentiates between "fancy" and "invention"; "invention" is more of the word-producing faculty), 130; Shadwell (Spingarn) II. 150 ("wit and invention [are] required in finding out a good humour"). (2) The creative power of a poet (or painter) expressed in a work of art. Without invention, "a painter is a copier, a poet is a plagiarist" (II. 195). Invention shows the scope and quickness of the imagination. In poetry, invention (as well as fancy and elocution) is one of the three happinesses of imagination (I. 98), and as such is embodied in writing (see Imagination and Fancy). Correspondingly, the three principal parts of painting are "invention, design or drawing, and colouring." Invention is the most important of the three parts. Contained within it are (a) disposition of the work (following the rules and tradition of a genre), (b) refusal on the part of the artist (or poet) to include unnecessary ornaments and descriptions, and (c) the force which heightens and beautifies the action. Invention in a great work of art is what overpowers the judgment of an audience, reader, or viewer, transporting his imagination: I.PAM 98, 98, II.PS 32, PPBPP 195, 195, 204, 208, PF 274, 275, 275, 290, 291, SS.XIV.DAVd 185, 186, 188, 189, 189, XVII.APa 349, 349, 391; Alexander (Spingarn) I. 182 ("witty inventions" are rhetorical adornments), 182 ("variety of invention" is found in "sentences," "witty conceits," and "generous rapture"), 183, 188; Phillips (Spingarn) II. 266 ("An epigram is . . . the fag end of poetry . . . [consisting] rather of conceit and acumen of wit than of poetical invention"; "invention" to Phillips is higher than "wit"), 267 ("invention" is "the grand part of the poet or maker, and verse, the least"), 267, 267 ("decorum is the well-management of invention"); Rymer (Z) 110 ("felicity of invention"). (3) The act of artistic creation, the act of combining images or ideas (II. 42), the act of thinking up something: I.PRL 7, PT 135, 135, II.ETV 16 (and translation), PAA 42, DCOPS 98, PPBPP 189, SS.XIV.DAVd 185, 187, XV.AP 241, XVII. AAEHL 101, APa 365. (4) A work of art, an idea, an image: I.PRL 142, GCT 242, POE 267, 267, II.PAA 36, DCOPS 82, 88, LJD 178, PPBPP 190, LL 212, DAV 224, PF 277, 277, 278, SS.XIV.DAVd 187, 189, XVII.APa 359; Peachum (Spingarn) I. 132.

J

JUDGE (sb.) A critic; one who gives an opinion on a literary work; one who passes sentence on a historical event, a historical figure, etc. "Judge" connotes nothing favorable or unfavorable. See Critic, Judgment. I.PRL 3, EDP 38, 41, 68, 69, 74, 76, 78, PSL 105, 107, 107, DEDP 119, 126, PWG 131, PTL 140, PrTL 143, 143, PEL 145, 147, DECG 179, PA 184, 188, AAHP 198, 200, 203, PAL 226, 226, 229, 230, GCT 243, 256, 258, POE 265, 265, 273, PSF 277, 278, II.PS 29, 33, PAA 39, 39, 40, 42, PDS 45, 46, 50, 50, CSE 59, PE 63, DCOPS 74, 74, 88, 94, 117, 125, 128, PEP 161, 162, 167, LWW2 174, PPBPP 200, 204, 208, 210, LL 214, DAV 233, 243, 244, 245, 252, 253, PRAV 258, LCM 265, PF 272, 273, 278, 280, 287, 294, SS.IV.DMLM 256, V.PAZd 189, 198, VII.VDG 199, VIII.DC 215, IX.TRAA 212, XIV.DAVd 178, 180, XV.AP 236, 249, 249, PNOEM 397, PHC 410; Jonson 87, 88, 89.

JUDGMENT (sb.) (1) The critical faculty (of any man); intellectual control. It is the faculty which discriminates between things which are similar in appearance. It is an active, not a passive faculty, unlike understanding (II. 39). Its capacity is innate, but it is able to be informed and educated (II. 90). Judgment is directly related to the traditional rhetorical term "dispositio"; it is the faculty in a poet which orders, controls, and maintains. It specifically orders plots, chooses characters, maintains what is chosen (and checks to see if a work fits into its genre or model, or pattern). Thus, for example, judgment regulates comedies of humour, but not farces (which are unnatural or grotesque). Judgment also regulates decorum, and the power of a poet's judgment reveals itself in a work of art primarily through decorum (II. 42). Judgment, for instance, manifests itself as decorum when it becomes a part of the second of the happinesses of imagination, for fancy is the "variation, driving, or moulding of [a] thought, as the 'judgment' represents it proper to the subject" (I. 98). Judgment opposes and tries to govern imagination (or fancy). The more fancy (or imagination) a poet has, the more judgment is needed to maintain coherence in his writing. Yet if one's judgment becomes too strong, one's poetic ability declines proportionately. See Decorum, Design, Disposition, Fancy (sb.), Imagination, Understanding, Wit. I.PRL 2, 3, 8, 9, EDP 13, 19, 68, 80, 91, 91, 91, 91, 91, 91, 91, 91, 91, 91, 91, 92, PAM 98, 103, PSL 105, 105, 105, 105, DEDP 119, 123, 129, PTL 140, PEL 145, 146, 146, 148, 148, 148, 155, DECG 178, 182, 182, PA 184, 187, AAHP 198, 201, 207, GCT 247, 254, 255, 257, POE 265, PSF 275, 275, 275, 279, II.LP 10, PS 32, 33, PAA 42, PE 61, DCOPS 90, 90, 101, 119, 127, 139, PEL 156, 158, 164, 167, TCDD 170, 170, 172, LJD 180, PPBPP 182, 185, 193, 196, 206, 206, 207, LL 213, DAV 224, 230, 237, 244, 244, 244, 257, PRAV 261, LCM 266, PF 272, 280, SS.VII.DTC 247, 253, VIII.DAm 11, DKA 137, DC 213, 214, DLT 372, XIII.SAVPMF 310, XIV.DG 2, 3, 3, 4, DAVd 171, 180, 204, XV.PNOEM 399, 405, 406, 406, XVII.APa 383, 387, 391, XVIII.CPd 45, LLd 79; Jonson 27, 28, 51, 52, 54, 55, 56, 57, 58, 59, 59, 67, 89, 91, 99, 100; Milton III. 303; Reynolds (Spingarn) I. 147 (the critical faculty); Alexander (Spingarn) I. 187 (a good work develops a reader's judgment), 189; Hobbes (Spingarn) II. 54 (the second part of the mind; the first is memory; the third is fancy), 59, 59 ("Judgment begets the strength and structure . . . of a poem"), 59, 70; Cowley (Spingarn) II. 90; Sprat (Spingarn) II. 125, 130; Shadwell (Spingarn) II. 153, 159 ("Fancy rough-draws, but judgment smooths and finishes"), 159 ("Judgment does indeed comprehend wit, for no man can have that who has not wit"); Sheffield (Spingarn) II. 287 ("Without judgment, fancy is but mad"); Rymer (Z) 3, 5, 18 ("Right judgment is higher than common sense"), 117 ("Judgment runs most-what by comparison: by purple we judge of purple"). (2) Discretion, good sense, common sense, reasonableness of thought: I.EDP 50, GCT 242, II.LP 6, DCOPS 93, DAV 230, 238, 243, 257, PF 280, SS.VIII.DLT 374, XIV.DAVd 175, XV.AP 229, XVII.LPd 74, PFAAP 339, XVIII.PDCW 5, XVIII.CPd 38; Alexander (Spingarn) I. 183 ("The deep judgment and grave sentences of Horace and Juvenal"), 184. (3) Criticism (especially literary) ranging from simple liking or disliking to the act of formally asserting opinions and applying critical principles: I.EDP 38, 63, 77, 81, 86, PSL 105, PrSL2 109, DEDP 130, OHP 159, 160, PA 189,

PAZ 191, AAHP 196, 197, 197, 199, HAR 212, 212, 215, 218, PAL 225, 225, EO 236, 236, GCT 260, II.LP 11, PS 29, PDS 50, CSE 57, DCOPS 109, 128, PEP 164, LWW2 174, PPBPP 182, DAV 240, 257, LCM 266, PF 271, 281, 286, SS.II.DIE 288, V.DSI 103, 103, PAZd 197, IX.TRAA 211, 214, X.PHP 114, XVII.LPd 70, 71, PFAAP 340, 341, XVIII.CPd 24, 29, 41, LLd 65. (4) Moral condemnation: I.PEL 146, SS.VIII.PC 219.

JUST (adj.) (1) Appropriate, describing that which preserves decorum, is suitable, well-balanced, proportionate. The English meanings of "just" (right, exact, proper, equitable, etc.) were relatively restricted in a literary sense. In French, the literary uses of *juste* are important and widespread. Dryden uses the French meanings. "Just" concerns appropriateness, the application (of words), correct proportion and design (*dessein*), and proper decorum. The appropriate expression, the "just" expression, is the most decorous, the one which best fits tone and subject. Without the French influence of *juste*, Lisideius' definition of a play as "a 'just' and lively imitation of human nature" (I. 25) would make little sense. To Dryden, a "just image" (of human nature) is a decorous, apt, appropriate, well-balanced, proportionate, suitable image. It is not an exact or mirror image of nature, but is one which reflects human nature as it probably is or as it should be. The *Dictionnaire de l'academie française* (1694) says, "juste–1° adj.–Qui va bien, où rien n'est de trop, où rien ne manque. Se dit aussi de . . . choses qui ont la mesure et la proportion requise, qui est tout à fait convenable." La Bruyère (*Oeuvres*, Paris, Editions of les grands écrivains de France, 1865, p. 141) uses *juste* in this way: "Mais il est égal, soutenu, toujours le même partout, soit pour dessein et la conduit de ses pièces, qui sont justes, régulières, prises dans le bon sens et dans la nature" (he speaks of Corneille). Corneille ("Au lecteur," *Le Menteur* in *Oeuvres Complètes*, Paris, 1963, p. 337 [written in 1641]) says, "Elle est toute spirituelle depuis le commencement jusqu'à la fin, et les incidents si juste et si gracieux qu'il faut être, à mon avis, de bien mauvais humeur pour n'en approuver pas la conduit et n'en aimer pas la representation." Boileau ("L'art poétique," *Oeuvres*, Paris, 1872, p. 302) writes, "Enfin Malherbe vint, et, le premier en France,/ Fit sentir dans le verse un juste cadence,/ D'un mot mis en place enseigna le pouvoir,/ Et réduisit la muse aux règles du devoir." I.EDP 25, 51, 87, DEDP 122, OHP 158, HAR 212, 217, GCT 239, 254, POE 273, PSF 275, 277, II.PAA 43, DCOPS 81, 82, 140, PEP 162, PPBPP 184, 190, PPV 219, DAV 231, 237, 251, 256, PF 275, SS.V.PAZd 198, VIII.DAm 9, XIV.DAVd 162, XV.AP 227, 228, 230, 232, 233, 241, 243, XVII.DPL 8; Wilmot (Spingarn) II. 283 ("Just, bold strokes are good, although in Shadwell's work unfinished"); Rymer (Z) 74, 84, 85. Juster: SS.XV.AP 240. Justly: I.DEDP 111, HAR 219, PSF 278, 279, II.PAA 35, 37, DCOPS 73, 94, LL 215, SS.VIII.DLT 375, XIII.SAVPMF 315, XIV.DAVd 162, XV.PNOEM 399. Justness: I.EDP 27 (of plot), HAR 216, PSF 278, II.CSE 57, SS.XVIII.PDCW 5. (2) Right, exact, correct, proper, equitable. In English, "just" had more ethical and moral uses than literary: I.PAM 102, II.PE 62, DCOPS 127, PPBPP 199, LL 213, SS.III.DEL 234, XIII.SAVPMF 315, XIV.DAVd 159, XV.AP 247, XVII.LPd 70, XVIII.CPd 30. Justly: I.PAM 101, DEDP 129, HAR 212, PEL 144, GCT 259, POE 265, II.DCOPS 112, 125, 128, 130, LL 215, PPV 220, PRAV 259, LCM 266, PF 293; Jonson 35, 46, 93 ("In every action which is the subject of a just work, there is required a certain proportional great-ness"); Milton I. 331 (tragedy should "temper and reduce them [the passions] to just measure with a kind of delight"), II. 187.

K

KIND (sb.) "Kind" can be plural or singular. (1) A literary genre (such as satire, tragedy, heroic opera, epic, pastoral, comedy). Watson says there are no clear-cut examples of this meaning before Dryden: "Webbe in *Elizabethan Critical Essays*, I. 262, is ambiguous": I.EDP 15, 23, 38, PSL 105, 106, PTL 159, PAZ 191, AAHP 199, 203, HAR 218, PAL 231, II.PS 25, 32, 32, PAA 39, DCOPS 81, 96, 102, 109, 115, PPBPP 191, 207, PPV 220, DAV 224, PF 290, SS.XV.PNOEM 408. (2) Type, sort (in general): I.EDP 53, 85 (of plot), 92, PSL 105 (of writer), DEDP 114, PEL 146, 149, 151, DECG 179, 180, PAZ 203, HAR 219, PAL 226, 256, II.LWW1 52, DCOPS 113, 113, 136, 148, 149, SS.VIII.DKA 136, DLT 375. (3) Type of style (in verse, prose, stanza form, etc.): I.EDP 79, 80, 81, 81, 84, 85, 87, 89, PAM 96, PSL 105, II.DCOPS 147, 150.

L

LABOURED (ppl. adj.) Describing a work of art or a part of it which is success-ful because of painstaking revision: I.EDP 80, ECG 167, SS.V.DA 8, XV.AP 227, 237.

LANGUAGE (sb.) To Dryden, language, especially the English language, is a living, dynamic entity, always changing by the elimination and addition of new words, expressions, and modes of speech. The language during the Restoration was improving because of the influence of polite society on poets (something the Elizabethan poets lacked). Poets, according to Dryden, make any language what it is. The principal gift of Restoration writers was that they eliminated gross, low words and expressions, and in style imitated the easy, cultured, highly polished conversational language of an accomplished upper class. In 1685, Dryden introduced "diction" as an English word, largely taking the place of def. (1). See Diction. (1) Diction; choice of words, phrases, and expres-sions; way of expression: I.PRL 5, EDP 40, 40, 58, 69, 69, 70, DEDP 119, PEL 154, 155, DECG 170, 170, 170, 171, 171, 173, 176, 178, 182, PAL 231, GCT 241, 241, 253, 253, POE 266, II.PS 25 (and thoughts), CSE 57, DCOPS 81, 83, DAV 235, 238, 247, 248, PRAV 259, PF 283, SS.V.DSI 322, VII.VDG 177, XIII.SAVPMF 315, XV.AP 229, 229, XVIII.LLd 81; Alexander (Spin-garn) I. 182 ("The apparel of poesy, which may give beauty but not strength"); Rymer (Z) 127 (in Waller, "the language [is] clean and majestic"). (2) The whole body of words and the methods used to combine them em-ployed by a nation, a people, etc. (as English language, Roman language, etc.). Dryden also uses "language" as the literature written in a specific language: I.PRL 5, EDP 14, 30, 31, 38, 39, 69, 70, 71, 80, 81, 83, 83, 90, PAM 95, 96, 100, DEDP 111, 115, 116, 118, PEL 145, 154, 154, ECG 167, DECG 170, 171, 171, 176, 176, 177, 178, 182, AAHP 206, 206, GCT 239, 246, 259, POE 262, 268, 269, 269, 271, 271, 271, 272, 272, 273, II.LP 2, 3, 3, 3, 3, 3, 11,

PS 20, 23, 23, 23, 24, 30, 31, 32, PAA 36, 37, 37, 37, 39, 40, 40, 40, CP 65, DCOPS 80, 81, 81, 86, 90, 97, 107, 111, 111, 116, 118, 151, 152, 152, 154, PEP 161, 166, PPBPP 200, 201, LL 214, 214, 214, 215, PPV 218, 220, 220, 222, DAV 235, 235, 235, 237, 238, 240, 246, 246, 246, 247, 248, 250, 251, 251, 252, 252, 252, 256, PRAV 258, PF 270, 271, 271, 272, 274, 276, 286, 287, 287, 288, SS.II.CIE 322, V.DSI 104, VI.DKK 6, DTC 250, 251, 252, 252, 253, VII.VDG 180, 188, VIII.DC 215, XIV.DAVd 161, 162, 189, 204, XV.AP 231, PHC 410, XVI.AARLSFX 9, XVII.DPL 7, LPd 25, 26, 33, 55, 55, 63, DHL 83, DPWDY 210, XVIII.CPd 30, 31, LLd 81, 81, 81, 81, 81; Sprat (Spingarn) II. 112 ("Elegance of language comes from the city"), 113; Phillips (Spingarn) II. 263 (on refinement of the English language).

LAST PERFECTION (1) Elocution. In a poem, "elocution" consists of diction, elegance of diction (SS.XIV. 204), and rhetorical ornamentation (II. 150); in a play, "the words and discourses" (I. 157, 219). Elocution is the last perfection because it is the last thing to be accomplished or considered in the composition of a poem or play (and therefore placed last in the rhetorical trivium, inventio, dispositio, elocutio), and because it is the least important consideration. Dryden, who follows Aristotle's precepts about elocution, says, "Aristotle . . . places [the parts of elocution] in the last rank of beauties; perhaps only last in order, because they are the last product of the design, of the disposition or connection of its parts; of the characters, of the manners of those characters, and of the thoughts proceeding from those manners" (I. 219–20). Elocution therefore by itself is less important than its appropriateness to the thoughts, manners, etc. Thus, Dryden criticizes Hobbes for saying that diction is the first beauty of an epic poem (II. 275) (when it is the last), and he overlooks diction entirely when he prefers Chaucer to Ovid, for Chaucer's diction is "given up, as a post not to be defended" (II. 278). See Diction, Elocution. I.OHP 157, HAR 219, II.DCOPS 150, SS.XIV.DAVd 204; Sprat (Spingarn) II. 112 (of the English language). (2) The finishing improvement (in a work of art or in an artistic or literary genre): II.DCOPS 86 (of the design of an epic poem), 139 (of satire).

LAST RANK OF BEAUTIES See Last Perfection, def. (1). I.HAR 219.

LAWS (sb.) (1) The neoclassical precepts or rules governing the correct execution of a work of art, such as the unities, decorum of the stage, liaison des scènes, etc. "The fundamental law" of art is "imitation of nature" (I. 56, 136). For a more complete treatment, see Rules. I.EDP 44, 56, 56, 63, 63, 66, 66, PSL 105, DEDP 123, PrT 136, PEL 150, 150, OHP 159, II.PDS 47, PPBPP 201, 201, SS.VII.VDG 159, 162, XIV.DAVd 180. (2) The King's example (of good conversation): I.DECG 181. (3) Precepts governing the writing of history, such as recording events impartially and accurately: I.PAM 95, SS.XVII.LPd 63, AARHL 95.

LAZAR (sb.) A grotesque image of a person, a deformed person. From Lazarus, a leper: I.PAM 101, DEDP 115, PAZ 190, II.PPBPP 190.

LEARNED (sb.) Those knowledgeable in Ancient literature, history, art, etc.: I.DEDP 117, AAHP 200, II.DCOPS 108, LL 209, PRAV 262, PF 271.

LEARNED (ppl. adj.) (1) Educated, formally or naturally (as Dryden says

Shakespeare was [I. 67]); widely read; erudite; knowledgeable, especially by means of study. To be learned usually means to be knowledgeable in the lore of the Ancients. It is often used in conjunction with either judicious or ingenious. See Ingenious. I.EDP 67, 69, HAR 218, II.PS 29, DCOPS 96, 101, 113, 114, 124, 136, 142, LJD 178, PPBPP 183, 200, LL 209, 211, PPV 216, 219, DAV 245, 252, 253, 254, 257, PF 270, 272, 280, 283, SS.VI.DKK 8, XVII.DPL 7, LPd 29, AARHL 97, XVIII.CPd 30, LLd 67. (2) A work or time which exhibits learning. See Learning. I.PAM 95, LD 209, II.PAA 37, DCOPS 152, DAV 235, SS.XV.AP 235.

LEARNING (sb.) (1) The store of knowledge or erudition gained by study, especially in the lore of the Ancients. Although a poet should be learned, Dryden once says learning and poetry are separate (SS.XVII. 23), perhaps indicating that learning consists of historical and philosophical information. To Dryden, learning is usually an admirable thing to have. Learning alone, however, is not enough for an able man or a poet. Along with learning, he must also apply wit (I. 55, 273, II. 159, SS.XVII. 6, XVIII. 78), art (II. 30), care (I. 76), merit (II. 82), genius (II. 83, 85), elocution (SS.XV. 399), judgment (SS.XVIII. 78), and parts (SS.XVIII. 80). These qualities concern faculties of the mind, or innate abilities of which learning (which is acquired) is not a part. In one place Dryden speaks scornfully of learning, but only when it becomes a "wretched affectation" (II. 291): I.EDP 67, 96, PEL 155, DECG 176, PA 187, PAL 229, 231, POE 266, 267, 273, 273, II.LP 10, PS 20, 30, PAA 36, PDS 45, DCOPS 73, 81, 81, 82, 83, 85, 96, 96, 119, 120, 120, PEP 157, 159, 163, LJD 178, PPV 220, PF 291, SS.IX.EWTM 430, XIV.DG 10, DAVd 181, XV.AP 245, PNOEM 399, 407, XVII.DPL 6, 6, 6, LPd 23, 23, 55, XVIII.CPd 31, LLd 74, 78, 78, 80. (2) The act of gaining knowledge: SS.XVII.LPd 25.

LIAISON DES SCÈNES "The continuity or joining of the scenes." One rule of the neoclassical French theater is the connection of scenes in each act. The stage is never empty until the end of an act. A new scene is formed when one or more people leave the stage or join those already onstage. In the French theater, each act is what the English would call a single scene: I.EDP 29, 37.

LIBERAL ARTS AND SCIENCES A carry-over from the liberal arts of the medieval trivium (rhetoric, logic, grammar) and quadrivium (arithmetic, geometry, music, astronomy). Dryden names some of the liberal sciences (moral philosophy, mathematics, geography, history). Those subjects studied by gentlemen and poets, not by narrow professionalists: II.DCOPS 90, DAV 225, SS.XIV.DG 6 (philosophy is a liberal science), XVII.APa 361 (only arts), XVIII.LLd 63 (only sciences).

LICENTIOUS (adj.) (1) Describing poetic license: II.PEP 165 (of the Greeks), SS.XV.PNOEM 405 (wildness and extravagance of an uncontrolled fancy). (2) Lewd, obscene: II.PF 290.

LIVELINESS (sb.) Lifelikeness, quality of a painting in which the painter appears to be "the living hand of nature": SS.XVII.APa 379.

LIVELY (adj.) (1) Lifelike, probable, natural, having the appearance of being lifelike (not of being life itself). Related to "enargeia" and "hypotyposis":

I.EDP 33. Bodies: SS.XVII.APa 375. Colors: II.PEP 167, SS.XVII.APa 377, 377. Description: I.PAM 98, GCT 259. Expression (of the subject): SS.XVII. APa 351, 363. Figures (characters): II.PS 278. Image: PTL 139 (of piety), AAHP 203. Image of human nature: I.EDP 25, 87, 87, DEDP 122. Imitation (of truth): II.PPBPP 194. Impression: II.LP 7. Touches: I.GCT 247. Wolsely (Spingarn) III. 21 (Lively, here, is related to both "energia" and "enargeia": "Poetical wit [is] . . . a true and lively expression of nature. . . . This expression of nature must be true that it may gain our reason, and lively that it may affect our passions"), 22, 23; Rymer (Z) 127 ("The expression being more lively, free, elegant, and easy"; here, too, "lively" is related to both "energia" and "enargeia"). (2) Fresh, animated: Agitation: II.DCOPS 130. Delicacy: II.PS 27. Fire (of a vein): SS.XVII.APa 345. Imagination: SS.XIII. SAVPMF 315. Narration: SS.XV.AP 243, XVI.AARLSFX 10.

LIVELY (adv.) In a lifelike manner, in a probable manner: I.EDP 51, 51, 69, 73, AAHP 203.

LOFTY (adj.) Often a synonym for "sublime." Dryden uses "lofty" only once before 1674 (I. 90), the year of Boileau's "Traité du sublime," and it is only after this date that Dryden started thinking about the sublime. Dryden usually thinks of "lofty" and "sublime" in terms of style or the thoughts contained within style, or in other words, he thinks of it primarily as a rhetorical rather than an aesthetic term. See also Sublime, Great, and Majestic. (1) Sublime, great, sonorous, elevated, soaring. Dryden uses "lofty" to describe a style of writing, a poem, a finished work of art. A lofty style employs "bold figures," elevated diction, and the discourses of noble characters: I.EDP 90, GCT 238, 254, 277, II.PAA 35, DCOPS 130, 150, PEP 163, PPV 218, DAV 232, 233, SS.XV.AP 231, 232, 236; Milton III. 238, IV. 286 (the three kinds of style are "lofty, mean, or lowly"); Peachum (Spingarn) I. 128 ("The loftiness of sound"), 129, 130; Wilmot (Spingarn) II. 283 ("lofty" language). Loftier: SS.XV.AP 241. Loftiest: SS.XV.AP 229, 253. Loftily: I.DEDP 116, SS.XVII. PPBPPd 298. Loftiness: I.PSF 277, II.LP 9 (of general history), PS 25 (of expression), PAA 35, PDS 46, DCOPS 144, 149. (2) Describing genius: I. GCT 254. (3) Describing the empty grandeur of "rant" or "fustian": II.DAV 229.

LOW SATIRE Low, commonplace subjects satirized in a commonplace style. Horatian as opposed to Juvenalian satire: II.DCOPS 136, 143.

LUSCIOUSLY (adv.) Fulsomely (pejorative): SS.XVIII.LLd 71.

LUXURIANT (adj.) Describing what is so profuse it transgresses reasonable bounds. A luxuriant poet, for example, overwrites, becoming redundant and repetitious. A luxuriant fancy is exuberant and difficult to control. It produces a superabundance of whims, frivolous words and thoughts, unnecessary similitudes, etc.: I.PRL 8 (poet), EDP 80 (fancy), 90 (poet), 92, 92 (fancy), POE 272 (fancy), II.DCOPS 61 (fancy), 130 (poet), PEP 163 (fancy and expressions). Luxuriance: I.DECG 178 (of writing). Luxuriancy: I.EDP 92 (in verse), DECG 173 (of fancy). Luxurious: II.DCOPS 82 (style).

LYRIC (adj.) Pertaining to poetry, or parts of it, which is meant to be sung or which could be sung. Lyric poetry, therefore, includes such extremes as small, light ditties and great odes like Dryden's own "Alexander's Feast." A great ode is part of an important genre; little songs such as sonnets or madrigals, are not: I.PRL 7, EDP 17, 23, 84, II.PS 32, 32, 32, PAA 39, DCOPS 75, 80, 81, 82, DAV 234, 248.

M

MACHINE (sb.) (1) Any kind of supernatural invention (in an epic poem or a play), but especially a divine person or character that intervenes in the earthly affairs of men. Rymer, in 1674, could be the first to use "machine" in English in conjunction with divine intervention in an epic poem (Thomas Rymer, *Critical Works*, ed. C. Zimansky [Yale, 1956], p. 8). Rymer, who is against Christian machines argues that they will not move readers, because their distance from earthly practices and everyday beliefs is so great that they lack human attributes. Human heroes cannot hope to imitate Christian celestial beings. Rymer is thinking of *Paradise Lost,* where (he thinks) all principal actions are carried on by machine. Dryden, taking issue with Rymer, says that a poet should use Christian machines in an epic poem, provided he uses the proper machines (Dryden suggests "guardian angels"). Dryden discusses Christian machinery in II. 86–92, and 178: II.DCOPS 84 (Milton), 86, 87, 87, 88, 88, 90, 92, LJD 178, 178, 178 (Virgil), PF 276 (Agamemnon's dream in the *Iliad*), SS.XIV.DAVd (except where noted, all the following are about Virgil) 175, 175, 175, 197, 198, 198, 198, 199, 200, 200 (Horace on stage machines), 200 (Dryden on Horace), 201, 202. (2) Any mechanical or theatrical device which the Ancient theater used to bring a god onstage: I.EDP 35, II.CP 69. (3) A device for show, a decoration on the stage. Dryden connects "machine" closely to "scenes [scenery], songs, and dances," but only in the Preface to *Albion and Albanius*: II.PAA 35, 36, 36, 41, 42; Flecknoe (Spingarn) II. 96 (mechanical device). (4) A force in a play which moves emotion in an audience (as terror, pity, etc.): I.PAL 222, EO 236. (5) Any literary device or trick: II.PF 279. (6) A political plot, intrigue, contrivance: SS.VII. VDG 189.

MACHINING PERSONS Supernatural beings who intervene in the action of an epic poem (as in Milton's *Paradise Lost*): II.DAV 233.

MACHINING WORK Activity of supernatural beings in an epic poem (as in Virgil's *Aeneid*): SS.XIV.DAVd 176.

MADMAN (sb.) (1) One who likes disconnected flights of fustian: I.PSF 277. (2) An inspired poet. See Aristotle, *Poetics*, Chapt. XVII on the madness of a poet who is afflicted with the rages he tries to express. Castelvetro claims Aristotle held the poet to be mad as well as divinely inspired. Rapin (Chapt. V) and Dryden deny that the poet is mad. See Enthusiasm, Fury, Rage, Inspiration, Fancy (sb.). I.GCT 255, 255.

MAJESTIC (adj.) The most important synonym for "sublime" (after 1674). Grand, dignified, stately, sublime. See Great, Lofty, Sublime. I.EDP 24 (Denham), II.PS 21 (Virgil), DCOPS 144 (style), DAV 251 (beauty), 256 (mien), SS.X.PRLaici 32 (expressions), PHP 117 (turn of heroic poesy). Majestical: II.PAA 35 (expressions), PEP 166, DAV 224 (part of a series with "grave" and "sublime"), SS.XVII.PPBPPd 299. Milton usually sees something "majestic" as a concrete image whether it is a landscape or a personification. Milton: II. 48 (Satan), 432 (Jove's "majestic brow"), 463, III. 238, 471. Otherwise, Milton's usage is the same as Dryden's: II. 472 ("majestic, unaffected style"), IV. 69; Peachum (Spingarn) I. 128, 128, 128 ("the majesty of Vergil's verse"); Hobbes (Spingarn) II. 56 ("majesty of stile" is in hymns; "majesty" is "sublimity"); Cowley (Spingarn) II. 90; Sprat (Spingarn) II. 131 ("the majesty of style" in Cowley's Pindaric odes), II. 135; Phillips (Spingarn) II. 265 (Spenser's stanza is "majestic"), 269, 271 (Spenser is full of "poetic majesty"): Rymer (Z) 8, 118 ("the weight and majesty of tragedy"), 127 (in Waller, "the language . . . [is] majestic").

MANAGE (v.) "Manage" is very close to the French *ménager* which shares meanings with the English word and also has some meanings that are different (which Dryden uses on occasion). (1) To arrange discourses or arguments. It comes from the French *ménager*: "disposer avec art" (E. A. Horsman, "Dryden's French Borrowings," *RES* n.s. I [1950], 346–51). Littré says, "ménager les termes, les expressions, parler avec une grande circonspection": I.PAL 150, AAHP 200, 203, II.DCOPS 147, 149, DAV 230, 235, SS.VII.VDG 152, VIII. DLT 374, 374, XIV.DAVd 157; Rymer (Z) 8 (Cowley could "manage his digressions"). Management: I.PSL 107, DEDP 111, PSF 274, II.DCOPS 145, DAV 242, SS.XVII.APa 393. Managing: I.EDP 38, 54. (2) To regulate parts of a work of art (a function of the judgment): I.EDP 61, PO 234, GCT 252 (a character in a play), II.CSE 58 (a character) DCOPS 90, 137, PF 293, SS.XVII.APa 367 (lights and shadows). Management: SS.XV.PNOEM 399. Manager: I.POE 266. (3) To handle, to conduct: I.EDP 79 (a play), II.PAA 35 (provinces, areas of influence), SS.V.DAL 323. (4) To carry on (a conversation): I.EDP 60, PO 234. Management: II.DCOPS 108. (5) To manage business, to carry out affairs, etc., to carry out (the business of a play): I.PRL 4, II.PEP 161. (6) To husband economically or carefully (both an English and French meaning). "Administrer, gérer, conduire son bien, sa fortune avec raison et jugement" (from A. Furetière, *Dictionnaire universel*, 1690 [as quoted by Cayrou]): I. EDP 69 (his strength). Managing: I.GCT 256.

MANNERS (sb.) (1) The chief qualities of a person's character (in a work of art) (SS.XIV. 163). The manners of Aeneas, for example, are "piety to the gods and a dutiful affection to his father, love to his relations, care of his people, courage and conduct in wars, gratitude to those who had obliged him, and justice in general to mankind" (SS.XIV. 161). Manners always have to be appropriate and consistent to characters, and as such are closely connected to decorum and correctness (see also Humour). The general English literary use comes from the French *moeurs*. "Les partisans de Terence . . . l'élevent avec raison au-dessus de tous les poètes comiques, pour l'élégance de sa diction et pour les vraisemblances de moeurs" (Racine, Preface in *Bérénice*). Dryden points out that tragedy depicts the passions, while epic displays manners. A comedy of manners shows off and investigates the qualities, motives, and actions of the characters. In 1679, Dryden includes anger, hatred, love, ambition, etc., under "manners," but he excludes terror and pity which, he says, "are to be moved in the audience by the plot" (I. 253). In 1700, he extends the meaning to include all the passions as well as the descriptions of the characters (II. 278). See GCT 247–49 for definition and causes of "manners." See Passion, Decorum, Just, Proper. I.EDP 73, HAR 211, 216, 217, 217, 219, 220, GCT 247, 248, 248, 248, 248, 248, 249, 249, 249, 249, 249, 249, 249, 249, 250, 250, 250, 251, 251, 251, 251, 251, 251, 251, 253, 260, II.DCOPS 108, 115, TCDD 169, 170, PPBPP 186, 186, 189, 189, 189, 190, 198, DAV 228, 228, 242, PF 275, 275, 275, 278, 290, SS.XIV.DAVd 146, 157, 161, 161, 163, 186, XV.PHC 410; Jonson 35 ("From moral philosophy, it [poetry] took the soul, the expression of senses, perturbrations, manners, when they would paint an angry person, a proud, an inconstant, an ambitious, a brave," etc.); Hobbes (Spingarn) II. 56 (the subject of an epic poem), 56 ("Manners [are] presented, not dictated"), 56; Rymer (Z) 50, 134 ("Character and manners" should be natural and proper to the actors). (2) Behavior of a person or people, collectively. One sometimes travels to observe the manners of various peoples in different countries. "Correct manners" only refer to proper, polite behavior in society. A poet must know the manners of men before he can be successful: I.PTL 139, 139, PEL 146, 152, 153, DECG 181, 183, PA 186, AAHP 205, HAR 213, 217, PAL 223, 224, 224, 224, POE 263, II.LP 12, PS 20, DCOPS 79, 98, 130, 138, 144, 155, 155, 155, 155, PEL 159, 162, PPBPP 183, 190, PPV 221, DAV 234, 234, PF 274, 274, 277, 284, 285, 292, 293, SS.VII.VDG 154, VIII.DLT 374, XIII.SAVPMF 315, XIV.DG 8, XV.AP 250, PNOEM 406, XVII.LPd 29, 68, 71, XVIII.LLd 64; Sprat (Spingarn) II. 128; Rymer (Z) 19, 64.

MASCULINE (adj.) (1) Describing a style where thoughts and ornaments are bold, comprehensive, vigorous, etc. The product of a daring genius or a bold fancy. See Bold. I.EDP 66 (fancy), GCT 247 (Shakespeare), II.PS 25 (thoughts), PDS 45 (tropes and figures), DCOPS 130 (Juvenal), DAV 238 (English), SS.III.DEL 234 (style); Sprat (Spingarn) II. 129 ("The feminine kind [of beauty in poetry] is smoothness and beauty. . . . Strength is the chief praise of the masculine"). (2) Distinct (pronunciation). See Effeminacy. II.PAA 35.

MECHANIC (adj.) See Rule, Humour. (1) Pertaining to the unities of time, place, and action. The mechanic beauties of a play are the unities: I.GCT 247. Mechanic unities: SS.VII.DLT 375. Mechanical rules of unity: II.PDS 49, DCOPS 96, PEP 161, LWW2 173, PPBPP 188, DAV 227, SS.VIII.PC 220; Rymer (Z) 18 ("The mechanical part of tragedies [the unessential part] consists of the proportions, the unities, and outward regularities"). (2) Describing dogmatic rules in general: (a) Mechanic beauties of heroic verse: II.DCOPS 152. (b) Mechanic rules of poetry: SS.XIV.DAVd 181. (c) Mechanical rules of versification: II.DAV 236. (3) Describing qualities which belong to the lower classes of people: (a) Mechanic people: I.EDP 69. (b) Mechanic trade (stonecutter): SS.XVIII.LLd 63. (c) Mechanic humor (in Jonson's comedies) deals with low people: I.ECG 167.

MEMORY (sb.) (1) One of the faculties; the faculty that stores thoughts, which are then drawn out (from the memory) at an appropriate time (by the fancy, for example); the faculty that remembers. See Hobbes on the faculties (Spingarn II. 59). See also Imagination, Fancy (sb.), Judgment. I.PRL 3 (fancy, memory, and judgment), 8, PAM 98, 98, DECG 181, II.LP 4, DCOPS 90, PF 289, 290, SS.XVII.LPd 30; Hobbes (Spingarn) II. 54 (Memory is the first part of the mind; the second is judgment; the third is fancy), 59 ("Memory [is] the mother of the muses. . . . Time and education beget experience; experience begets memory; memory begets judgment and fancy"), 59, 59, 60, 63 (a person has "images of nature in the memory distinct and clear"), 70. (2) A remembrance, a recollection (of something): SS.VII.VDG 201.

MENIPPEAN SATIRE "Menippean satire" is distinguished only by its use of "several sorts of verse" and by its purpose, which is diversion through "tales and stories." See Satire, Varronian Satire. Varro, says Dryden, calls his own satires "Menippean" because he "imitated in his works the manner of Menippus the Gadarenian." Dryden's examples of Menippean satire are Petronius' *Satyricon*, Lucian's *The History*, Apuleius' *Golden Ass*, Spenser's *Mother Hubberd's Tale*, and Dryden's own *Absalom and Achitophel*. Actually, this definition, or description, does not fit *Absalom and Achitophel*. Dryden makes "Menippean satire" a general classification distinguished from formal verse satires (as found in the satires of Juvenal, Horace, and Persius, where satirists deliver a kind of secularized sermon): II.DCOPS 113, 114.

METAPHRASE (sb.) "Word by word, and line by line" translation. See Translation. I.POE 268, II.DAV 246.

METAPHYSICS (sb.) Dryden uses this important word only once (II.DCOPS 76). For further information see Watson's Gloss and A. H. Nethercot, "The Term 'Metaphysical Poets' before Johnson," *MLN*, XXXVII (1922). See Hard, Conceit.

MODERN (sb.) An author living in the present or one living in the modern ages as opposed to the ancient (i.e., Greek and Roman); one who thinks and lives in modern times; one of the party who advocates the supremacy of the present age over that of the ancient Greeks and Romans. There is no real battle between the Ancients and Moderns in England (unlike France) until the argument between Sir William Temple, Bentley, and Boyle in the Phalaris controversy. Dryden examines the differences between the Ancients and Moderns in the "Essay of Dramatic Poesy": I.EDP 23, 24, 24, 24, 32, 32, 42, 44, 58, DEDP 121, 122, 122, 124, 125, OHP 159, AAHP 199, II.DCOPS 74, 75, 85, 90, 115, 138, 141, 142, PEP 161, PPBPP 191, 201, SS.XIV.DAVd 192, XV.PNOEM 408, XVIII.LLd 81.

MONSTROUS (adj.) Describing anything unnatural, outside of nature, distorted. Dryden does not use it to refer to something horrible. See Absurd, Grotesque, Ridiculous. I.EDP 27, PEL 146 (farce), GCT 249, PSF 278, II.PEP 167 (length of verse); Rymer (Z) 3 (unbridled fancy gives conceptions which are "monstrous and have nothing of exactness, nothing of resemblence or proportion"). Monster: Rymer (Z) 57 (Seneca's Phaedra is a monster; she can stir neither pity nor terror because she is unnatural; no one can identify himself with her), 64, 170.

MYTHOLOGIES (sb.) Allegorical or symbolic meanings. "These [Ovid's *Metamorphoses*] . . . have also deep learning and instructive mythologies couched under them": SS.XIV.DAVd 181.

N

NATURAL (adj.) (1) Reasonable, fitting, appropriate are the most usual meanings of "natural." Anything which appears or sounds good is called "natural." "Natural" as it refers to verse, for example, means that the idioms, diction, and expressions are appropriate to the subject or character. "Natural" as it describes art means that the art closely approximates that segment of nature it is imitating: I.PRL 7, EDP 43, 55, 71, 73, 81, 81, 82, 82, 82, 82, 82, 82, 83, 84, 84, 85, 91, PAM 100, DEDP 112, 113, 120, 123, PEL 146, 147, OHP 157, 157, AAHP 203, HAR 217, 220, PAL 223, 223, PO 234, GCT 244, 244, 244, 247, 248, 248, 254, 258, 259, POE 265, II.LP 5, PS 19, 25, 30, PAA 40, 41, LWW1 53, PE 61, CP 67, DCOPS 98, 139, PEP 163, 167, PPBPP 184, 187, 201, PF 281, SS.V.PAZd 197, 198, VIII.PC 220, X.PRLaici 32, XIII.SAVPMF 311, XIV.DAVd 147, XV.AP 225, 226, 246, PNOEM 401, XVII. PPBPPd 293, 293, 294, 294, 297, 299, APa 347, 361, 369, 381, 385, XVIII. CPd 25. Naturally: I.PRL 2, EDP 51, 51, 64, 73, 75, 76, 80, 80, 80, 82, 89, PAM 99, DEDP 128, 128, 128, 129, HAR 217, GCT 244, 244, 253, 254, POE 265, 266, PSF 277, II.LP 10, PS 25, PAA 34, PDS 49, SS.XV.AP 246, PNOEM 399; Rymer (Z) 85, 134. (2) A natural day is twenty-four hours; an artificial day is twelve hours. This special use helps classify terminology in the neoclassic, dramatic unities. See Corneille's third "Discours" for the origin of this definition. See also Artificial Day. I.EDP 70, DEDP 129, II.DCOPS 95, 96, DAV 226. (3) "Natural" also describes that which is innate in a person from his birth, or is innate in something: Beauty (of flowers): SS.XVII.APa 385. Disadvantage (of English): II.PAA 38. Disposition (of someone's mind): SS.XVII.APa 349. Endowments (of a poet): II.DCOPS 90, 96, 139. Gifts (talents): I.EDP 68. Harshness of the French: II.PAA 38. Humanity (of Plutarch): II.LP 12. Inclination: II.PF 274, 276. Modesty: SS.XIV.DG 4. Poetry: II.DCOPS 98. Qualification: II.LL 215. Reservedness (of the English): I.DECG 181. Temper: II.PPBPP 198.

NATURE (sb.) "Nature" as it is imitated in neoclassical as well as ancient times is the basis for all art (see also Aristotle, *Poetics*, and Horace, *Ars Poetica*). Dryden says, "The imitation of nature is therefore justly constituted as the general, and indeed the only, rule of pleasing, both in poetry and painting" (II. 193). See also Imitation, def. (1). For Dryden's justification of the rules for imitation of nature see II. 193. For general information see A. O. Lovejoy, "Nature as Aesthetic Norm," *History of Ideas* (1948); C. S. Lewis, *Studies in Words* (1960), Chapt. II. (1) That which is probable. Dryden usually uses "nature" as the world, the universe, and all things as they usually appear in their free, imperfect, untouched, untrammeled, natural state. He says "[Nature] is a thing infinite and boundless as can never be fully comprehended but where the image of all things are always present" (I. 3). Nature is the world as it appears or as it usually appears. Thus, nature is that which is probable. A play, for example, imitates human nature or people as they probably are: I. PRL 3, EDP 27, 32, 33, 35, 38, 39, 56, 67, 67, 78, 79, 79, 82, 83, 84, 86, 86, 87, 87, 87, 88, 88, 88, 88, 89, PAM 98, 99, 100, 101, DEDP 113, 114, 120, 122, 122, 122, 122, 122, 122, 122, 123, 124, 129, PTL 140, PEL 146, 146, 152, OHP 159, 162, 165, AAHP 198, 200, 200, 200, 203, 204, 204, HAR

214, 215, PAL 226, PO 233, GCT 246, 247, 251, 253, 254, 260, POE 265, 267, PSF 278, II.ETV 14, 14, 15, PAA 35, 38, 40, 40, DCOPS 76, 82, 93, 94, 96, 97, 106, 119, 129, 140, 143, 159, PPBPP 184, 184, 189, 190, 190, 190, 191, 193, 193, 193, 193, 193, 193, 193, 193, 194, 194, 194, 195, 195, 196, 197, 207, PPV 219, 220, DAV 226, 229, PF 275, 280, 280, 285, SS.II. DIE 287, VII.VDG 199, VIII.PC 221, DLT 374, XIV.DAVd 185, 187, 187, 187, 187, XV.AP 240, 245, 246, 247, XVII.DPL 6, 16, PPBPPd 293, 293, 293, 294, 294, 297, 297, 298, 299, APa 345, 345, 347, 349, 351, 359, 359, 363, 381, 385; Hobbes (Spingarn) II. 61, 62 ("Beyond the actual works of nature a poet may now go; but beyond the conceived possibility of nature, never"), 62, 63; Rymer (Z) 68 (Aspatia in *The Maid's Tragedy* is from "romance but not nature"), 134, 163 ("Philosophy tells us it is a principle in the nature of man to be grateful. . . . History may tell us that [some persons] were ungrateful; poetry is to follow nature; philosophy must be his [the poet's] guide: history and fact in particular cases . . . are no warrant or direction for a poet"). (2) Dryden says that art improves nature; to him, "nature" never means idealized nature of "la belle nature" unless he qualifies it with perfect, best, etc. (see "perfect nature" [discussed below] and Imitation, def. [1b]). Dryden says, "The poet adorns truth and nature, but does not alter them" (I. 120). He also says, "Nature . . . is always the same, though in different dress" (from André Dacier). (See S. H. Monk, "Dryden's Eminent French Critic in a 'Parallel of Poetry and Painting,'" *N and Q*, n.s. II [1955] 433). The following citations are where Dryden talks about perfect nature or what nature should be: I.EDP 87, II.PPBPP 183, 185, 194, SS.II.DIE 287, XVII. APa 296; Wolsely (Spingarn) III. 21 ("Nature [is] . . . not only . . . all sorts of material objects and every species of substance whatsoever, but also general notions and abstracted truths, such as exist only in the minds of men and in the property and relation of things one to another—in short, whatever has being of any kind"). (3) "Nature" personified (for artistic conceptions of nature, see Jean Hagstrum, *The Sister Arts*): I.PRL 4, EDP 42, PrAZ 192, II. PS 27, SS.XVII.APa 359. (4) Inclination (of a person's mind) such as ill- or good-natured: I.PTL 140, PEL 145, 152, DECG 181, PA 187, GCT 247, 260, II.PDS 44, DCOPS 74, 74, 75, PEP 156, 162, LJD 178, DAV 225, PF 284, 284, SS.VIII.DAm 7, 11. (5) The force which makes things and people what they are. Dryden separates nature from God on II. 267: I.EDP 62, OHP 157, DECG 181, II.LP 9, DCOPS 136, PPBPP 190, LET 267, SS.XVII.LPd 71, PPBPPd 293. (6) Art of the highest order is nature itself. This is the highest compliment a poet can receive, and Dryden gives it outright only once: "[Shakespeare] is that nature which they [other poets] paint and draw": I. PrT 136. (7) Kind, genre, function, essence, description, inherent characteristics (as "the nature of tragedy"). In Dryden's writings, this is the second most used meaning (from Latin, *natura*). See Kind. I.EDP 37, 63, 86, 87, PSL 104, DEDP 114, 118, 119, 120, 120, 128, 129, PTL 138, 142, PEL 145, OHP 158, AAHP 196, 199, 204, 204, 204, 206, HAR 211, 218, PO 232, GCT 244, 252, 254, 257, 260, PSF 275, 279, II.LP 3, 8, PAA 35, 38, 40, 40, 41, PE 61, DCOPS 82, 91, 95, 101, 102, 102, 112, 120, 125, 142, PEP 162, PPBPP 189, 201, LL 215, PPV 219, DAV 235, PF 278, 285, 290, SS.VIII.DLT 376, XV.PNOEM 406, XVII.APa 359, 361.

NOBLE (adj.) "Noble" is a honorific descriptive term used for anything that Dryden wants to praise or heighten. He uses it to modify over fifty different terms. It means impressive, of noble birth, lofty, great, dignified, distinctive, illustrious, morally elevated, etc. The following quotation illustrates Dryden's general use of the term: "Chaucer is now become an original; and I question not but that the poem has received many beauties by passing through his noble hands" (II. 291). "Noble," however, is never synonymous with "sublime": I.EDP 71, 78, 90, PAM 95, 97, PSL 105, PrSL2 108, DEDP 111, 116, PEL 152, OHP 160, 162, DECG 171, 178, AAHP 196, HAR 216, GCT 238, PSF 279, II.PS 25, 31, 33, 37, PDS 46, LWW1 53, DCOPS 81, 96, 104, 109, 130, 137, 140, 148, 149, 150, 153, 153, PEP 167, PPBPP 182, 187, 188, 191, 193, 193, 193, DAV 251, 251, PF 290, 291, SS.II.DIE 285, 285, III.DEL 235, V.DA 5, XIV.DAVd 146, 148, 176, 189, XV.AP 235, 236, 240, 249, 250, 251, 251, XVII.PFAAP 339, APa 349, 353, 381, 387. Nobleness: I.EDP 14, GCT 259, II.DCOPS 94, SS.XVII.APa 345, 363, 365, 393. Nobler: I.PAZ 191, PSF 278, II.ETV 16, PAA 38, DCOPS 90, 108, PPBPP 194, SS.XV.AP 243, 250. Noblest: I.EDP 52 (elevated), 87 (highest), PrO 235, GCT 245, SS.XV.AP 243 (art), 249 (flights), XVII.DPL 6, PPBPPd 296 (pages). Nobly: II.DAV 249. Rymer (Z) 127, 136.

NOVEL (sb.) A story in prose or verse. "Both [Chaucer and Boccacio] writ novels" (II. 289). An extended fictitious work in prose: I.EDP 57, PEL 153, 154, 154, II.PDS 48, DAV 224, 250, LPe 263, PF 271, 285, 289.

NUMEROUS (adj.) Measured, rhythmical: II.DCOPS 84, 130.

NUMEROUSNESS (sb.) Strang says Dryden is the first to use the word; she says OED records first use in 1712. See "numerosity" below, for meaning: II.PS 31 ("of . . . verse"). Numerosity (regular meter flowing well in sound and sense): Cowley (Spingarn) II. 86 (qualities of good poetry are "sweetness and numerosity"); Rymer (Z) 4.

O

OCTAVE RHYME Ottava Rima: an eight-line stanza rhyming ABABABCC. Watson says this is "an unparalleled translation": II.PF 271.

ODE (sb.) A lyric poem, a song, written in the high style. See SS.XV. 232, 232 for a description. Otherwise, Dryden mentions three kinds: (1) Horace's odes: I.DECG 177, AAHP 198, II.PS 18, 30, 31, 31, 31, DCOPS 80, 93, 104, 104, 125, 125, 135, 144, PPBPP 203, SS.VIII.DC 215, 215, XIV.DG 3, DAVd 160, 204. (2) Cowley's odes: I.AAHP 203, II.LJD 179, DAV 238. (3) Pindar's odes: I.POE 270, II.PAA 36.

OPERA (sb.) A dramatic, musical entertainment. "A poetical tale or fiction, represented by vocal and instrumental music, adorned with scenes, machines, and dancing" (II. 35). Watson says Evelyn naturalized the word in 1644 (Diary, 19 November, 1644): I.OHP 158, AAHP 195, II.PAA 34, 35, 35, 35, 36, 36, 37, 37, 37, 38, 39, 39, 39, 40, 40, 41, 41, 41, 41, 42, 42, 42, 43, DAV 230, SS.VIII.DAm 9, DKA 129, 136.

OPINIATRE (adj.) Stubborn. Watson says the word is a French borrowing. It is used by Milton and Pepys before Dryden, but first recorded use is 1591: I.PEL 145. Opiniaster (adj.): Milton III. 169.

ORNAMENT (sb.) An embellishment, a decoration, an adornment. (1) That which makes something stand out: I.PAM 100. (2) That which stands out, as a man in his profession, jewels in their setting, etc.: II.PEP 162, DAV 244, 257, SS.XIV.DAVd 162, XV.AP 231. (3) In drama and in poetry ornaments usually have to do with words or diction or elocution, the last perfection of art. An ornament is also "the child of fancy" (I. 105), thus emanating from the faculty of the imagination (or fancy). (a) In drama, ornaments can be verse, descriptions, narrations, stage machinery (II. 41), prologues (SS.XV. 411), and what Dryden calls "urbana, venusta, salsa, faceta" (the language of learning and cities which is graceful and charming, piquant and witty, polished and elegant): I.EDP 27, 31, 79, PEL 149, 153, II.PAA 41, PPBPP 202, SS.XV. PHC 411. (b) In poetry, ornaments almost entirely have to do with words. Dryden names as particular ornaments "language and elocution" (I. 154), turns on thoughts and words (II. 238), words (I. 272), "pomp of figures" (II. 5), "choice of words, the numbers of periods, the turns of sentences" (II. 10), "lofty figurative and majestical expressions" (II. 35), figures (SS.XV. 241), "dignity of expression" (Virgil's "chief ornament") (II. 75), fictions (SS.XIV. 182), similitudes (SS.XIV. 192), and machines or gods (SS.XIV. 201): I.PSL 105, DEDP 114, PEL 154, AAHP 196, POE 272, 272, 272, II. LP 5, 10, 10, PAA 35, DCOPS 75, 96, 113, PPBPP 196, 196, LL 214, DAV 238, 245, 252, 255, 258, PF 274, SS.VII.VDG 147, XIII.SAVPMF 311, XIV. DAVd 182, 192, 201, XV.AP 241, 241, 241, 242, 242, XVII.APa 345. (4) Colors are to painting what words are to poetry, but Dryden also mentions other parts of paintings as ornaments: drapery (II. 196), background or portraits (SS.IX. 422), and decorative badges (SS.XVII. 361): II.PPBPP 196, SS.IX.EWTM 422, XVII.APa 361, 363, 391. (5) As ornaments of history, Dryden mentions "proverbial sayings, epigrams, epitaphs, apophthegm" (SS. XVII. 30): SS.XVI.AARLSFX 9, XVII.LPd 30.

P

PANEGYRIC (sb.) (1) An elevated poem of praise or celebration. A branch of the genre of epic poetry (I. 101): I.EDP 20, PAL 228, II.PE 61, 62, DCOPS 75, 127, PPBPP 202, 202, SS.III.DEL 234, V.DSI 106, PAZd 190, VI.DKK 8. Panegyric (adj.): I.PAM 101. Panegyrical (adj.): II.PS 31. (2) High flown praise in poetry or prose: I.PSF 279, II.PPBPP 202, SS.VII.VDG 173, 212, XI.DF 199, XVI.DLSFX 4.

PAPER (sb.) (1) Poem: II.PF 272, SS.X.PRLaici 11, 31. (2) Treatise, discourse, essay, preface, collection of poems: I.DEDP 130, II.DCOPS 79, 110, SS.IX.EWTM 425, XVI.AARLSFX 11, 11, 11. (3) Manuscript: SS.XVII. PFAAP 339.

PAPER OF VERSES A short poem, or poems (probably in manuscript form): I. EDP 87, PAM 101, POE 264, II.DCOPS 103, 110, SS.IV.DMLM 257.

PARAPHRASE (sb.) Dryden says paraphrase is "translation with lattitude, where the author is kept in view by the translator, so as never to be lost, but his words are not so strictly followed as his sense, and that too is admitted to be amplified, but not altered" (II. 268). See Translation, Metaphrase, Imitation. I.POE 268, II.DCOPS 152, 152, DAV 246, 246.

PARODY (sb.) A serious passage (from a work by a great poet) which is inserted into a satire and made amusing by turning the sense into something ridiculous: II.DCOPS 103, 104, 104, 115, 148.

PASQUIN (v.) To abuse (someone) by means of lampoons, libels, satires, etc.: SS.VII.DDG 16.

PASSION (sb.) To move an audience or reader through concernment (or empathy or involvement), a poet or painter must represent the passions accurately and with understanding. He should feel the passion he represents (or expresses) and make it natural, believable, or probable. (1) Strong and violent (II. 278) feelings, emotions, or inclinations found in plays, poems, paintings, nature, or in the poet himself. Dryden mentions love (the most frequent and important of his passions), lust, cruelty, friendship, honor, ambition, and revenge (Dryden calls the last three the "stronger passions"). Passions may vary in intensity. Dryden feels, "To represent these [passions] is the poet's work" (I. 48). See also Manners (Dryden at one point (II. 278) says that passions come under "manners"): I.PRL 4, EDP 25, 41, 41, 42, 48, 51, 52, 52, 56, '59, 60, 69, 73, 74, 87, 87, 87, PAM 98, 99, 99, PSL 106, PEL 155, OHP 159, 164, 164, 165, EAZ 193, AAHP 200, 200, 203, 203, HAR 212, 212, 213, 213, 216, 216, GCT 241, 241, 242, 246, 247, 248, 248, 250, 250, 253, 254, 255, 255, 257, 257, 257, 257, 259, 259, 260, 260, 260, 260, PEO 263, 265, 265, 265, 265, PSF 278, II.LP 9, PS 26, 27, 30, 30, PAA 37, PDS 48, DCOPS 85, 129, 140, PEP 167, LWW2 174, PPBPP 189, 194, 196, 197, 201, 201, 201, 201, 201, 202, PPV 217, 221, DAV 228, PF 278, 279, 279, 279, SS.II. DIE 285, VI.DTC 249, VII.VDG 197, XIII.SAVPMF 312, XIV.DG 10, DAVd 176, 188, 190, XV.AP 239, 240, 247, XVII.PPBPPd 297, 298, APa 363, 363, 363. Passion, in general: I.EDP 41, 45, 58, 59, 89, OHP 157, PrAZ 192, AAHP 203, GCT 254, 257, II.PS 26, SS.III.DEL 236. (2) The believable emotion used in a work of art to beget concernment in a reader, an audience, or a viewer. Dryden says that the audience should feel the same passions that the poet describes (I. 265). He is most concerned about tragedy and the passions of fear and pity (from Aristotle and his interpreters). Other passions he names are terror, horror, compassion, detestation, joy, indignation, contempt, grief, and admiration. See also Concernment. I.EDP 60, 60, 69, DEDP 114, HAR 213, 213, 214, 214, 214, 215, 216, 216, PAL 222, GCT 243, 245, 245, 245, 247, 254, 256, 258, 258, POE 265, II.LP 4, PAA 39, DCOPS 143, PEP 166, PPBPP 194, DAV 227, 228, 233, 234, SS.V.DA 5, X.PRLaici 33, XV. 234, 237, 239.

PASTORAL (sb.) (1) A kind of play or opera with shepherds, shepherdesses, and a rural setting, such as Fletcher's *The Faithful Shepherdess*, or Guarini's original *Il Pastor Fido*: I.EDP 66, 77, II.DCOPS 145. (2) The genre of poetry excelled in by Theocritus, Virgil, and Spenser. Theocritus is the model. A pastoral poem consists of low diction, rural scenes and beliefs, shepherds, shepherdesses, idealized existence, etc. See Eclogue. II.PS 18, 30, PPV 217, 218, 218, 219, 219, 220, DAV 236, 242, LET 268, SS.XIII.DAVPMF 313, XV. AP 224, 228, 231. Pastoral dialogue: A part of a play where shepherds and shepherdesses fancifully exchange sallies: SS.VIII.DAm 10. Pastoral letter: A letter from a Bishop to the divines in his diocese: II.DCOPS 123. Pastoral opera: Guarini's *Il Pastor Fido*: II.PAA 37. Pastoral tragedy: Euripides' *Cyclops*: II.DCOPS 103.

PATHOS (sb.) That which moves a pleasant pity or sadness in an audience. Dryden says, "There is a certain . . . pathos in their [Beaumont and Fletcher's] serious plays, which suits generally with all men's humours": I.EDP 69.

PERFECT (adj.) Describing idealized nature as found either in art or in the mind of the artist, as in perfect nature, perfect shape, perfect example, perfect idea, etc., Dryden says that nature itself is imperfect. "Perfect" also denotes something which is faultless, exact, and complete: I.PRL 2, 7, EDP 32, 66, PSL 105, 105, PEL 150, OHP 158, DECG 174, 182, 182, PAL 222, PO 234, GCT 239, 246, POE 267, II.LP 7, 8, 8, PAA 41, DCOPS 70, 74, 76, 83, 83, 90, 94, 95, 109, 145, 152, PPBPP 182, 183, 184, 184, 185, 185, 185, 185, 186, 186, 186, 194, 200, 204, 207, LL 212, PPV 219, DAV 228, 228, 254, PF 273, 281, 291, SS.II.DIE 287, VI.DTC 251, XIV.DAVd 163, 166, XV.AP 229, XVII. PPBPPd 293, 293, 293, 296, 296, 299, APa 349, 383, XVIII.PDCW 7, CPd 29.

PERFECTIONATE (v.) To make an idea or image in one's mind ideally perfect by selecting only "the most elegant natural beauties" in its formulation: SS. XVII.PPBPPd 297.

PERSON (sb.) (1) Dramatic, fictionalized character in a play, poem, opera, dialogue, painting, etc. Falstaff is a person in Shakespeare's *Henry V*. Adam is a person in Milton's *Paradise Lost*. In a poem, a person also can be the poet as the speaker (I. 99): I.PRL 9, EDP 33, 35, 37, 37, 50, 52, 61, 61, 61, 61, 61, 71, 73, 73, 73, 74, 75, 76, 78, 79, PAM 98, 99, PSL 106, DEDP 123, 123, 126, 127, 127, 128, 128, 128, 128, PEL 146, 150, 150, 152, 154, 155, OHP 159, DECG 179, 180, 182, 182, HAR 212, 213, 218, PAL 222, 222, PO 234, 234, GCT 240, 240, 244, 245, 246, 248, 248, 248, 249, 249, 249, 249, 249, 250, 250, 251, 251, 252, 253, POE 265, 265, 267, PSF 278, II.PAA 37, 37, DCOPS 84, 102, 103, 121, PEP 161, LWW2 174, PPBPP 186, 189, 189, 189, 190, 195, 197, 198, 198, 198, 198, LL 211, PPV 219, 219, DAV 229, 229, 233, PF 275, 278, 278, 284, SS.II.CIE 321, V.DA 8, VIII.PC 374, 375, XV.AP 238, PNOEM 398; Davenant (Spingarn) II. 17, 18; Hobbes (Spingarn) II. 64. (2) An actual living or historical being: I.EDP 62, 69, 73, 78, 81, 87, 87, DEDP 128, PEL 147, AAHP 199, POE 263, II.DCOPS 92, 110, PPBPP 193. (3) Someone's physical appearance: I.DEDP 130, OHP 166, DECG 179, GCT 253, 253, 253, II.PF 284, SS.VII.VDG 153, XVII.PPBPPd 296.

PICTURE (sb.) (1) A painting, a portrait, an image on canvas: I.PAM 101, DEDP 114, PT 134, GCT 249, POE 272, PSF 275, II.LP 8, PS 21, 33, PE 62, PPBPP 187, 188, 189, 189, 193, 195, 196, 196, 197, 198, 199, 199, 200, 200, 200, 202, 203, 206, DAV 256, SS.IX.TRAA 213, XIV.DAVd 188, XV. PNOEM 407, 407, 407, XVII.PPBPPd 293, 296, 296, APa 343, 351, 355, 363.

(2) A play or a scene, a part or role in a play (which imitates nature): I.PRL 2, PTL 139, PAL 224, GCT 252, II.DCOPS 78, PEP 159, DAV 228, SS.XV. AP 247. (3) An image captured by words; a description; a poetic imitation (of nature): I.EDP 75, PAM 99, PAL 226, POE 265, SS.VIII.PC 226, IX. EWTM 422, XVIII.LLd 73.

PINDARIC (adj.) (1) Describing verse with lines of unequal length, in imitation of the verse form of Cowley's so-called imitations of Pindar's odes: I.EDP 84, II.PS 31. (2) A kind of elevated lyric verse, with intense passions, bold panegyrics, and ecstatic praise, which tries to capture the swelling and decline of emotions and passions by a changing length of line (in imitation of Pindar's spirit and Cowley's verse form in imitating him). Cowley describes this kind of ode in the "Preface of Poems" (1656): "The digressions are many and sudden, and sometimes long. . . . The figures are unusual and bold, even to temerity. . . . The numbers are various and irregular, and sometimes . . . seem harsh and uncouth" (Spingarn II. 86): II.PS 32, PE 61, LJD 179. (3) Phillips (Spingarn) II. 265 (a poem consisting of "stroph, antistroph, and epode." This is the classic form of a Pindaric ode. See Thomas Gray's "The Bard" as an example).

PINDARIC (sb.) An "Alexandrine," although Dryden (II. 238) says this use is improper: II.DAV 238, 247.

PINDARIC LINE An "Alexandrine": II.DAV 247.

PITY (sb.) (1) The concernment and compassion an audience feels for a tragic hero. Pity is one of the ends and part of the scope of a tragedy (I. 245). (The other end, Dryden says, is usually terror; he also includes fear and horror.) A writer of a tragedy tries by means of plot and his audience's concern for the good (I. 213, 253) to move and to rectify or purge pity. See Aristotle, *Poetics*, Chapt. VI. See Concernment. I.PEL 152, HAR 211, 211, 212, 213, 213, 213, 215, 215, 216, 216, 216, 217, 218, 218, 218, 218, 218 (here, Dryden includes love as the "best commonplace of pity"), 219, 219, PAL 222, 222, EO 236, GCT 243, 244, 245, 245, 245, 246, 246, 246, 246, 247, 247, 250, 250, 250, 250, 253, 259, II.PPBPP 199, 202, SS.XV.AP 237; Rymer (Z) 27 (pity is moved in an audience by punishment which exceeds an error), 57, 69 (pity is separate from "poetical justice"). (2) Compassion (in an epic, in painting, in life in general): II.PEP 166, 167, 167, PPBPP 197, IX.TRAA 214.

PLACE (sb.) (1) Imaginary location of a play, an epic, or a painting. "Place" is one of the three unities (see Corneille, "Discours des trois unités" [1660]) and wherever Dryden discusses "place," he also discusses "unity of place." "Unity of place" in a play means that the scene of a play remains unchanged. Dryden is moderate in his views on unity of place (see I. 127), but says the more it is kept, the more realistic a play will be. He finally calls unity of place a "mechanic beauty" of a play (I. 247). He drops the discussion at about the middle of his career, referring to it only casually thereafter. (a) Unity of place in a play: I.EDP 28, 29, 29, 29, 29, 29, 29, 29, 29, 35, 45, 64, 64, 64, 70, PrSL 108, DEDP 123, 123, 124, 125, 125, 125, 125, 125, 125, 125, 125, 125, 125, 125, 125, 125, 125, 125, 127, 127, 127, 127, 127, 127, 127, 127, 141, 222, 247, II.DCOPS 95, 95, TCDD 171, PPBPP 188, SS.VII.VDG 162, VIII.

PC 220, DLT 375 (Dryden here calls place a "mechanic unity"), 375, 375, XV.AP 237, 237. (b) Unity of place in an epic. Dryden comes to no conclusion on unity of place in the epic: II.DCOPS 82 (in Tasso), 96 (in *Iliad*), PPBPP 188 (in *Iliad*). (c) Unity of place in painting. Dryden says it is similar to tragedy: II.PPBPP 188. (2) A passage in a treatise, poem, etc.: I.EDP 83, PEL 147, AAHP 196, II.DAV 245. (3) Station, position, employment (in ranks, patterns, arrangement, fitness of things, etc.): I.AAHP 201, GCT 259.

PLAY (sb.) (1) A work of art destined for the stage, a dramatic production. Dryden (or rather Lisideius) says, "A play ought to be a just and lively image of human nature, representing its passions and humours, and the changes of fortune to which it is subject, for the delight and instruction of mankind" (I. 25). It differs from an opera in that it depends neither on music nor on supernatural characters: I.PRL 2, 2, EDP 24, 25, 27, 29, 30, 30, 30, 31, 43, 43, 44, 45, 45, 46, 46, 47, 47, 48, 48, 50, 54, 55, 56, 57, 57, 58, 58, 59, 60, 60, 61, 61, 61, 61, 62, 64, 64, 65, 65, 65, 65, 66, 66, 66, 68, 68, 69, 69, 70, 70, 71, 71, 71, 74, 75, 75, 76, 77, 77, 77, 78, 79, 79, 81, 81, 82, 82, 84, 85, 85, 86, 87, 88, 90, 91, PAM 94, 100, PSL 104, 104, 105, 106, 107, 107, PrSL 107, 108, PrSL2 109, 109, DEDP 111, 112, 113, 115, 115, 115, 116, 118, 120, 120, 120, 120, 122, 125, 125, 127, 127, 128, 128, 129, 130, PWG 131, 132, PT 133, 134, 134, 134, PrT 136, 137, 137, PTL 138, 139, 140, 140, 141, 141, 141, 141, PrTL 143, 143, PEL 144, 144, 145, 146, 147, 148, 150, 150, 150, 150, 151, 153, 153, 153, 154, 154, 154, 154, 155, OHP 165, 165, 166, ECG 167, 167, DECG 169, 170, 172, 172, 172, 180, 181, 182, PA 184, 185, 185, 188, PAZ 191, PrAZ 192, EAZ 193, HAR 213, 213, 213, 214, 215, PAL 222, 227, 230, 231, PrO 235, EO 236, 236, GCT 239, 240, 240, 240, 240, 243, 243, 244, 244, 244, 247, 251, 252, PSF 274, 274, 278, 279, 279, II.PAA 35, 41, PDS 44, 47, 48, 48, 49, 50, 50, 50, 50, 51, 51, DCOPS 102, 107, 108, 108, 109, 109, 109, 109, 110, 142, 142, 142, 142, 142, 150, PEP 160, LWW2 174, 174, 174, 175, 175, PPBPP 190, 196, 198, 199, 200, 201, 207, PF 293, 293, 294, 294, SS.II.DIE 285, III.DTL 374, 375, IV.DMLM 253, 256, 257, V.DA 8, PAZd 199, 200, VI.DKK 5, DTC 247, 253, VII.DDG 13, 14, VDG 147, 148, 148, 149, 149, 149, 150, 152, 153, 153, 155, 160, 160, 162, 163, 163, 164, 165, 166, 166, 172, 197, 198, 199, 200, 200, 201, 202, 202, 203, 205, 209, 211, 215, 216, 216, 216, 218, 218, VII.DAm 9, 11, DKA 132, DC 213, 217, 217, PC 219, 219, 220, 221, 222, 227, 227, DLT 374, 374, XV.AP 236, 237, 237, 237, 239, 245, 246, 249, PNOEM 397, 398, 398, 399, 400, 401, 401, PHC 409, 410, 410, 411, 411. (2) Same meaning as def. (1), but here Dryden talks of a theoretical play and what qualities it should theoretically and practically have (such as the unities, liaison des scènes, etc.). See Tragedy, Comedy, Farce, Tragi-comedy, Drama, Heroic Play. I.EDP 25, 25, 25, 33, 33, 33, 34, 34, 38, 45, 45, 46, 47, 48, 49, 50, 50, 50, 50, 52, 54, 55, 55, 56, 57, 59, 60, 61, 61, 62, 62, 64, 65, 66, 78, 78, 78, 79, 79, 79, 82, 82, 83, 84, 87, 87, 88, 91, PAM 98, PSL 106, 107, PrSL 108, DEDP 112, 113, 114, 114, 114, 115, 119, 120, 122, 122, 122, 123, 125, 127, 128, 128, PTL 141, PEL 155, OHP 156, 156, 157, 157, 158, 159, 162, 162, 163, PO 233, 234, PrO 236, GCT 243, 244, 246, 247, 248, 248, 249, 250, 253, 255, PSF 275, 275, 278, 278, II.PAA 41, PDS 49, DCOPS 145, 145, 145, PPBPP 184,

195, 198, 198, 202, 203, SS.VII.VDG 163, XIV.DAVd 200, XV.AP 240, 249, XVII.APa 357. (3) Gambling: I.PrSL2 109, PrAZ 192.

PLEASANT (adj.) (1) Agreeable (the most important meaning), that which is pleasing to the mind (and senses). That which is pleasant promotes serenity and appeals to one's sense of well-being and of what is fitting or suitable. Therefore, the judgment is the important faculty in creating or appreciating pleasantness: I.EDP 58, 69, PT 135, PEL 145, 148, 148, OHP 159, 162, PA 186, PAL 231, II.LP 8, DCOPS 138, 152, DAV 226, SS.XV.AP 240, XVII. LPd 159, 162. Pleasantly: I.PEL 148, II.ETV 15, DCOPS 94, SS.II.DIE 247, XVII.APa 383. Pleasantness: I.PEL 148. Peachum (Spingarn) I. 127 (Horace's "invention" is "sweet and pleasant"); Sprat (Spingarn) II. 135 (in Cowley's Latin poems there are three forms of spirits: majestic, passionate, and pleasant; pleasant is the lowest). (2) Merry, gay, laughable, amusing: I.PEL 155, AAHP 199, PSF 274, II.DCOPS 107, 119, PPV 222, SS.XV.AP 235, XVII. LPd 63. Pleasantly: II.DCOPS 138.

PLEASANT (sb.) That which is agreeable (see Pleasant [adj.] def. [1]), neither so elevated as sublime nor so strict as severe, neither loosely ordered nor low. The "golden mean": SS.XV.AP 225, 226, 250.

PLEASE (v.) To delight, gratify, satisfy (the sight, the imagination, the mind, the ear, etc.). To "please" is usually the primary end or purpose of poesy or painting (note, however, II. 186 where the chief end of poetry is to instruct, painting to please). See Instruction. (a) As an end in poetry: I.DEDP 116, HAR 214, 219, II.LP 10, PS 28, PAA 35, PPBPP 186, 186, 191, PF 285, SS. V.DSI 101, XV.AP 250; Rymer (Z) 75 ("The end of all poetry is to please"), 75 ("Some sorts of poetry please without profitting"), 75 ("Whoever writes a tragedy cannot please but must also profit; 'tis the physick of the mind that he makes palatable"). (b) General meaning: I.EDP 51, 51, 80, 82, DEDP 120, 120, 120, PEL 145, 145, 146, 155, PrAZ 192, EAZ 193, 193, AAHP 200, 200, 200, 200, 202, 203, HAR 214, 214, 214, PAL 224, 225, 226, 226, PO 232, GCT 246, 254, PSF 276, 278, II.LP 10, 10, 12, PS 27, 31, PAA 42, 42, PDS 44, PE 64, CP 68, DCOPS 75, 127, PPBPP 191, 193, 193, 194, 194, 194, 194, PPB 217, DAV 230, 231, 245, 251, 253, PF 291, SS.VIII.DAm 9, IX.TRAA 212, 212, XIV.DAVd 156, XV.AP 227, 231, 239, 244, 245, 247, 247. Pleasing: I.EDP 41, 47, HAR 216, II.ETV 15, PS 26, DCOPS 82, 154, LL 211, DAV 245, 251, PF 270, 274, 274, 281, 290, SS.XIV.DAVd 182, XV. AP 228, 235, 237, PNOEM 408, XVII.PPBPPd 296. Pleasingly: II.LL 211.

PLEASURE (sb.) (1) Enjoyment, delight. See Instruction. I.EDP 73, PAM 97, DEDP 115, 129, PA 186, EAZ 193, AAHP 199, 200, HAR 219, GCT 244, 246, PSF 279, II.PS 22, 24, 29, 30, 33, PDS 49, CP 66, 66, DCOPS 74, 87, 96, 119, 130, 130, 130, 131, 147, 153, 153, 155, PEP 167, LWW2 173, PPBPP 186, 193, 194, 194, LL 211, 211, PPV 217, 221, DAV 224, 229, LET 267, PF 276, 276, 283, 293, SS.V.DA 5, VIII.DLT 376, XIV.DAVd 199, XV.AP 236, 242, 251, XVI.AARLSFX 11, XVII.LPd 75, PPBPPd 298, PFAAP 338, 339, 339, 340, APa 343, XVIII.LLd 71. Pleasure as the chief end of comedy: I.PEL 152. Pleasure as secondary end of poetry: II.DCOPS 153. As one of two ends of poetry: I.PTL 138, II.DCOPS 127, 129, 130, 140, 150. As one end of tragedy: I.HAR 219. As one end of biography: II.LP 7, 7. As one end of history: II.LP 4. (2) The source of delight, or a source of delight: I.EDP 35, 73, DEDP 126, II.DCOPS 131, 132, PPBPP 194, SS.XV.AP 234, 243. (3) A diversion: I.PRL 3, PSF 279, II.PPBPP 190, PPV 222, DAV 256, SS. XV.AP 238, 246, 246. (4) Desire, will (to do something), choice: I.PRL 3, II.PDS 46, SS.V.PAZd 197.

PLOT (sb.) The story, plan, design, or scheme of a play (which is made up of accidents, intrigues, and actions). A plot as one of the "living beauties" of a play (I. 108) moves "pity and terror" (I. 253). The "mechanic beauties" of a plot are observance of the three unities (I. 247), especially that of action. Dryden equates action with plot on I. 159. Although a plot exists by itself (and may be borrowed), it is the foundation of a play (I. 247), and its design, order, or adaptation is a function of the playwright's judgment. There are two main kinds of plots, regular and irregular. A regular plot consists of a single story. Dryden describes Greek and French plays as regular. An English play is ordinarily irregular, usually consisting of a main plot and an underplot. It provides more variety, more diversion. See main plot (I. 45), Spanish plot (fast moving and chaotic) (I. 48, 244), French plot (I. 56, 59, 128), English plot (I. 59, 66). See also Under-plot, Under-part, Fable, Action, Regular, Unity, Pity, By-concernment. I.PRL 2, 5, EDP 28, 33, 34, 35, 35, 35, 35, 37, 38, 45, 48, 48, 48, 49, 50, 50, 53, 54, 56, 58, 58, 58, 59, 59, 61, 64, 65, 65, 65, 66, 68, 68, 74, 75, 76, 81, 85, 87, PSL 106, PrSL 108, DEDP 123, 128, 128, 128, 129, PWG 132, PT 134, 135, PTL 141, OHP 158, 159, DECG 172, 173, 182, HAR 212, 212, 219, EO 236, GCT 240, 243, 244, 246, 246, 247, 247, 247, 247, 253, PSF 274, II.PDS 46, CP 68, DCOPS 145, SS.VIII.PC 220, XV.PNOEM 398.

POEM (sb.) An artistic, literary composition. Dryden says it is primarily a product of wit or the imagination (I. 98). The "most perfect poem," Dryden says, is the *Aeneid*. (1) A literary composition in general. See also Historical Poem, Satire, Opera. I.PRL 7, PAM 93, 93, 94, 95, 95, 95, 95, 96, 97, 97, 97, 98, 100, 100, 102, DEDP 111, PEL 154, 154, OHP 158, 158, 160, 160, 160, 160, 162, DECG 170, PA 185, PAZ 191, 191, AAHP 196, 197, 199, 203, 206, 207, HAR 217, PAL 227, GCT 248, 249, 249, 261, POE 264, 265, II. ETV 15, PS 26, 29, PE 61, 62, 63, DCOPS 75, 76, 76, 79, 80, 82, 83, 83, 84, 84, 86, 86, 90, 91, 95, 96, 96, 96, 97, 98, 98, 98, 103, 103, 103, 105, 105, 107, 112, 112, 112, 112, 112, 113, 114, 114, 115, 115, 116, 121, 122, 137, 143, 145, 147, 148, 148, 150, 150, 151, PEP 156, 160, 166, LJD 178, PPBPP 183, 186, 187, 187, 188, 188, 188, 193, 193, 195, 199, 199, 201, 203, 206, 206, 208, DAV 223, 224, 224, 224, 224, 225, 226, 226, 227, 227, 227, 227, 228, 228, 228, 229, 230, 231, 231, 232, 233, 233, 236, 238, 238, 244, 247, 248, 249, 252, 254, 254, LCM 266, LET 267, PF 272, 275, 275, 275, 275, 275, 279, 285, 290, 291, 292, 292, 293, SS.III.DTL 375, IV.DCG 11, V.DSI 103, PAZd 197, DAL 324, VI.DTC 250, VII.VDG 149, 210, VIII.DC 215, IX. DAM 89, TRAA 209, 211, 213, 214, EWTM 422, 428, X.PRLaici 10, 13, 32, 32, PHP 109, 113, 117, XI.DF 198, 198, XIII.SAVPMF 310, 314, 315, XIV. DG 2, 2, DAVd 146, 146, 146, 148, 153, 156, 158, 161, 163, 175, 177, 182, 185, 185, 189, 191, 193, 193, 194, 198, 200, XV.AP 229, 234, 241, 242, 244,

245, 250, PNOEM 405, 407, 407, 408, XVII.PFAAP 339, 339. (2) A play in general: I.PRL 3, EDP 47, 54, 76, PSL 104, 106, PWG 131, PT 136, PTL 138, 140, HAR 217, 219 (chief end is to instruct), PAL 222, 224, PO 233, PrO 235, EO 236, GCT 248, POE 275, PSF 278, II.LP 8, PDS 44, 45, 50, DCOPS 102, 102, 103, 103, SS.II.DIE 286, 287, 288, 288, CIE 321, 322, IV. DMLM 252, V.DAL 325, VII.DDG 12, VDG 166, VIII.DAm 7, DC 214, PC 227, DLT 371, 376, XV.AP 237. (3) An opera: I.AAHP 195, 196, 204, SS. V.DSI 107, VIII.DKA 129, 136, 136. (4) A heroic poem, or a poem in general, as strictly differentiated from other literary genres: I.EDP 79, 87, 87, 87, PAM 94, OHP 159, 159, 159, 159, 162, II.PPBPP 198. (5) A tragedy: II. DCOPS 80. (6) A literary composition (of a genre higher than a "paper of verses," ditties, etc.): I.EDP 87. (7) A genre of poetry: II.DCOPS 143, 144, DAV 229.

POESY (sb.) Poetry, poetry in the abstract, poetry as an art or subject, all that pertains to kinds of poetry and their composition. See Kind, Heroic poesy. Except for three minor exceptions, Dryden stops using the term in 1672: I.PRL 6, 7, 7, EDP 18, 20, 23, 23, 24, 24, 24, 24, 25, 26, 32, 32, 35, 56, 56, 67, 76, 83, 83, 83, 86, 86, 87, 90, PAM 101, 101, PSL 105, DEDP 111, 113, 113, 114, 119, 120, 121, 121, 121, 122, 123, 128, PTL 138, 139, 139, PEL 144, 151, 153, SS.IV.DCG 11, 11, DMLM 257, X.PHP 117, XVII.APa 343, 343.

POET (sb.) (1) God (as the "almighty poet"), a manipulator of people, a maker, a creator, etc.: I.PRL 4. (2) Author of a play or plays, a playwright (usually of tragedy). He affects the soul, excites the passions, moves admiration, manipulates characters, images men's minds, and makes men laugh: I.PRL 4, EDP 31, 34, 35, 37, 38, 41, 42, 42, 44, 45, 46, 47, 49, 51, 52, 53, 53, 55, 60, 61, 61, 61, 62, 64, 67 (Shakespeare), 67, 68, 68, 69, 70, 70, 73, 74, 74, 75, 76, 77, 78, 79, 80, 87, 88, 88, 89, 91, PSL 104, 105, 105, PrSL 108, 109, 109, DEDP 114, 114, 115, 117, 119, 120, 120, 120, 120, 120, 125, 125, 129, PWG 131, PT 133, 134 (Shakespeare), 134, PTL 138, 139, 140, 141, PrTL 143, 143, 143, 143, PEL 145, 146, 146, 147, 147, 147, 148, 149, 150, 151, 152, 152, 153, 154, 155, 155, 155, 155, OHP 158, 162, ECT 167, 167, 167, 167, DECG 170, 172, 177, 178 (Shakespeare), 178, 178, 178, 180, 182, 182, 183, PA 185, 185, 186, 188, PrAZ 192, EAZ 193, 194, AAHP 200, LD 209, HAR 211, 211, 212, 212, 212, 213, 213, 214, 214, 214, 215, 215, 216, 217, 217, 217 (Shakespeare), 218, 219, 219, PAL 223, 223, 224, 225, PO 233, EO 236, 236, 237, GCT 238, 239, 239 (Shakespeare), 243, 244, 247, 248, 249, 249, 249, 250, 251 (Shakespeare), 251, 251, 252 (Shakespeare), 253 (Shakespeare), 254, 255, 256, 257 (Shakespeare), 257, 258, 259 (Shakespeare), 260 (Shakespeare), 260, 261, PSF 278, 279, II.PDS 44, 45, 47, 47, 48, 49, 49, 51, 51, CP 67, DCOPS 67, 79, 102, 104, 108, 115, PPBPP 184, 185, 188, 189, 191, 196, 196, 198, 198, 199, 200, 200, 201, DAV 225, 226, 231, 234, PF 293, SS.V.DA 5, VI.DKK 10, VII.VDG 147, 148, 150, 153, 163, 179, 184, 199, 200, 204, 218, VIII.PC 220, DLT 374, 375, 375, 376, XV.PNOEM 398, 398, 398, 399, 400, 401, 401, 402, 402, 402, 402, 402, 403, 406, 406, 407, 407, 407, PHC 411, 411. (3) A writer of verse, a writer of poetry, a versificator, manipulator of language, rhymer, etc.: I.PRL 7, EDP 39, 69, 69, 76, 79, 81, 82, 82, 84, 85, 86, 90, 90, PAM 94, 95, 96, PrSL 108, DEDP 112, 121, OHP 162,

DECG 170, 177, PA 185, 185, 188, AAHP 200, 202, 205, 206, 207, PAL 222, 226, 226, 226, 226, 227, 227, 227, 227, 227, 228, 229, GCT 242, POE 263, 263, 264, 265, 266, 267, 268, 270, 271, 271, PSF 275, 276, 277, 277, II.PS 19, 20, 20, 20, 21, 21, 21, 21, 22, 23, 23, 25, 29, 29, 31, 31, 32, 34, 36, 38, 39, 39, 40, 40, 40, CSE 57, 58, 58, 59, 59, PE 62, DCOPS 77, 79, 80, 82, 83, 83, 85, 86, 86, 86, 88, 88, 88, 91, 91, 93, 93, 97, 97, 103, 104, 107, 116, 116, 116, 118, 119, 124, 125, 125, 126, 127, 128, 131, 131, 134, 135, 136, 136, 136, 141, 143, 144, 144, 146, 146, 148, 153, 153, PEP 156, 157, 157, 157, 157, 158, 158, 159, 159, 161, 161, 162, 163, 164, 164, 165, 165, 165, 167, 167, LWW2 173, 173, LJD 178, 178, 179, 179, 180, PPBPP 185, 186, 186, 187, 187, 187, 188, 190, 191, 191, 191, 191, 195, 195, 195, 196, 197, 197, 201, 204, 204, 205, 206, 206, 207, PPV 217, 218, 219, 220, 220, DAV 224, 224, 225, 225, 228, 228, 228, 229, 229, 229, 232, 232, 233, 233, 235, 236, 237, 238, 239, 239, 239, 240, 241, 242, 243, 244, 245, 246, 248, 248, 248, 250, 251, 254, 255, 256, 257, PRAV 258, 259, LCM 265, 266, LET 268, PF 269, 270, 271, 271, 271, 274, 275, 276, 276, 277, 278, 278, 279, 280, 280, 281, 282, 282, 283, 283, 284, 285, 287, 292, SS.II.DIE 286, 287, 287, 288, III.DEL 234, 235, 235, DTL 374, IV.DCG 11, 11, DMLM 255, V.DSI 100, 101, 101, 103, 103, PAZd 190, DAL 316, 318, VI.DKK 6, 6, 6, 9, 9, VII. VDG 179, 180, 198, 198, 198, 205, 210, 210, 210, 216, DDS 301, 303, 304, VIII.DKA 136, 137, DC 214, 214, X.PRLaici 32, XI.DF 203, XIII.SAVPMF 310, 312, 313, 314, 315, XIV.DG 2, 5, 9, DAVd 147, 152, 153, 157, 157, 157, 158, 159, 160, 160, 161, 162, 166, 167, 171, 174, 174, 175, 175, 177, 177, 178, 179, 179, 179, 181, 182, 184, 184, 184, 185, 185, 186, 187, 187, 187, 188, 191, 191, 194, 195, 196, 197, 199, 199, 201, 204, XV.AP 231, 232, 237, 242, 245, 248, 250, 251, 252, 252, XVII.LPd 25, 76, DHL 84, PPBPPd 298, 299, APa 343, 343, 347, 391, XVIII.LLd 73. (4) A writer full of imagination, fancy, force of spirit, inborn vehemence, copiousness of imagination, and genius. He controls these forces with judgment and learning. He sees into passions, imitates nature (usually human nature), and through mastery of the language and accuracy of expression (combined with genius of imagination) becomes a maker of great poetry. These citations refer to Dryden's discussions of the qualities and qualifications a poet must possess: I.PRL 8, 9, 9, EDP 43, 47, 47, 51, 80, 90, 91, 91, PAM 95, 98, 99, 99, 101, DEDP 121, PEL 149, 154, OHP 160, 161, DECG 173, PA 187, AAHP 198, 198, 199, 204, 204, GCT 248, 248, 254, 254, POE 263, 265, 265, 266, 267, II.PS 19, 20, 26, 26, 30, 32, DCOPS 85, 90, 90, 96, PEL 163, PPBPP 206, SS.XIV.DG 3, 3, DAVd 181, 181, 181, 184, 190, XV.AP 233, 241, 241, 243, 244, 251, PNOEM 405, 406, 408, XVII.PPBPP 294, 296, 297.

POETIC DRESS "Sounding" diction and elegant elocution. See Poetic Parts. II. DCOPS 154.

POETIC FIGURE A person in a painting who is derived from a poem (as Achilles from the *Iliad*): II.PPBPP 197.

POETIC FIT Silly behavior, exaggerated behavior. The state of mind (of someone) who so exaggerates virtues that they become vices: I.PA 224.

POETIC GENIUS A mind which innately gravitates toward poetry. Innate poetic ability (opposite of geometric genius): SS.XIII.SAVPMF 315. Poetical: II. PPBPP 204.

POETIC INFLUENCE The influence exerted by the stars at someone's birth causing him to possess the genius to be a poet: SS.XV.AP 224.

POETIC JUSTICE Rewards and punishments given judiciously to the characters at the end of the play. Punishments of wrongdoers at the end of a play, in accordance with the viciousness of their crimes. In English, probably first used by Rymer (Z) 22: I.HAR 215. Rymer (Z) 22, 26, 69 (poetic justice is separate from pity). Poetical justice: I.HAR 218, GCT 245, II.PDS 48 ("An involuntary sin deserves not death").

POETIC LICENCE "The liberty, which poets have assumed to themselves in all ages, of speaking things in verse which are beyond the severity of prose" (II. 205). In words, it is manifested in tropes; in "sentences and propositions" it is manifested in figures (II. 206). Its use varies according to the language and age in which an author writes (II. 206), but it should always be contained within reasonable bounds. See SS.XV. 406–8 for explanation. See also Horace, *Ars Poetica*, ll. 9–10: I.AAHP 205, 205, 206, 206, 206, 206, 206. Poetical: SS. XV.PNOEM 406. Hobbes (Spingarn) II. 62 ("The resemblance of truth is the utmost limit of poetic liberty").

POETIC PARTS (of a poem) (1) Of verse, the parts are diction and elocution: II.DCOPS 153. Poetical: II.PS 28, DCOPS 153. (2) Of a play, the parts are "descriptions, images, similitudes, and moral sentences": II.PDS 45.

POETIC PROSE Blank verse: I.EDP 84 (here, used disparagingly).

POETIC RAGE Wild, uncontrolled imagination or fancy (which has to be restrained by rules or judgment). See also Madman, Fury, Rage, Enthusiasm. SS.XV.AP 227.

POETICAL DESCRIPTION Beautiful or imaginative or impassioned description: I. PAM 96 (used to cover up ignorance of subject), II.PS 25, 26, SS.XIV.DAVd 201 (beautiful and imaginative).

POETICAL DICTION Tropes: II.PF 291.

POETICAL EXPRESSIONS Metaphorical expressions (used in translation to capture an author's style): II.PS 21, PPBPP 183.

POETICAL FICTION (1) Imaginary event or action used as the plot of a play: I.EDP 46, II.PAA 35. (2) An imaginary monster, a chimera: I.AAHP 204.

POETICAL TRANSLATION A work translated by paraphrase or imitation (not metaphrase) which shows at least some of the style of the original (besides the mere meaning): I.POE 268, II.PS 22.

POETRY (sb.) See Heroic, Heroic Poem, Heroic Poesy, Heroic Poetry, Lyric, Elegiac Poetry, Epic (adj.), Tragedy, Comedy, Satire, Sonnet, Farce, as different kinds of poetry. See Invention, Design (sb.), Elocution, etc. for how a poet makes poetry. See also Soames' *The Art of Poetry*, translated and Anglicized from Boileau's *L'Art Poétique*, and revised by Dryden (SS.XV. 224–53). It covers English literary history, the rules, descriptions of genres, etc. "Poetry" in 1672 takes over entirely what is included in "poesy." See Poesy. (1) The art of a poet and his productions: I.PWG 131, PEL 148, OHP 159, 160, 161, 161, 161, 162, DECG 169, 172, 178, PA 188, AAHP 197, 198, 198, 199, 199, 199, 200, 200, 201, 203, 203, 205, 205, 207, 207, HAR 213, 217, 219, PAL 225, 225, 226, 226, 228, 228, 228, 228, 230, 231, GCT 245, 245, 245, 246, 246, 248, 255, 255, 255, 258, 260, POE 262, 271, 271, PSF 276, 278, 278, II.LP 10, PS 19, 24, 29, 30, 33, PAA 34, 35, 35, 36, 37, 37, 38, 38, 38, 41, PE 60, DCOPS 73, 74, 74, 77, 78, 79, 79, 80, 81, 81, 81, 82, 82, 85, 86, 87, 88, 89, 93, 94, 95, 96, 97, 98, 98, 98, 98, 98, 99, 99, 99, 100, 100, 101, 102, 103, 104, 106, 106, 106, 106, 107, 124, 126, 127, 130, 131, 131, 132, 143, 149, 150, 151, 153, 153, PEP 156, 157, 161, 164, 164, 165, TCDD 171, LJD 177, 178, 179, PPBPP 181, 183, 185, 185, 186, 186, 186, 187, 189, 190, 191, 191, 192, 192, 192, 193, 194, 194, 194, 195, 196, 196, 196, 196, 199, 201, 202, 202, 203, 203, 208, PPV 217, 218, 222, DAV 229, 229, 229, 230, 230, 232, 233, 237, 238, 238, 239, 240, 242, 243, 245, 247, 252, 252, 257, 257, PRAV 258, LET 267, PF 274, 275, 277, 280, 281, 286, 289, 289, 289, 290, 292, 292, SS.III.DEL 233, 234, DTL 374, 375, IV.DCG 12, V.DAL 318, VI. DKK 9, DTC 247, 250, 250, VII.VDG 162, 173, 179, 181, VIII.DKA 135, 135, 136, 136, PC 219, 222, DLT 374, IX.TRAA 210, EWTM 431, X.PRLaici 32, XIII.SAVPMF 315, 315, XIV.DAVd 180, 181, 181, 185, XV.AP 224, 225, 228, 228, 232, 233, 235, 235, 242, 243, 243, 245, 248, 249, PNOEM 398, 405, 405, 406, 407, 407, 407, 407, 407, 408, PHC 410, XVII.DPL 6, LPd 23, PPBPPd 299, 299, APa 391. (2) The art of the playwright and his product (plays, usually tragedy): I.PRL 5, DEDP 119, PTL 140, OHP 157, 157, 157, 158, DECG 169, 173, PA 189, AAHP 195, 199, PAL 224, PO 233, GCT 248, 260, SS.VII.VDG 159.

POINT (sb.) (1) French *pointe*: "Pensée qui surprend par quelque subtilité d'imagination, par quelque jeu de mots" (Cayrou). "Trait d'esprit, pensée vive et ingenieuse" (Dubois and R. Lagane). The *OED* records this meaning as 1728. A "point" is epigrammatic in its compactness and sharpness. Thus, its style cannot be elevated: I.OHP 160, SS.XV.AP 234, 234, 234, 234. Points of epigram: II.DCOPS 82. Points of wit: II.DCOPS 150, SS.XV.PNOEM 399. Pointed: Rymer (Z) 76. (2) Proposition, idea, clause: I.DEDP 124, 128. (3) Specific end or purpose: I.HAR 215, POE 266, II.LP 7, DCOPS 146. (4) Consideration, particular, subject: II.PS 32, DCOPS 118.

POINT OF HONOUR "Point d'honneur." A quibble which, if given up, causes one to lose self-respect and reputation. Dryden criticizes its use in French drama, and differentiates between "honour" and the artificiality of "point of honour": I.OHP 164.

PREFACE (sb.) An essay attached to and preceding any kind of literary work (or translation). It may discuss the work to which it is attached, explaining its theme, genre, scope, and aim as a work or as a genre, or it may animadvert on some other subject. Dryden says, "The nature of a preface is rambling, never wholly out of the way nor in it. This I have learned from the practice of honest Montaigne" (II. 178). Elsewhere, where he contrasts his prefaces with those of Segrais, he calls his own "epistolary" (SS.XIV. 163). The resulting immediacy of Dryden's thought (which also emanates from his diction and his ability to capture his thoughts exactly in words) makes his style interesting. Thus, we see not only his style but the tone of his thinking in his prefaces. Dryden distinguishes between the two on I. 179: I.EDP 83, PAM 96, PSL 104, 107, DEDP 112, 117, 123, 130, 130, PWG 131, PT 133, PTL 138, PEL 144, 144, 150, DECG 169, PO 232, 233, 234, GCT 243, POE 271, PSF 279, II.PS 30, PAA 37, 41, 42, PDS 50, DCOPS 85, 116, 120, 151, 152, PEP 163, LWW2 174, LJD 178, PPBPP 183, 190, DAV 233, 240, 247, 254, 255, 256, 257, PF 273, 275, 278, 291, 293, 293, SS.VII.VDG 213, VIII.DKA 132, IX. EWTM 423, X.PRLaici 14, 14, 29, PHP 109, XIV.DAVd 162, 163, 204, XV. PNOEM 398, XVIII.CPd 25, 50.

PREFERENCE (sb.) (1) The act of favoring something over another or all others: I.AAHP 199, II.CP 69, DCOPS 83, 140, 145. (2) Superiority, precedence. This meaning emanates from def. (1). By using the word in this way, Dryden assumes an absolute standard of values in judging literary works. When a discerning, accomplished critic favors one work over another, the first is superior. The *OED* does not record this meaning until 1798: I.HAR 219, II.PS 29, CP 70, DCOPS 96, 129, DAV 231, SS.XIV.DAVd 164, 180.

PREPARATION (sb.) (1) The action of introducing material about a character or event in a play, and working up to the actual entrance of the character or the happening of the event. The greater the event or the more important the character, the more elaborate the preparation has to be. See Act. II.PDS 45, 51, SS.VIII.DLT 374; Rymer (Z) 61 (act one, or the "parados"). (2) An inferior literary composition served up to the reader (pejorative): II.DCOPS 153 (of morals).

PREVENT (v.) To anticipate: II.DCOPS 147, SS.XIV.DAVd 162.

PREVENTION (sb.) A preformed conclusion or prejudice: SS.XVII.PFAAP 341.

PROBABILITY (sb.) Likelihood, naturalness, that which is likely to happen or to be true (but not historical truth [SS.II. 288]). See Probable, Imitation, def. (1b). I.EDP 29, 55, 62, 62, 64, 78, 79, 83, DEDP 126, AAHP 202, GCT 240, 245, 260 (in fiction), POE 264, II.PDS 45, 47, DCOPS 152, PPBPP 198, PF 277, SS.II.DIE 288, V.PAZd 198, XIV.DAVd 198, XVII.LPd 51, XVIII. CPd 45, LLd 69; Rymer (Z) 6.

PROBABLE (adj.) Likely. Dryden says that "imitation of nature" is the only foundation of dramatic poesy (I. 122), as it is for all art. To imitate nature is not to reproduce it, but to produce a probable likeness of it. Dryden says, "'Tis not necessary that there should be historical truth in it [a play or poem]; but always necessary that there should be a likeness of truth, something that is more than barely possible, 'probable' being that which succeeds or happens oftener than it misses" (I. 245). About "probable" and the purpose of art, Dryden says, "That which is not probable will not delight a reasonable audience" (see Delight [sb.], def. [1]). See I. 161 on when a heroic poet is not bound to what is "probable." See also Imitation, def. (1). I.EDP 47, 85, DEDP 122, 123, PEL 146, OHP 161, PAL 223, GCT 243, 245, 245, 245, 255, PSF 279, II.PAA 36, DCOPS 88, 108, 110, LL 210, SS.XIV.DAVd 148, 181, 193, 194, XV.PNOEM 408, XVI.AARLSFX 12. Probably: II.PDS 50. Davenant (Spingarn) II. 11 (an epic about a historical person is a "probable fiction"); Rymer (Z) 24, 134 ("Nothing is more odious in nature than an improbable lie").

PROFESSOR (sb.) One who practices an art: II.PPBPP 184.

PROPER (adj.) Distinctively appropriate, suitable, correct. "Proper" is not as important a term as "just," but Dryden uses it fairly often and with approximately equivalent meanings. He differentiates it from "just" when "just" assumes English meanings and "proper" means "appropriate." "Proper" is the adjective form of "propriety," and as such is related directly to the concept of "decorum" which plays such an important role in determining style, design, characterization, taste, etc. Dryden says, "Nothing is truly sublime unless it is just and proper" (I. 277). That which is proper appeals to and is a product of judgment (see SS.VI. 247–48). Dryden uses "proper" as a substantive once: he speaks of "the bounds of just and proper" (SS.VI. 248). See Decorum, Just, Propriety, Improper. (1) Correct, appropriate, fitting, well-timed, well-placed, well-chosen, etc.: I.EDP 74, PEL 145, 153, DECG 171, AAHP 206, HAR 213, PAL 225, 231, PO 233, GCT 246, POE 268, II.PS 20, PAA 34, 35, DCOPS 88, 90, 117, 127, 136, 143, 147, 147, PEP 166, PPBPP 187, PPV 222, DAV 226, 238, 248, 254, SS.VII.VDG 168, XV.AP 226, XVIII.CPd 25; Rymer (Z) 85, 134. Properly: II.LP 10, DCOPS 116, 142, 143, 146, PF 279. (2) Describing the appropriate manners, speech, and behavior of characters in a play, poem, or painting (as to what they should be): I.PRL 2, PEL 149, 150, DECG 182, HAR 217, 217, GCT 250, PSF 277, II.DCOPS 108, PPBPP 185, 186, PF 286, SS.XV.AP 239, XVII.PPBPPd 296, APa 355. Properly: I. DECG 178. (3) Describing the appropriate placement or arrangement of parts in a work (of art): I.PEL 155, AAHP 203, GCT 259, II.DCOPS 94, 103, PPBPP 195, 201, SS.XIV.DAVd 175, XVII.APa 363. Properly: II.DCOPS 102. (4) Pertaining to appropriateness of hyperbole and description: I.AAHP 205, II.PS 22, LL 211. (5) Suitable (as a function or duty). Not strictly a literary usage: I.AAHP 201. (6) Grammatically correct: II.LWW1 53, 53. (7) Successful, adequate: Properly: I.DEDP 125, 125, 126.

PROPORTION (sb.) (1) Properly corresponding size and emphasis in each part of the human body as it appears in itself or as it is imitated by art. See Imitation, def. (1). (a) In painting: I.EDP 35, II.PS 19, SS.XV.PNOEM 407, XVII.PPBPPd 299, APa 381. Proportionable: SS.XVII.PPBPPd 298. (b) In sculpture: I.EDP 88. (c) In Plato's abstract conception of beauty: SS.XIII. SAVPMF 313, 313. (d) In tragedy or heroic poesy (where characters appear as larger than life-size): I.EDP 87, PAM 101, SS.X.PRLaici 33; Rymer (Z) 3, 18. (2) Properly corresponding size (in general). (a) Tragedy to epic: II. DAV 226. (b) Of an engine to the weight it can move: I.GCT 247. (3) Amount (of something) in comparison to (its) other parts (which altogether make up a whole): I.EDP 91 (of judgment), GCT 253 (of the seven deadly sins), II.DAV 235 (vowels to consonants). (4) Correspondence of time of a play on stage to imaginary time in the play: I.DEDP 127, 129, GCT 241. Proportionable: I.DEDP 126.

PROPORTIONED (adj.) Equally distributed (correspondences between a tragedy and actual life): II.DCOPS 95.

PROPOSITION (sb.) (1) A conclusion, an assertion, a rule: I.DEDP 122, 122, 124, 125, 129, II.PAA 35, DCOPS 95, 108, 138, 154. (2) A statement, a unit of expression which contains a complete thought: I.AAHP 206. (3) The opening of an epic which contains the statement of what will be treated: II.DAV 228.

PROPRIETY (sb.) Decorum, appropriateness, fitness, suitability. "Propriety" usually refers to the appropriateness of words and thoughts to a particular subject. This, of course, is Dryden's well-known definition of wit (see I. 207). "Propriety" of thought is "that fancy which arises naturally from the subject, or which the poet adapts to it" (II. 34). "Propriety of words is the clothing of those thoughts with such expressions as are natural to them" (II. 34). "And from these, if they are judiciously performed, the delight of poetry results" (II. 35). "Propriety" is a synonym for "the proper meaning" of a word in SS.XV. 251 and XVII. 55. Dryden says he derived the concept of propriety of words and thoughts from the "arch-poet," Virgil (I. 207). See Wit, Proper, Diction, Decorum. (1) Appropriateness of words to subject: I.EDP 31, PEL 155, II.PAA 34, DCOPS 94, 143, SS.VI.DTC 251, XVII.LPd 55. Of thoughts and words: I.AAHP 207, PSF 278, II.PS 22, 22, 24, PAA 34, PEP 163, LL 210. Of style: II.LP 13. Of sound: II.PAA 40. Of thoughts: II.PAA 34, PF 274, SS.XIV.DAVd 204. Of language: I.PEL 155, POE 272, II.LL 214, SS.XIII. SAVPMF 315. Jonson 42 ("And herein is seen their [figures] elegance and propriety, when we use them fitly and draw them forth to their just strength and nature by way of translation [which is the making of figures] or metaphor"); Hobbes (Spingarn) II. 69 ("The character of words that become a hero are propriety and significancy"). (2) A standard which gives intellectual pleasure, such as "proprieties of history" (truth of matter, method, and lack of obscurity of words or expression): II.LP 5. Wolsely (Spingarn) III. 23 ("Propriety" is "true expression" [natural or lifelike expression]). (3) Decorum. The consistent expression of a person's distinctive and appropriate qualities, abilities, humors, likes, dislikes, etc.: II.PAA 35, LJD 177, PF 278. (4) Distinctive quality. "Laughter is indeed the propriety of a man": II.PPBPP 190. (5) The correct word (for something): II.DAV 254.

PROSE (sb.) The written language (without metrical structure) or all works written in this way. To Dryden, prose is severely literal (I. 205), admitting no tropes (II. 10), but providing a writer with liberty of thought and easier expression (II. 290). (a) Dispute about whether to use rhyme or prose in serious plays: I.PRL 6, 7, 7, EDP 76, 79, 83, 83, 84, 84, 84, 86, 92, PAM 101, DEDP 113, 113, 113, 114, 114, 115, 115, 115, OHP 157, 157, II.ETV 15. (b) General reference: I.PTL 138, OHP 160, AAHP 205, 206, PrO 235, II.LP 10, PAA 38, PE 63, DCOPS 78, 97, 106, 113, 115, 147, PEP 164, DAV 245, 245, 254, PF 271, 272, 272, 290, SS.VI.DTC 251, VII.VDG 181, VIII.DKA 137, XIV.DAVd 184, 204, XV.AP 234.

PROTAGONIST (sb.) (*OED* says first recorded use in English). "Chief person of [a] drama," the main character of a play: I.PEL 150.

PROTATIC PERSON A character in a play, appearing in the protasis, who either "hear[s] or give[s] the relation" (or narration). It may be a character central to the play (as used by the French) or someone who takes little or no part in the subsequent proceedings. This is a French borrowing, the first and almost only use in English. Corneille uses "personnage protatique" in "Examen de *Rodogune*" and "Discours du Poème Dramatique." See Act. I.EDP 50.

PURE LANGUAGE Words and expressions which are both clear to the understanding and exactly appropriate to the subject or person to which they apply. Also "pure style" (SS.XVIII. 75). In the following citations Dryden refers only to Shakespeare and Boileau: I.PAL 231, GCT 241, II.DCOPS 81, DAV 248, SS.XV.AP 229.

PURGE (v.) (1) To rectify, to harmonize or balance (our) passions (as the instruction or purpose of tragedy). Dryden says, "The end or scope of tragedy is to rectify or purge our passions, fear and pity" (I. 245). After having its passions purged by a tragedy, the audience supposedly loses false pride; and therefore, its outlook on the world should be more balanced. Purging is a violent process, and "the effects of tragedy are too violent to be lasting" (II. 227). To "purge" also has the connotation of cleansing by the expulsion of something bad. Dryden uses it once with this definition as the primary meaning. He says, "To raise, and afterwards to calm the passions, to purge the soul from pride, by the examples of human miseries, which befall the greatest; in few words, to expel arrogance, and induce compassion, are the great effects of a tragedy" (II. 227). See Fear, Pity, Catharsis. I.GCT 245, 245, II.DAV 234. Purging: I.GCT 243. (2) To cleanse, to purify, to rectify (pertaining to the language and purpose of satire): II.DCOPS 104, 112, 143. Purging: II.DCOPS 143. (3) To correct, to expunge (violently) errors from verses: II.LCM 265, LET 268.

PURITY (sb.) The quality found in something which measures up to standards of perfection. Dryden primarily uses "purity" to describe words and phrases which are appropriate to the subject and clear to the understanding (thus, correct, concise, and exact). In the English language, he would like "certainty of words and purity of phrase" (SS.VI. 251). (1) Appropriateness, propriety, clarity (as a standard of perfection in expressions): I.EDP 31 (of style), 66 (of rhyme), PSF 278 (of phrase), II.PS 20 (of English), 31 (of Horace's expressions), 32 (of English), PAA 40 (of English), CSE 57 (of language), DCOPS 131 (of words), DAV 246 (of style), 248 (of diction), PF 272 (of Boccace), 277 (of English), SS.VI.DTC 251 (of phrase). (2) Exactness of meaning, as found in the French language. Dryden describes the French as afraid of metaphor: II.PAA 38, DAV 238, 247. (3) Clarity of thoughts and words: II.CP 66 (of conceptions), SS.XVIII.LLd 61 (of words and conceptions). (4) The exactness of words, in propriety and meaning, in the Latin of the golden, Augustan age: II.LP 6, DCOPS 118, 118, 125, SS.XVII.LPd 75. (5) Decorum (of manners) in a play: II.TCDD 170.

Q

QUANTITY (sb.) The length of a syllable as a metrical unit (in Greek or Latin poetry): I.EDP 83, PAM 95, II.PAA 40. (a) Syllable length (contrasted with English "accent"): I.EDP 83. (b) Rhyme in English replaces quantity: I.EDP

88. (c) Length of syllables in English and other modern languages: II.DAV 237, 237.

QUIBBLE (sb.) A pun: II.DAV 243.

QUIBBLE (v.) To pun: Quibbling: I.EDP 22, SS.XV.AP 234, 247. Quibbler: SS.XV.AP 234.

QUICK (adj.) (1) Vigorous, energetic, fast producing. Describes fancy and imagination in poets (and once in a painter: SS.XVII. 389): I.EDP 80, PT 135. Quickness (of imagination or fancy): I.PAM 98, II.PS 25, DCOPS 147, SS.XVII.APa 389. (2) Lively, vivid, energetic (wit or speech in repartee): I.EDP 89, PEL 149. Quickness (of wit in repartee): I.EDP 68, 79, PAM 99, DECG 182; Jonson 100. (3) Intelligent: II.LP 4 (reader). Quickness (intelligence): II.DCOPS 138. (4) Fast, rapid: I.EDP 65 (turn in a play), II.DCOPS 147 (return of rhyme).

QUICKEN (v.) To stimulate, to inspire: I.EDP 26, PrSL2 109 (fancy).

R

RAGE (sb.) (1) Poetic rage (furor poeticus). See Poetic rage, Fury, Inspiration. The passion (invariably accompanying inspiration) which a poet feels for his subject. To be effective, rage must be controlled by judgment or rules. I.GCT 258, SS.XV.AP 227, 251. (2) "Poetic rage" as transferred to a work of art which in turn incites a similar passion in an audience or reader: II.PEP 167, SS.XV.AP 237 ("pleasing rage"). (3) Sexual passion (*OED* says first recorded use is 1697): SS.XIII.SAVPMF 311.

RAIL (v.) To satirize in a heavy-handed manner. To use abusive language, to use invective, to declaim against something. Juvenal "rails" at vice. See Raillery, Rally. I.PrSL2 109, II.DCOPS 137, 138, SS.VII.DDG 17, VDG 172, 177, 177, 216, IX.EWTM 428, XV.AP 235. Railing: II.PS 31, DCOPS 97, SS. VI.DKK 9, X.PRLaici 27, 27, XV.PNOEM 399, XVII.LPd 75, AARHL 99.

RAILLERY (sb.) Dryden first uses "raillery" to mean coarse, rough, heavy-handed satire or jesting (I. 21), but by 1671 he means light, refined abuse, usually in the dialogue or repartee of comedy. Thereafter, when he wants "raillery" to mean coarse satire or abuse he uses a qualifying adjective or context. "Raillery" becomes a key term in satire. Dryden says, "The nicest most delicate touches of satire consist in fine raillery" (II. 136). "A wise man is tickled while he is hurt in this manner, and a fool feels it not" (II. 137). Dryden thinks that Restoration satire and drama excel in raillery (I. 181) because it is the product of a polite, refined, cynical age. He links "raillery" to the French, from whence its meaning probably came. See Fine raillery, Rally, Repartee. (1) Coarse satire or jesting: I.EDP 21, DEDP 116, II.DCOPS 99, 100, 103, 107, 110, 138, PF 293; Cowley (Spingarn) II. 79; Sprat (Spingarn) II. 130. (2) Witty, refined abuse: I.PEL 145, DECG 172, 181, PA 186, II.DCOPS 107, 136, 137, LL 212, 215 (and Attic salt), SS.XIII.SAVPMF 312, XVIII.LLd 74, 75 (which the French call Attic salt). (3) An instance or passage of witty abuse: II.DCOPS 102, 109, 110.

RALLY (v.) To ridicule in a light way, to banter. Horace laughs and rallies, Juvenal declaims and rails (II. 31). "Railing" moves indignation; "rallying" moves laughter (II. 138): II.PS 31, DCOPS 129, 138, 138.

REASON (sb.) (1) The intellectual, discriminating faculty which thinks or judges. It is the rational (not the imaginative) faculty. See Judgment. I.EDP 78, DEDP 126, 126, 126, 126, 126, 126, 126, 127, PEL 148, II.PPBPP 182, SS.XV.AP 232, 249, 251, 251. Reasonable (man): I.DEDP 126, AAHP 199, 202, DAV 225, 232, GCT 256. Reasonable (describing a thought well thought out or a man as thinking): I.DEDP 126, AAHP 197, 207, PAL 222, 233, GCT 242, 245, 250, 256, II.PS 288. Hobbes (Spingarn) II. 70 ("Men more admire fancy than they do either judgment, or reason, or memory"); Rymer (Z) 20 ("Fancy is like faith in religion; it makes for discoveries, and soars above reason, but never clashes or runs against it"), 20 ("In the contrivance or oeconomy of a play, reason is always principally to be consulted. Those who object against reason, are the fanaticks of poetry, and are never to be saved by their good works." See also Enthusiasm. Rymer is alluding to the difference between religion of reason found, for example, in sermons by Tillotson, and the religion of extreme dissenters as found in the followers of George Fox.), 20. (2) An argument, a fact; argument in general. Thus, a reason gives a justification for what is asserted: I.EDP 78, DEDP 127, 129, PEL 145, 147, 151, AAHP 204, HAR 216, GCT 244, POE 263, 270, 272, 273, II.PS 27, PAA 36, 37, 40, DCOPS 98, DAV 233, 249, SS.XIV.DAVd 176. (3) Probability, truth, common sense. The rules promote verisimilitude because they represent common sense (or reason). "The Art of Poetry" gives "reason's" rules for drama: "Your humble style must sometimes gently rise;/And your discourse sententious be, and wise:/The passions must to nature be confined;/And scenes to scenes with artful weaving joined./Your wit must not unseasonably play;/But follow business, never lead the way" (SS.XV. 247): I.DEDP 126, 126, 126, PEL 146, AAHP 200, HAR 214, II.PAA 35, SS.VI.DTC 253, XV.AP 225, 225, 225, 237, 247, 247. Reasonable (within the bounds of reason): I.EDP 55, DEDP 124, 126, AAHP 199, 202, PAL 225, PO 232, GCT 261, SS.VII.DLT 376. Reasonably: I.PEL 147, HAR 214, 215, 217, II.PS 33. (4) Thought or logic: I.PEL 151, AAHP 200 ("right reason"), II.PAA 35, LL 212, SS.XV.AP 233. (5) Basis, fundamental principle: I.GCT 243.

REFINE (v.) (1) To improve a language by "rejecting such old words and phrases which are ill-sounding, or improper, or in admitting new, which are more proper, more sounding, and more significant" (I. 171). Refinement comes from freedom of conversation and employment of wit in discourse: I.PAM 100, ECG 167, DECG 170, 177, 177, GCT 239, II.PS 24, PAA 38, 38, PF 271, SS.XV.AP 228. Refinement: I.DECG 171, 171. Refiner: I.DECG 177 (Horace). Refining: I.DEDP 176, II.DCOPS 152. (2) To revise and improve an art or work of art by eliminating flaws or roughness: I.EDP 66, 92, GCT 241, II.DCOPS 110, DAV 236, PF 290, SS.XIV.DAVd 165, XV.AP 252. Refinement: I.DECG 178. Refining: I.PEL 145. (3) To improve, to polish, to add polish (in general): I.DECG 172, II.PAA 36, SS.XIII.SAVPMF 312. Refining: SS.XIV.DAVd 149.

REFLECTION (sb.) (1) Censure, invective, abuse, or a censure, a libel, an invective: II.DCOPS 104, 109, 116 (equated with the French *médisance* and with satire), 136, SS.V.PAZd 186, 190, VI.DKK 10; Rymer (Z) 76. (2) Thought, meditation: I.OHP 158, II.PPBPP 204, SS.XVII.PFAAP 338, APa 385; Rymer (Z) 17, 129. (3) Thought or meditation written down, a remark: I.GCT 242, 260, II.LP 10, DCOPS 132, SS.VII.VDG 186, XVI.DLSFX 6, XVII.LPd 70. (4) Act of coloring, gilding, brightening (something which is flat and unimaginative): I.PSF 275. (5) A criticism, a critical statement: II. DCOPS 83.

REGULAR (adj.) (1) Describing a play written according to the rules. See Rules. I.EDP 58, 65, 65, 66, 66, 68, PSL 105, PAL 222, 231, GCT 243, 247, POE 271, II.PDS 49, DCOPS 108, TCDD 171. Regularly: I.EDP 35, 56, 61, PWG 131. (2) Well-organized, proportionate, easily understood, logical (in development or arrangement): II.DCOPS 82, SS.XIII.SAVPMF 313, 315. Regularity: II.DAV 247, SS.XVII.APa 355.

RELATION (sb.) See also Fable. (1) Narrative in a play, action described rather than acted out. There are two kinds: that which describes events antecedent to the play and that which describes events which take place behind the scenes. The second causes the debate which emanates from the question of whether English or French plays are superior. French plays narrate the outcome of battles, murders, etc., while English plays show them on the stage. Neander, in EDP (I. 63), argues for compromise. A poet should avoid the two extremes of omitting something beautiful and charming (or striking and exciting) and of including something incredible or "undecent": I.EDP 50, 50, 50, 51, 53, 53, 54, 62, 63, PO 234, GCT 249, SS.VIII.PC 220 (an example of what should or should not be omitted). (2) Story, the telling of a story: I.EDP 47, PA 184, II.DCOPS 103. (3) Telling or narrating history, or a story from history: II.LP 5, 7, PDS 49, CP 68, SS.VII.VDG 158, 191, XVII.LPd 54, AARHL 96, 96. (4) Connection: II.LP 8, SS.XVII.PPBPPd 299 (between poetry and painting).

REPARTEE (sb.) (1) A sudden, smart, short reply (I. 8), produced by "quickness of wit" (I. 68, 99). It is connected with argumentative discourse: I.PRL 8, EDP 68, 79, 88, 88, 88, 89, PAM 99, DEDP 116, II.PPBPP 198. (2) "A chase of wit kept up on both sides [by two characters], and swiftly managed" (I. 60). It is "the soul of conversation," "the greatest grace of comedy, where it is proper to the characters" (I. 149). It is found in comedy of wit (I. 149) and is noted for its "quick and poignant brevity" (I. 89): I.EDP 60, 89, PEL 149, PAL 223; Shadwell (Spingarn) II. 150 (Shadwell disagrees with Dryden; he says "repartee" is not "wit").

REPRESENT (v.) (1) To imitate nature through the art of the theater; to deceive by imitation. A play and the stage it is played on replace (or represent) real or probable actions, places, times, and characters which embody human nature or personate actual people, with all their passions, humours, and sudden thoughts. The line differentiating "narration" and "representation" is sometimes vague. Hobbes says that "representation" is "narrative" (Spingarn II. 55). "Representation," however, applies to that which can be visualized, whether on the stage, in a painting, in a poetic image, or in the narrative of an action. See Relation. I.EDP 29, 41, 48, 51, 51, 51, 51, 52, 55, 62, 62, 64, 69, 69, 71,

73, 73, 74, 80, 88, PSL 107, DEDP 113, 113, 125, 126, 126, 126, 127, 127, 127, PTL 139, PEL 147, 152, OHP 162, DECG 178, AAHP 191, 199, 203, HAR 218, 219, PAL 223, GCT 243, 243, 245, 249, 252, 252, 252, PSF 278, II.PDS 48, 49, DCOPS 100, 108, 142, PPBPP 184, 189, 190, 195, DAV 226, 228, 229, 230, SS.VII.VDG 147, 148, 160, 163, 166, 168, 168, 169, 216, VIII. PC 222, Hobbes (Spingarn) II. 55; Rymer (Z) 88. Representing: I.EDP 25, DEDP 114, DECG 178, II.PDS 46, SS.VII.VDG 160. (2) To imitate nature in poetry by means of description, expression of emotions, narration, personation: I.PAM 98, 98, 100, II.CSE 58, DCOPS 92, 107, 135, PPBPP 197, PPV 219, PF 291, SS.II.DIE 288, V.PAZd 197, XVIII.LLd 73. Representing: II.DCOPS 137. (3) To depict (something) in a painting: II.PPBPP 189, 197 (an emotion), SS.XVII.PPBPPd 292, 293, 298, 298, 299, APa 353, 363. (4) To imitate actions in opera: II.PAA 35, 42. (5) To express (something) through "vocal and instrumental music": II.PAA 35. (6) To describe or narrate in history (or in other prose or speech): II.PPBPP 202, SS.II.DIE 288, SS.VIII.PC 220, X. PHP 114, XIII.SAVPMF 312, XVII.LPd 23, AARHL 100. Representing: SS. VIII.PC 219. (7) To serve as an example (as one person may represent many): II.DAV 243.

REPRESENTATION (sb.) (1) A stage or play as an imitation (or deceptive and artistic representation) of nature (I. 2, 82). Also, the acting out on stage of a play or a part of a play. See Represent, def. (1). Tragedy, for example, is "a delightful representation of human life in great persons" (I. 213), while "comedy is a representation of human life in inferior persons and low subjects" (II. 189): I.PRL 2, EDP 47, 51, 54, 62, 82, 87, DEDP 123, 126 (def. of deceit of a play), 127, 128, PTL 139, 141, 142, PEL 146, 148, 152, 155, OHP 162, PA 184, HAR 213, POE 265, II.PDS 46, DCOPS 99, 110, PPBPP 189, 189, SS.VII.DDG 13, VDG 188, 203, VIII.DAm 9, DLT 375. (2) Description either of concrete reality or of an image invented by the mind (in poetry): I.OHP 161, 161, SS.IV.DCG 12, IX.EWTM 422, XVII.PPBPPd 297.

RESEMBLANCE (sb.) (1) Likeness. Art is a resemblance of two kinds of nature: actual and probable. (a) In a resemblance of probable nature, the closer a work of art is to nature, the better it is (I. 27, II. 193). The perfect work of art which imitates probable nature is that which is a perfect resemblance of the perfect image of nature found in the mind of the greatest poet or painter (SS.XVII. 295). Thus, art which is a perfect or close to a perfect resemblance of nature becomes like nature itself (see Nature), and as one work of art resembles another which is nearly perfect, it too comes close to nature. In drama, the rules help achieve resemblance to nature (I. 127): I.EDP 27 (Ancients are nature), 41 (Shakespeare is like nature), DEDP 127, 127, II.PPBPP 186, 193, 193, 196, SS.XVII.PPBPPd 295; Hobbes (Spingarn) II. 62 ("The resemblance of truth is the utmost limit of poetical liberty"); Rymer (Z) 3. (b) In the resemblance of actual nature, a likeness or resemblance which is too exact is inferior (I. 114). When a poet or artist imitates nature, he should strive to achieve a flattering resemblance of the whole by smoothing out the blemishes. A portrait should not be too exact: I.DEDP 114, 114, II.PE 62, PPBPP 184, DAV 256, SS.IV.DCG 15. (2) Likeness. A property of manners. The manners of a particular hero must always be the same in any work of art.

Achilles' manners, for example, must always resemble the significant characteristics set by Homer (I. 249): I.GCT 249, II.LP 8, CSE 57. (3) Likeness or parallel of a person or thing to something else, as a historical person or events are parallel to, or a likeness of, a person or incident in a play: II.PF 272, 289, SS.VII.VDG 156, 179, 216, 217, 217, 218, 219, DDS 301, XIV.DAVd 183, 183, XVII.LPd 69, DHL 89, 89, XVIII.LLd 68. (4) Likeness of one genre or work of art (or part of either) to another: I.PSF 277 (fustian to loftiness), II.PS 23 (translation to the original), DCOPS 102, 106, PPBPP 190 (grotesque painting to farce), 191 (art to poetry), 203, 204 ("strong glowing colours" to "bold metaphors"), PF 290, SS.XIV.DAVd 188.

RETRENCH (v.) See Alter, Correct (v.), Judgment. (1) To revise and improve writing by deleting or reducing the literary products of fancy or imagination. The judgment, by retrenching, controls and corrects the imagination: I.EDP 25, 69, DECG 170, POE 265, 272, II.PE 61, DAV 254. (2) To reduce the fullness of explanation by revising. To cut back the sense in order to give the imagination of a reader more play: Retrenchment: II.DAV 242.

RHAPSODY (sb.) An extravagant effusion of sentiment with no thought content to support the words. Dryden calls Settle's *Empress of Morocco* a "rhapsody of nonsense": I.PAZ 191, SS.XV.PNOEM 397; Phillips (Spingarn) II. 270 (Phillips is against rhyme and calls a work a "rhapsody of rhyming couplets").

RHETORIC (sb.) (1) Eloquent expression: I.PRL 9, SS.XIII.SAVPMF 316 (Virgil's rhetoric). (2) The art of expression (such as the proper use of tropes and figures in general or hyperboles, catachreses, etc., in particular), the art of eloquence and oratory, the art of persuasion (all of which fall under the heading of "rhetoric"): I.AAHP 201, II.LP 4, SS.XV.PNOEM 408, XVIII.LLD 63, 63, 64, 74.

RHODOMONTADES (sb.) Bragging, extravagant speeches: I.OHP 165 (of Almanzor).

RHYME (sb.) Dryden mentions "rhyme" in two contexts. The first is the reiterated statement that rhyme is inferior to the quantities of the Ancients (I. 95, 269, II. 15). The second is the discussion of whether "rhyme" is superior to "blank verse." From 1664 (PRL) through 1672 (OHP), Dryden says rhyme sounds more natural and more effectual than blank verse, at least for heroic poesy and tragedy. He is not entirely sure of his position, however, and considers his defense of rhyme to be the weakest part of EDP (I. 112). In the second phase of his attitude toward rhyme Dryden vacillates. In 1676 (PrAZ) he says, "[I grow] weary of [my] long-loved mistress, Rhyme," because it is too confining and unnatural (I. 192), and in 1678 (PAL) he says he will use whichever form best suits his material (I. 231). But in 1693 (DCOPS), Dryden criticizes Milton for not using rhyme in *Paradise Lost* (the reason, Dryden says in II. 84, is that rhyming was not Milton's "talent"). Finally, in 1697 (DAV), Dryden unequivocally favors blank verse. He says, "He who can write well in rhyme can write better in blank verse" (II. 240). (1) Verse marked by a set pattern of agreement in the terminal sounds of its lines. See also Burlesque, Double Rhyme, Female Rhyme, Octave Rhyme. I.PRL 6, 7, 7, 7, 7, 8, 8, EDP 55, 65, 66, 66, 77, 78, 78, 78, 78, 79, 79, 80, 80, 80, 80, 81, 81, 81,

81, 81, 81, 82, 82, 82, 82, 82, 82, 83, 83, 83, 83, 84, 84, 84, 84, 85, 85, 86, 86, 87, 87, 87, 88, 88, 88, 88, 88, 89, 89, 89, 89, 89, 90, 90, 90, 91, 92, PAM 95, 95, 96, PrSL 108, DEDP 112, 113, 113, 113, 113, 115, 115, 115, 115, OHP 157, 157, 157, 157, DECG 175, PAZ 190, PrAZ 192, EAZ 193, PAL 231, POE 269, II.ETV 15, 15, 15, PAA 35, DCOPS 84, 85, 85, 147, 147, 147, 148, DAV 240, 240, 240, 240, 248, 256, SS.VII.VDG 199, XV.AP 224, 225, 225, 226, 233, 233, 234; Milton II. 6 (Milton argues against rhyme: it was invented in a barbarous age to help lame meter; it hinders poets who without rhyme will have more freedom in writing heroic poems; and it was rejected by the Italians, Spanish, and Ancients who hated the jingling sound of like endings); Hobbes (Spingarn) II. 57 (rhyme is too confining). (2) A single example of def. (1): I.PRL 6, 8, 8, 8, EDP 79, 82, 82, 82, 90, PAM 95, 96, 96, II.PAA 38, 40, 40, 40, LWW1 54, 54, 54, DCOPS 147, DAV 247, PF 271, SS.XV.AP 227, 233, 234, PNOEM 399. (3) A piece of poetry, a poem: I.EDP 90, SS.XV.AP 228, 230, 235, 240, 244, 249. (4) The action of writing poetry: SS.XV.AP 224.

RHYMER (sb.) A poet (pejorative) who elevates rhyme over sense: II.PAA 41, DCOPS 85, SS.IX.EWTM 431, XV.AP 249.

RHYTHMUS (sb.) Rhythm, meter, and harmony in either music or speech. "Homer and Virgil . . . amongst all the poets, only understood that which was called 'rhythmus' by the Ancients": II.PAA 40.

RIDICULE (sb.) (1) An absurdity, an absurd thing: I.AAHP 205, II.DCOPS 108, 119, 132. Ridiculum: I.EDP 73. (2) Mockery directed toward something which is thought to be absurd: II.DCOPS 140, SS.VII.VDG 185.

RIDICULOUS (adj.) Pleasantly or unpleasantly unnatural, preposterous, absurd. See Absurd, Monstrous, Grotesque, Nature. (1) Describing a play, a part of a play, a poem, etc., which is unpleasantly unnatural (which lacks verisimilitude or probability): I.EDP 47, 51, 65, DECG 172, GCT 254 ("a great passion out of season"), II.DCOPS 86 (fables), DAV 230. Ridiculously: I.EDP 49, DEDP 123. (2) Pleasantly laughable, preposterous (but within the realm of possibility) owing to the deformity of a humour, affectation, etc. (in a comedy, satire, etc.): I.EDP 71, 72, 72, 72, PEL 146 (figures and grimaces), 148, 152, 152, 155, PAL 190, AAHP 199, II.DCOPS 137 (Zimri as a caricature of George Villiers), 146. Ridiculousness: I.PEL 145 (of his habit and his grimaces). (3) Pleasantly preposterous (in general): I.DECG 172 (raillery), II. DCOPS 103 (meaning), 115, SS.VIII.DLT 375. (4) Unpleasantly preposterous, laughable, inadequate, absurd (in general): I.EDP 82, 90, DEDP 113, PRL 140, PEL 155, PA 186 (descriptions), PAL 226, GCT 261 (mistakes), II.DCOPS 112, LL 212, SS.IV.DMLM 255, V.PAZd 199 (accidents), VII. VDG 174 (accusation), XV.PNOEM 402 (description), XVIII.CPd 48.

RIGHT REASON Reason which avoids being seduced by prejudice, and which follows common sense or nature, and is thus able to distinguish between truth and falsehood. Dryden says, "Good nature, by which I mean beneficence and candour [freedom from partiality], is the product of right reason" (II. 74): I. AAHP 200, II.DCOPS 74, 140, SS.XV.AP 239. Rightly: I.AAHP 203.

RISIBILITY (sb.) From French *risibilité* (not in *OED*). The ability to laugh (which distinguishes man from all other creatures). The *Dictionnaire de l'academie* says, "La faculté distinctive de l'homme": II.DCOPS 143.

ROMANCE (sb.) (1) A loose, rambling, fictitious tale of adventure, love, passion, etc., different from a novel or play (I. 153), relatively unconfined by rules, and written only for amusement. "In a romance those errors [transgressions of rules] are excused/There 'tis enough that, reading, we're amused:/ Rules too severe would there be useless found" (SS.XV. 240): I.PRL 3, EDP 42, PEL 153, 154, SS.XV.AP 240; Rymer (Z) 68 (Aspatia in *The Maid's Tragedy* is from "romance but not nature"), 117 ("That wild-goose-chase of romance"). (2) The literary genre made up of romances: SS.V.PAZd 198.

ROUND (adj.) (1) Too assertive ("Here the sense flags, and your expression's round"): SS.XV.AP 230. (2) Complete: SS.XVIII.LLd 75 (periods).

RULES (sb.) Precepts, principles, models as precepts. By "rules," Dryden usually means precepts (see, for example, I. 200, II. 207), but sometimes he means models as precepts. Thus, classic poems are rules (II. 207), and "ancient statues . . . are the rule of beauty and gracefulness" (SS.XVII. 353). Dryden is consistent in his attitude toward rules of art, especially in the drama. He says that rules are not a "Magisterial prescription on poets" (I. 260, from Rapin, *Reflexions*, XII). They can be broken at any time that a poet feels it is necessary to gain greater beauties (II. 49). From the beginning of his career, Dryden says that servile obedience to rules kills beauties (I. 63), and later he calls rules "mechanic" (II. 161). He says, "Better a mechanic rule stretched or broken than a great beauty were omitted" (II. 227). There is only one rule that never can be broken or stretched: all art is an "imitation of nature" (I. 122, II. 193). In sum, the rules help the judgment follow nature, and are therefore exceedingly important (I. 260). But the rules are not enough (I. 193) and the greatest beauties come from the artist's imagination which occasionally breaks the rules (I. 66, 193, 200, 212, II. 49, etc.). (1) Precepts of dramatic poesy. Mostly the unities of time, place, and action, but also "liaison des scènes," decorum of the stage, poetic justice, probability, reason, etc.: I.EDP 30, 32, 36, 44, 48, 63, 66, PrSL 107, DEDP 122, 122, 124, 125, 128, PEL 147, EAZ 193, AAHP 200, HAR 212, 215, 217, GCT 244, 246, 250, 260, 260, PSF 279, II.PAA 39, PDS 47, 49, 50, DCOPS 73, 74, 95, 96, 145, PEP 161, LWW2 173, PPBPP 188, 191, 191, 191, 207, DAV 227, SS.VIII.PC 220, DLT 375, XV.AP 237, 239, 247, 247, 252. (2) Precepts of heroic or epic poetry (such as decorum, unity of action, Homer as a model, etc.): I.OHP 160, 162, GCT 248, II.DCOPS 82, PPBPP 193, DAV 240. (3) Precepts of prosody (such as cadences, rhyme, etc.): I.EDP 82, 83, 83, 84, II.PAA 40, DAV 237, SS.XV. AP 230, 233, 237, 238, 244. (4) Precepts of translation (see I. 273): I.POE 273, II.ETV 15, 15, 16, PS 19, 19, LL 215, 215. (5) Precepts of receiving words into the language: I.EDP 39, II.DCOPS 84. (6) Precepts of logic: I. EDP 58. (7) Precepts of music: II.PAA 38. (8) Precepts of poetry (in general): SS.VIII.DKA 136, XIV.DAVd 181, XV.AP 232, 249, 250. (9) Precepts of art (mostly imitation of nature): I.DEDP 122, 122, AAHP 200, II.PPBPP 193, 193, 193, 194, 194, DAV 226, SS.XV.AP 232, 233, 240, PHC 411. (10) Precepts of satire (such as unity of action and theme): II.DCOPS 145, 146. (11) Precepts of painting (all rules are in Dryden's translation of "De Arte

Graphica"): II.PPBPP 193, 193, SS.XVII.PFAAP 337, APa 353. (12) Precepts of history (such as accuracy): SS.VII.VDG 162. (13) Precepts in general: I. EDP 75, DEDP 118, PEL 147, OHP 165, AAHP 199, PAL 230, PSF 275, II.PS 32, DCOPS 125, SS.XVII.APa 253.

RUN (sb.) The flow of verse or of thoughts and images expressed in verse. "Run of verse" refers to the speed and energy of the cadence of a line. Dryden uses "run of verse" twice. He once defines it as "a kind of cadence" (II. 164), and once distinguishes it from other parts of versification when he says, "[Lucilius] minded neither his style nor his numbers, nor his purity of words, nor his run of verse" (II. 131). See Numerousness. II.DCOPS 131, PEL 164, DAV 238 ("run and measure of trimeter").

RUN (v.) To flow or move. Verse, or the flow of thought, images, and meter moves or "runs" (at a certain speed). "Running" thus becomes an English equivalent of *enjambement*. Dryden calls *enjambement* "running the sense into another line" (I. 84). See also Well-running. I.PRL 7, GCT 254, 255, II. DCOPS 84, 110, DAV 238 (French Alexandrines run "with more activity than strength"), LET 268, PF 272. Running: II.DCOPS 84, SS.XV.AP 233 ("Set rules for the just measure and the time,/the easy running and alternate rhyme").

S

SATIRE (sb.) See also Burlesque, Fescinnine, Raillery, Rally, Saturnian, Satyric. (1) Ridicule, verbal attack, invective, reflection, raillery (against folly, vice, or a wicked person). This is "satire" in its most general use. Crude invective is the lowest kind of satire; the highest is "fine raillery." Dryden says, "There is still a vast difference betwixt the slovenly butchering of a man, and the fineness of stroke that separates the head from the body and leaves it standing in its place" (II. 137). "The best and finest manner of satire . . . is that sharp, well-mannered way of laughing a folly out of countenance" (II. 147): I.EDP 49, DEDP 119 (the delight of comedy), AAHP 199 (in comedy), PAL 223, 229, GCT 243, II.LP 12, DCOPS 77, 81, 87, 97, 101, 101, 110, 112, 116, 116 (modern use), 116, 116, 131, 134, 136 (fine raillery), 140, PEP 164, LCM 265, PF 283, SS.V.DSI 106, VI.DKK 10, VII.VDG 169, 204, DDS 305, 305, VIII. PC 219, 222, IX.TRAA 212, EWTM 429, X.PRLaici 27, PHP 118, XIV.DAVd 178, XV.AP 234, 235, XVIII.PDCW 7. Satirical: II.DCOPS 107, 109 (plays from Old Comedy), 142 (nature), 142 (plays are like Old Comedy), PEP 162 (age), PF 282. Satirically: II.DCOPS 103, 104, 125. Satirize: SS.IX. EWTM 429, XVIII.LLd 67. Satirizing: SS.XVIII.LLd 65. (2) A poem, usually a formal verse satire (but in three instances a play). A satire, Dryden says, "Ought only to treat one subject; to be confined to one particular theme; or at least, to one principally. If other vices occur in the management of the chief, they should be transiently lashed, and not be insisted upon so as to make the design double" (II. 145). Dryden derives this conception of a formal verse satire from Juvenal, Persius, and Boileau: I.DECG 170, 170, AAHP 198, 199, GCT 240, II.PS 31, DCOPS 76, 78, 78, 80, 95, 95, 95, 104, 104, 104, 106, 106, 109, 110, 110, 110, 110, 111, 111, 112, 112, 112, 112, 112, 113, 113, 114, 114, 114, 114, 115, 115, 115, 115, 120, 121, 123, 123, 124, 125, 126,

128, 130, 130, 131, 132, 133, 135, 140, 140, 143, 144, 144, 145, 145, 146, 146, 146, 146, 148, 149, 152, SS.V.PAZd 190, VI.DKK 9, 9, X.PRLaici 27, XIV.DG 3, DAVd 204, XVII.LPd 75, AARHL 98. (3) The genre of poetry in which the purpose is to "lash" vice into reformation (I. 199, SS.IX. 214). "Satire is of the nature of moral philosophy, as it is instructive" (II. 122). Dryden usually means Roman formal verse satire as practiced by Juvenal, Horace, and Persius (see II. 63–115 for Dryden's version of its origin and development), but also includes other species of satire, such as tragical, declamatory Juvenalian satire, as different and developing from Horatian satire (II. 140); the low satire of Horace (and Dorset) which does not declaim but wittily rails (II. 136, 137, 140); "private satire" which is more often called abusive invective (II. 146); Varronian or Menippean satire which consists of several sorts of verse mixed with prose (the modern counterpart of which is Hudibrastic satire [II. 113, 114, 147]); and mock heroic satire which, to Dryden, is "the most beautiful and most noble kind of satire." Using Boileau's *Lutrin* as a model (of mock heroic satire), Dryden says, "Here is the majesty of the heroic, finely mixed with the venom of the other; and raising the delight, which would otherwise be flat and vulgar, by the sublimity of the expression" (II. 149): II.PE 63, DCOPS 76, 81, 85, 95, 96, 96, 97, 97, 97, 97, 98, 98, 102, 102, 103, 104, 104, 104, 104 (of Roman origin), 105, 105, 105, 107, 107, 109, 109, 109, 109, 110, 110, 110, 110, 111 (Roman satire), 111, 111, 111, 111, 111, 112 (several sorts of verses), 113, 113, 113 (of Lucilius), 113 (Varronian or Menippean satire), 113, 113, 113, 113, 114, 114, 115 (end of the history of Old Roman, Roman, and Varronian kinds of satire), 122 (Roman satire is Horace, Juvenal, and Persius), 122, 125, 125, 131, 131, 132, 136, 136, 136, 137, 140, 140, 140, 141, 142, 142, 142, 142, 143, 143, 143, 143, 143, 143, 143, 144 (modern satire), 145, 146, 146, 146, 146, 147, 149, 149, 149, TCDD 170, LL 211, PRAV 259, SS.XV.AP 235 (an essay on satire), 253, XVII.DPL 8. (4) A satyr (half goat, half man): II.LWW2 174.

SATIRIST (sb.) One who writes satires; not one who coarsely rails: I.EDP 39, II.PS 30, DCOPS 110, 111, 122, 124, 132, 132, 135, 139, 143, SS.XIII. SAVPMF 315, XVIII.LLd 71.

SATURNIAN (adj.) Describing rough, rude, extemporaneous raillery (in crude verse). The satire of ancient Rome. See Fescinnine. II.DCOPS 99, 106, 106, 106.

SATYRIC (sb.) A satyric tragedy or poem: II.DCOPS 102, 103.

SATYRIC (adj.) Describing a Greek (not a Roman) kind of tragedy (or other kind of play) which includes satyrs or clowns (who represent satyrs) who hurl invective, rail, etc. "Satyric" also describes a poem of this nature which is annexed to a tragedy: II.DCOPS 101, 102, 102, 103 (poem), 103, 103. Satyrical: II.DCOPS 98.

SCENARY (sb.) Scenario, a sketch or plan for a play (meaning not in *OED*). Both Watson and Strang think the word sounds current (in Restoration jargon): II.PPBPP 200, SS.VII.VDG 203.

SCENE (sb.) (1) A single action, incident, episode, encounter, dialogue (in a play). See Liaison des Scènes, Unbroken Scenes. I.EDP 29, 37, 37, 38, 41 (of passion), 41, 45, 49, 49, 55, 58 (of great passion), 58 (of mirth), 59, 64, 64, 64, 64, 64, 65, 69, 71, 74, 74, 75, 79, 84, 88, PSL 107, 107, PrSL 108, PWG 132, PT 135, PTL 141, OHP 158, ECG 167, DECG 182, 182, EAZ 193, PAL 231, PO 234, GCT 240, 241, 241, 241, 241, 241, 242, 242, 242, 243, 243, 251, 254, 259, II.PDS 49, SS.III.DEL 235, IV.DMLM 257, V.DA 8, VII.VDG 146, 147, 149, 162, 167, 167, 209, VIII.PC 220, 220, 220, 220, 220, 221, DLT 375, XV.AP 237, 237, 240, 247, 247, 247, PHC 410. (2) A specific division or part of an act (of a play) which may consist of a single encounter, an action, an incident, or a change of place. See Act. I.EDP 33, 37, 45, DEDP 126, 126, PEL 155, OHP 159 ("scene" compared to "canto" of an epic), DECG 178, PAL 222, GCT 244, II.PDS 50, SS.VII.VDG 147, 149. (3) The imaginary location of a play (where the action takes place). See Unity. I.EDP 29, 29, 62, 64, 64, 70, DEDP 125, PTL 140, GCT 240, 251, 255, II.PDS 49, PPBPP 195, SS.XV.PHC 411. (4) The stage or theater: I.PT 134, II.DAV 229, 230, SS.III.DEL 236. (5) "Behind the scenes" (an innovation by Dryden): I.EDP 50, OHP 162. (6) Scenery (of a play), which designates place or location, and is usually painted: I.EDP 29, 80, DEDP 125, PSF 275, II.PAA 35, 41, 41, 42, SS.XV.PNOEM 397. Flecknoe (Spingarn) II. 96. (7) Location, place (of a painting): SS.XVII.APa 363. (8) An encounter, an action, an incident, episode, etc., written for the stage or for a poem: I.PRL 5, 8 (either play or poem), 9 ("of argumentation or discourse," in either a play or poem), EDP 87, PAM 100, SS.XIV.DAVd 193 (in the *Aeneid*). (9) The geographical, literal surroundings: II.PPV 222. (10) The place where things happen, the world (as the "scene of history"): SS.XVII. CPd 24.

SECOND NOTION An unnatural image or idea which results from the combination of natural images. A centaur is thus a second notion: I.AAHP 204.

SECRET (adj.) (1) Describing a quality, device, or idea in a work of art meant not to be easily discerned or explained. A secret or hidden beauty in a play, for example, might be a moral contained within a character, requiring thought to recognize and explain (II. 50): I.PTL 139 (veneration), POE 266 (gracefulness), II.PS 31 ("secret happiness" is equated with "curiosa felicitas" in choice of words), PDS 50 (beauties), DCOPS 76 (graces), PPV 220 (charm), DAV 234 (force in expression), SS.XIV.DAVd 168 (beauties), 176 (reasons); Davenant (Spingarn) II. 17 ("secret graces" are a part of the second beauty of an epic; the first is morality). (2) Clandestine, concealed: I.GCT 251 (passage), II.PPBPP 189 (intrigues).

SENSE (sb.) (1) Meaning (of a work, phrase, sentence, line, work of art, etc.), thoughts (of an author): I.PRL 7, 8, 8, 8, EDP 21, 25, 81, 82, 82, 82, 82, 82, 90, PAM 95, 96, DEDP 117, 117, 129, PTL 141, OHP 157, DECG 174, 178, HAR 213, GCT 239, POE 265, 268, 268, 270, 270, 272, 272, 273, 273, PSF 276, II.LP 10, ETV 16, PS 21, 21, 21, 22, 22, 22, 23, 24, 24, 33, PAA 39, PDS 46, LWW1 54, 54, 54, 54, CP 66, 70, DCOPS 81, 84, 103, 103, 116, 119, 121, 139, 139, 149, 152, 154, 154, 154, 154, PEP 164, LJD 179, PPBPP 188, 206, 207, LL 214, 214, 215, 215, DAV 233, 234, 238, 240, 240, 241, 241, 242, 246, 247, 247, 249, 250, 250, 251, 253, 255, PF 274, 278, 286, 287, 287, 288, 289, SS.VI.DTC 251, VII.VDG 158, IX.EWTM 429, X.PRLaici

18, XIII.SAVPMF 312, XIV.DAVd 185, 198, 201, 202, 202, XV.AP 225, 226, 227, 228, 230, 232, 233, 233, 234, 234, 244, PHC 411, XVII.LPd 34, 71, PFAAP 340, XVIII.LLd 78, 81. Senseless: SS.XV.PNOEM 398. (2) Judgment, reason, good sense, common sense, wisdom. Dryden says that sound without sense is madness, bombast, etc. (I. 259). A mediocre artist can only write sense, a genius (who combined sense and sound) rises to sublimity: I. EDP 42, DEDP 112, PTL 142, 142, 143, PEP 161, DECG 171, 173, PA 187, PAL 224, GCT 258, 259, POE 269, II.PAA 39, LWW1 54, DCOPS 74, 78, 79, 80, 93, 102, 127, 147, 153, PEP 161, PPBPP 190, LL 213, DAV 243, 243, 244, LCM 266, PF 274, 280, 281, 286, 288, 289, 292, SS.IV.DMLM 255, VII.VDG 153, 160, DDS 299, VIII.DAm 7, DKA 132, IX.EWTM 431, XIV.DG 4, 9, 10, XV.AP 225, 229, 235, 235, 236, 245, 249, 249, 250, PNOEM 399, 401, 402, 402, 402, 402, 403, 405, 406, 406, 407, 408, XVIII.CPd 25. Senseless: SS.XV.AP 236. (3) One or all of the five senses. That which perceives in a sensate way: I.EDP 58, PTL 139. Senseless: SS.AP 225. (4) A feeling perceived in the mind, the heart, etc.; irrational realization, understanding, etc.: I.PTL 139, II.PS 26, DCOPS 134, SS.V.DA 5, XVII.APa 387 (connected to the sublime). (5) Genius, talent: SS.XV.AP 224, 252.

SENSIBLE (adj.) (1) Intellectually aware or conscious: I.PAM 100, PSF 276, II.LP 2, PS 33, CSE 57, DCOPS 88, 120, 137, 150, PPBPP 183, LL 212, PPV 218, DAV 249, PF 285, SS.III.DEL 235, VIII.DC 217, XI.DF 198. (2) Aware (through or by means of the five senses): II.DCOPS 73. (3) Intelligible, understandable (to others): SS.VI.DTC 251. Sensibly: SS.XIV.DAVd 147. (4) Sensitive (describing someone), capable of refined feelings: SS.XIII.SAVPMF 312. Sensibility: SS.XIV.DAVd 174. (5) Able to be perceived by the senses, able to influence the senses: SS.XVII.APa 371, 375.

SENTENCE (sb.) (1) A pithy saying, precept, maxim, aphorism: I.PAM 98, OHP 160, 160, PO 233, GCT 256, 256, II.LP 5, 10, PDS 46, DCOPS 128, 128, 136, DAV 243, SS.XV.AP 229, 230, 233; Alexander (Spingarn) I. 182, 183. (2) A complete thought, unit of syntax: I.DEDP 117, DECG 174, AAHP 206, POE 270, II.LWW1 53, 53, DCOPS 115, 141, SS.VI.DKK 6, VII.VDG 163, 199, XVII.LPd 34. (3) Literary verdict or judgment: I.PTL 140 (favorable), II.DAV 249, SS.X.PRLaici 24, XIV.DAVd 179. (4) A passage in a play, poem, oration, etc.: II.DCOPS 114, SS.XVIII.LLd 75.

SERIOUS (adj.) (1) Grave, earnest, opposite of jocular: I.PA 186, II.DCOPS 115, 124, 140, PF 279, 279, 284, 290, SS.V.DA 8, X.PRLaici 10, XIII. SAVPMF 315, XVII.LPd 63, PPBPPd 299. (2) Tragic. (a) Describing a play which is not a comedy (I. 56, 120), which is either a tragedy or a heroic tragedy. See Tragedy. Here, "serious" modifies "play" unless otherwise stated: I.EDP 56, 57, 69, 70, 74, 78, 81, 86, 87, 91, DEDP 112, 113, 114, 115, 115, 115, 120, 120, PEL 155, 155, OHP 156, 157, II.DCOPS 109 (piece). (b) Describing the tragic part of a tragi-comedy: I.PSL 107, PSF 274, II.PDS 51, DCOPS 103, PPBPP 202. (c) Describing qualities and effects of tragedy: I. DEDP 113 (subject), 113 (subject), 114 (subject), DECG 172 (concernment).

SIGNIFICANT (adj.) (1) Expressive, as in "significant language" (not in OED): I.EDP 90, DEDP 116, GCT 241, II.PEP 166. (2) Meaningful. Describing a word or words used for precise meaning, rather than for ostentatious display: I.EDP 25, PAM 98, DECG 171, II.DCOPS 84, 112, DAV 252; Hobbes (Spingarn) II. 69 ("The character of words that become a hero are propriety and significancy"); Rymer (Z) 15 ("signification").

SIMILITUDE (sb.) Simile, image (used as a simile or analogy). A "similitude" is one of the most poetical parts of poesy (II. 46), and Dryden compares it to a metaphor by saying, "A metaphor is . . . a kind of similitude comprehended in one word" (SS.XIV. 190). For Dryden's discussion of when and where to use similitudes, see SS.XIV. 189–91. A similitude can be used to explain something or to heighten and beautify poesy. See Figure (sb.). (1) Used for explanation: I.EDP 59, DEDP 127, II.LP 4, DCOPS 140, PPBPP 204, SS.IV. DMLM 256, VIII.DKA 134, XIV.DAVd 187. (2) Used to heighten or beautify poesy: I.PEL 155, GCT 254, II.PS 30, PE 61, PPV 219, SS.XIV.DAVd 189, 190, 190, 190, 190, 190, 191, 191, 191; Hobbes (Spingarn) II. 65. (3) Milton uses "similitude" in four ways: (a) Most often he means "image," a reflection of an original object, essence, or idea: II. 91 ("Begotten son, divine similitude of God"), 230, 264, III. 254, V. 116. (b) He also means similarity: III. 51. (c) Sometimes, he uses it to mean a comparison, as a simile, which is a rhetorical figure: III. 311, IV. 214. (d) Once, he means a formal comparison in logic: III. 324.

SMOOTH (adj.) Describing verse which avoids "synalaephas" (or other difficult pronunciations), employs consistent meter, and avoids extremes of passion and complex thought. Dryden says it is difficult to write smooth verse in English (II. 40). Although smoothness in itself can be an admirable quality (II. 13, SS.XV. 232, 243, XVII. 353), it is of limited importance. Dryden thinks Ovid is a limited poet who "avoids . . . all synalaephas . . . so that minding only smoothness, he wants both variety and majesty" (II. 22). About one of his own "papers of verses" Dryden says, "I affected the softness of expression and smoothness of measure rather than height of thought" (I. 102). See Numerousness, Run (sb.), Vowel. II.LP 13, PS 22, PAA 40, SS.XV.AP 232, 243, XVII.APa 353; Phillips (Spingarn) II. 263 (a "smooth" style was thought to be a Restoration achievement, a result of the lately refined and purged language); Rymer (Z) 12, 127. Smoothest: SS.XV.AP 229. Smoothly: II.ETV 15, LET 268. Smoothness: I.PAM 102, II.PS 22, 22, LWW1 53, PEP 164, SS.X.PRLaici 32; Sprat (Spingarn) II. 129.

SONNET (sb.) A poem of the same importance as madrigals and elegies (II. 238), in which a poet keeps strict "measure and time," uses "alternate rhyme," and does not allow a word to appear twice (SS.XV. 233). Dryden never explicitly defines the sonnet form: I.EDP 87, II.DCOPS 150, DAV 238, SS.XV. AP 233, 233, 234; Hobbes (Spingarn) II. 55 ("sonets . . . are but essayes and parts of an entire poem").

SONNETEER (sb.) A "little poet," one who writes minor verse: I.PAL 225.

SOPHISTICATION (sb.) An adulteration or perversion (of the language): I. DECG 176.

SOUL (sb.) (1) The animating force of a poet; genius; intellectual, inventive, and imaginative power of a poet. Dryden says, "Imaging is . . . a discourse which, by a kind of enthusiasm, or extraordinary emotion of the soul [of the poet], makes it seem to us that we behold those things which the poet paints" (I. 203): I.PRL 5, PAM 99, OHP 160, AAHP 203, PAL 228, GCT 260, II.PS 25, CSE 59, CP 69, DCOPS 85, 86, 106, 111, 153, LL 214, 215, DAV 223, PF 270, 272, 289, SS.XVII.DPL 6, PPBPP 294, XVIII.LLd 63. (2) The sensitive, mental faculties (judgment or understanding and imagination) of an audience, reader, or spectator; the innermost senses or feelings (of someone) which are stimulated and agitated by the re-creation of the fortunes of others. Dryden says, "The greater the soul [imagination] of him who reads, his transports are the greater" (II. 130). The judgment or understanding can have an equal share of the soul. Dryden also says, "The soul is but half satisfied when there is not truth in the foundation [of a poem]" (I. 121). The judgment apprehends truth; the imagination takes care of the rest. See Imagination, Judgment. I.EDP 39, 41, 41, 52, 89, PAM 99, DEDP 114, 121, 121, PTL 139, HAR 216, PAL 225, GCT 246, 256, II.LP 7, PDS 51, DCOPS 130, DAV 224, 227, 244, SS.V.PAZd 199, XV.AP 230, XVII.DPWDY 210. (3) The essence of poetry (which is "imitation of nature"): I.EDP 23, 56 ("imitation of humours and passions"), GCT 260 ("probability of fiction"), II.PS 32 (the "soul" of Cowley's imitation of Pindaric odes consists in "the warmth and vigour of fancy, the masterly figures, and the copiousness of imagination"), SS.XVIII.PDCW 5.

sound (sb.) (1) Resonance and harmony of words or verse (as related to sense or meaning). Dryden says, "Propriety of sound [should] be varied according to the nature of the subject" (II. 40). The poet who best relates "sound" to sense is Virgil, and Dryden says, "The sound of his words have often somewhat that is connatural to the subject" (I. 100). Sound without sense is fustian, and fustian is "an extravagant thought, instead of a sublime one, 'tis roaring madness instead of vehemence; and a sound of words instead of sense" (I. 259): I.PAM 100, DEDP 117, 117, GCT 259, PSF 277, 278, II.PAA 40, PDS 46, LJD 179, SS.XV.AP 229, 230, PNOEM 404, 405; Dillon (Spingarn) II. 307 ("The sound is still a comment to the sense"). (2) Euphony, resonance, harshness, noise (of words, phrases, etc.). Dryden usually implies that sound should be related to sense or meaning, but he also discusses sound alone. He says, "Nicety of hearing" is required in a poet so that "the discord of sounds in words shall as much offend him as a seventh in music would a good composer" (II. 40). He praises, for example, a line in one of Creech's translations by saying that "the many liquid consonants are placed so artfully that they give a pleasing sound to the words" (II. 245): II.PS 21, 22, 32, PAA 35 (loftiness of sound), 35 (masculine sound), 40, DCOPS 131, PEP 165 (synalaepha improves sound), 166, PPBPP 203, DAV 234, 234, 234, 251, PRAV 259, PF 288, SS.VIII.DKA 136, PC 226, XIII.SAVPMF 313, XV.AP 227, 231. (3) Rhyme, or sound of rhyme. Dryden says, "But these thoughts are never fettered with the number or sound [rhyme] of verse without study" (I. 78): I.EDP 78, 79, 83, 88, PAM 95, OHP 157, II.ETV 15.

sounding (adj.) Sonorous, resonant (describing words and expressions, sometimes by themselves, sometimes as appropriate to the subject). "For Virgil, above all poets, had a stock which I may call almost inexhaustible, of figurative, elegant, and sounding words" (II. 250): I.PAM 98, DECG 171, 175, GCT 260, II.DCOPS 84, 84, 112, 154, DAV 250, 252, 252, SS.VI.DTC 253 (language), XV.AP 229 (sentence).

SPIRIT (sb.) (1) Vigor and power of genius, imagination, fancy, or invention, as revealed in a work of art. "Too much labour often takes away the spirit by adding to the polishing, so that there remains nothing but a dull correctness" (II. 207). The nearest *OED* definition (IV. 3b) is "vigour or animation of the mind" (dated 1716). An older English usage (*OED* III. 4) is "A brisk or lively quality, vivacity, or animation in persons or things" (1588). These definitions are incomplete. The French conception of *esprit* is more attuned to Dryden's usage, and he appears to employ a combination of both the French and English. Littré (def. 26) quotes Bossu (Instr. II.): "L'esprit des grands écrivains doit se chercher non dans un passage seul, qui pourrait n'être qu'une faute d'impression, mais dans l'usage constant et uniforme auquel nous les voyons attachés partout ailleurs." Littré (def. 13) also quotes La Bruyère (XI): "Le mot esprit, quand il signifie une qualité de l'âme, et un de ces mots vagues, auxquels tous ceux qui les prononcent attachent presque toujours des sens différents: il exprime autre chose que jugement, génie, goût, talent, pénétration, étendue, grâce, finesse, et il doit tenir de tous ces mérites: on pourrait le défenir raison ingénieuse." Cayrou defines *esprit* (p. 350) as "intelligence, inspiration, talent." Neither the French nor the English definition wholly comprehends Dryden's use. The relation of spirit to genius, to the indefinable essence of a great work of art connects Dryden's use of "spirit" to Bouhours' "Je ne sais quoi," at least after 1671. See Bouhours, "Le Je ne sais quoi," *Les Entretiens d'Ariste et d'Eugene* (1671). See also Grace, Admiration, Genius, Happy, def. (2), Invention, Imagination, Fancy (sb.). I.EDP 24 (Cowley), 58, 65, 66, PSL 105, AAHP 198, GCT 254, POE 272, II.PS 20, 31, 33, DCOPS 83, 132, 153, PPBPP 207, 207, LL 214, 215, 215, 215, DAV 242, 250, LCM 265, SS.VIII.DKA 136, XIII.SAVPMF 315, XVII.DPWDY 210, APa 383 (in a painting); Rymer (Z) 5 (Spenser had "a large spirit"), 96 (the "spirit" of Aristophanes is best found in Rabelais). (2) Intellect, especially imagination, but sometimes both judgment and imagination as needed to comprehend fully a work of art. Dryden says, "The spirit of man cannot be satisfied but with truth or verisimility" (I. 47). The nearest *OED* definition (IV. 4) is "the faculties of perception or reflection" (1697). The French definitions are much closer. Dubois-Lagane calls it "intelligence, faculté de comprendre" (p. 203). Littré agrees in his def. 13: I.EDP 47, II.DCOPS 144, PPV 218, DAV 242, SS.III.DEL 232, V.PAZd 188, XVIII.LLd 78. (3) An intellect which is gay, perceptive, and witty (describing Charles II). Dubois-Lagane: "Le siège de la pensée, du souvenir, ou un certain brillant de l'intelligence propre aux reparties vives, aux sallies plaisantes" (p. 203): I.DECG 181. (4) The seat of the feelings or cast of mind, which may vary in outlook according to intellectual stimuli, events, circumstances, etc. "The continual agitation of the spirits [is] . . . a weakening of any constitution, especially in age" (II. 276): I.PAL 223, GCT 256, POE 265, II.PE 60, DCOPS 130, PF 276, SS.XVII.APa 363, 389. (5) Essence (of poetry). "Poetry is of so subtle a spirit that in pouring out of one language into another, it will all evaporate" (I. 271, quotation from Denham): I.POE 271, II.DCOPS 123. Sprat (Spingarn) II. 135

(in Cowley's Latin poems there are three kinds of spirits: "A majestic spirit, or a passionate, or a pleasant"). (6) A supernatural being: II.DCOPS 90, SS.XVII.PPBPPd 295.

STEAL (v.) To plagiarize without improving the stolen material. See Borrow. I.PEL 153, 153, II.PDS 49, SS.V.PAZd 190, XV.PNOEM 399, XVIII.LLd 78. Stealing: I.PrTL 141, PEL 153.

STING (sb.) A point (see Point), as found in an epigram, which hurts someone's feelings (I.PAM 98, OHP 160, DECG 179); as ascribed to sharp satire (SS.VII.VDG 169).

STROKE (sb.) (1) A part of a verbal description (in poetry), as a trope (or color), a figure, etc. "How bold, how masterly are the strokes of Virgil" (I. 99). "The boldest strokes of poetry . . . are those which most delight the reader" (I. 200). *OED* records this meaning as first used by Dryden. A "stroke" in painting is a line or perhaps a "brush stroke," so in poetry "stroke" refers to a noticeable phrase or a short passage: I.PAM 99, 99, AAHP 200, II.PPBPP 204, SS.VII.VDG 168 (a pun on blows), 168 (a pun on blows), 218; Wilmot (Spingarn) II. 283 ("Just, bold strokes" are good). (2) A crossing out, the line of a pen or pencil: I.PSF 275, SS.XVI.AARLSFX 12. (3) An addition or revision (to a poem): II.DAV 249, PRAV 261. (4) Authority. "He has a great stroke with the reader" (II. 292). The *OED*'s first record of this definition is 1731: II.PF 292. (5) A line (on a painting): SS.XVII.APa 379.

SUBLIME (adj.) Elevated and moving in the highest degree. Dryden describes a sublime passage of Shakespeare by saying, "The painting of it is so lively, and the words so moving that I have scarce read anything comparable to it in any other language" (I. 259). Boileau's translation of Longinus' *On the Sublime (Traité du sublime)*, which appeared in 1674, is the most important influence on Dryden's use of "sublime" and on the development of the concepts of the sublime in England. Dryden first uses "sublime" in 1677 (AAHP) and then to describe *Paradise Lost*, which, he says, is "one of the greatest, most noble, and most sublime poems which either this age or nation has produced" (I. 196). Dryden usually uses "sublime" as a rhetorical term, referring to the kind of words and thought a poet employs. Nothing can be sublime if majestic, elevated words are not matched by lofty thoughts (I. 257). "Sublime" is close to being purely an aesthetic term only in AP where that which is "sublime" is not "pleasant" (SS.XV. 225, 244); it has qualities about it which move, agitate, or even disturb readers or audiences. See also Elevated, Flight. (1) Describing the lofty, elevated combination of sound and sense which is found in the greatest works of art. "Nothing is truly sublime if it is not just and proper" (I. 277). Dryden says that Virgil's "thoughts and words are equally sublime" (II. 251). Sublime thoughts (or sense) are profound, exciting, masculine (I. 25). "Sublime" as a rhetorical term concerns more explicitly words and expressions as they contribute to sublimity. Dryden says that "boisterous metaphors" are "accounted" by Longinus as instruments of the "sublime" (II. 121). Plutarch, for example, "neither studied the sublime style, nor affected the flowery" (II. 10). Plutarch's lack of sublimity comes from his lack of "sounding words," because Plutarch, according to Dryden, excels in everything else. Dryden also says of mock-heroic satire that "the majesty of the heroic [is] finely mixed with the venom of the other [the satire]; and [raises] the delight, which otherwise would be flat and vulgar, by the sublimity of the expression" (II. 149). "Sublime" expressions are the boldest and most figurative (I. 207). See Bold, Lofty, Majestic. I.AAHP 196, 207, GCT 259, PSF 277, II.LP 10, DCOPS 130, DAV 224, 243, SS.XV.AP 225, 244, XVII.LPd 63; Milton III. 303, 328 ("Whatsoever in religion is holy and sublime"), IV. 286 ("Poetry is the sublime art"), 344; Phillips (Spingarn) II. 262 ("sublime tragedy"), 267 ("The more sublime the argument, the nobler the invention . . . [and] the greater the poet"); Dillon (Spingarn) II. 307 (the two extremes of writing are "sublime" and "low"). Sublimest: I.AAHP 207. Sublime (sb.): II.DCOPS 121. Sublimity (sb.): I.GCT 257, II.PE 61, DCOPS 149, 150, PEP 162; Jonson 38. (2) Describing the power of inventive genius or the freedom of an elevated spirit which can express its loftiness, majesty, and quickness through art or other kinds of works. A sublime genius is "capable of the greatest designs" (SS.XVI. 17). Dryden says of Virgil (as he appears in his eclogues), "Addressing [himself] to Pollio . . . he could not longer restrain the freedom of his spirit, but began to assert his native character, which is sublimity" (II. 218). Homer and Shakespeare are more often described as sublime, however, for as Dryden says, "Longinus has judiciously preferred the sublime genius that sometimes errs to the middling or indifferent one which makes few faults, but seldom or never rises to excellence" (I. 197). Dryden also describes the Greeks (SS.XVII. 351) and the English (over the French [II. 162]) as having a "sublime genius." See Genius, Happy, def. (2). I.AAHP 197, II.PS 25, SS.XVI.AARLSFX 17, XVII.APa 351, 387. Sublimity (sb.): I.AAHP 198, II.DCOPS 144, 150, PEP 162, LJD 179 (describing the faculties of John Dennis), PPV 218; Milton III. 294 ("[The] sublimest wits [have] largeness of . . . spirits"); Reynolds (Spingarn) I. 158 (a "sublime wit" is a man of the highest intelligence and understanding); Hobbes (Spingarn) II. 70 ("Sublimity of a poet is in fancy").

SWEETNESS (sb.) See also Numerousness, Run (sb.), Vowel. (1) A relatively precise quality of smooth-running, pleasant verse. Sweetness exists where many vowels are used to avoid harshness (II. 235) and where there are few if any open vowels or clashing consonants placed side by side. This kind of sweetness is important in lyrical verse (II. 32) and arias (II. 35). Ovid is usually the example of sweetness in verse (I. 121, II. 22). See II. 21 where Dryden lists the different kinds of sweetness, after saying, "There is a great distinction to be made in sweetness, as in that of sugar and that of honey" (II. 21): I. DEDP 121, DECG 175, II.PS 21, 22, 32, PAA 35, 38, 40, PEP 164, DAV 234, 235, 235, 237, 237, 237, 258; Sprat (Spingarn) II. 136; Rymer (Z) 4 (opposite from "grave" and comes from vowel sounds). Sweet (adj.): I.PS 23, II.DAV 234, 235, 235, 251. Sweetest (adj.): II.PAA 37. (2) A quality (in prose and verse) of brevity, preciseness, and exact placement of words for both meaning and sound. This, Dryden says, is the sweetness of Virgil: II.LP 10, SS.IX.TRAA 211; Peachum (Spingarn) I. 122 ("the sweetness and majesty of Virgil"), 127, 132; Drayton (Spingarn) I. 138 ("sweetness of Ovid"); Cowley (Spingarn) II. 86 (the qualities of good poetry are "sweetness and numerosity"); Rymer (Z) 127. (3) A pleasing quality of speech, such as rhyme, which is charming or soothing and therefore pleasant. Of Chaucer's poetry, Dryden says, "There is the rude sweetness of a Scotch tune in it, which is natural and pleasing, though not perfect" (II. 281): II.ETV 15, PS 30, DAV 240, PF 281, SS.XIV.DG 6; Jonson 34, 38; Peachum (Spingarn) I. 121, 122 (an enticing quality, the opposite of harshness). Sweet: II.PS 21. (4) A pleasing quality exuded by something or someone: II.TCDD 170, SS.VIII. DAm 11; Jonson 84. Sweetest: SS.XIV.DAVd 162.

SYNALAEPHA (sb.) "The cutting of one vowel when it comes before another in the following word" (II. 22). Examples are "th'Argive fleet" and "th'army" (II. 165): II.PS 22, 22, PEL 164, 165, 165, 165, 165.

T

TALENT (sb.) An ability or skill at which one excels and for which one has an inborn inclination. Shadwell's talent was drinking. Dryden says, "They who are only born for drinking . . . let both poetry and prose alone" (SS.VII. 181, see also II. 136). A talent comes from or is a part of someone's genius. Dryden says, "every painter . . . [should] cultivate those talents which make his genius, and not unprofitably lose his time in endeavoring that which she has refused him" (SS.XVII. 385). In his most comprehensive quotation about talent Dryden says, "The nicest, most delicate touches of satire consist in fine raillery. This, my lord, is your particular talent. . . . 'Tis not reading, 'tis not imitation of an author, which can produce this fineness: it must be inborn; it must proceed from a genius, and particular way of thinking which is not to be taught; and therefore not to be imitated by him who has it not from nature" (II. 136). The ability, talent, or skill in which one most excels varies from rhyme to invention. "Rhyme was not his [Milton's] talent" (II. 85). Horace had three talents. "He was a critic, a satirist, and a writer of odes" (II. 30). "Rafael had the talent of invention" (SS.XVII. 391). "Invention and design were the particular talents of Homer" (II. 204). See Happy, def. (2), Genius. I.EDP 73, PT 133, PEL 148, OHP 157, DECG 177, PAL 226, 228, POE 273, 274, II.PS 21, 30, PAA 39, CSE 59, PE 63, DCOPS 75, 85, 86, 94, 122, 129, 131, 136, TCDD 170, PPBPP 204, DAV 238, PRAV 259, PF 270, 274, SS.VII.VDG 181, 186, IX.EWTM 429, XV.AP 224, 248, PNOEM 399, 402, XVII.LPd 75, APa 385, 391.

TASTE (sb.) (1) Simple, personal likes and dislikes in spectators, readers, etc. Dryden says, "Let all men please themselves according to their several tastes" (I. 145): I.DEDP 119, 119, 119, 119, 120, 120, PEL 145, OHP 161, AAHP 198, 199, 207, PAL 226, II.DCOPS 74, 127, PEP 161, 161, LWW2 174, PF 286, SS.XV.PHC 410, XVII.PFAAP 340, APa 353. (2) Inclination on the part of the author: I.PrAZ 192, PAL 226. (3) Discrimination or perception (in a man). It can be good, bad, right, or wrong. "Sometimes conceited sceptics, void of sense,/ By their false taste condemn some finished part,/ And blame the noblest flights of wit and art" (SS.XV. 249). Taste is a function of the judgment, the faculty that discriminates between things. A good taste in poetry, for example, abhors fustian. See Judgment. I.HAR 214, II.DCOPS 130, PPBPP 193, SS.VI.DTC 247, VIII.DKA 136, X.PRLaici 11, XV.AP 249, XVII.LPd 70, APa 347. (4) A sample, a small part: SS.XV.PNOEM 401.

TERROR (sb.) One of the ends of tragedy (the other being pity) proposed by

Aristotle, Corneille, and Rymer and accepted by Dryden. Dryden says that terror is moved in us (the audience) by the plot (II. 253), by "some terrible example of misfortune, which happened to persons of the highest quality; for such an action demonstrates to us that no condition is privileged from the turns of fortune" (I. 245). The terror an audience feels is for themselves, for their own safety or well-being. Thus, Dryden says, a playwright should concentrate emotion in one person, the main character (I. 250), because to be moved to terror a member of an audience must identify himself with the principal character. Dryden, however, insists that terror is only a means; it leads to instruction (I. 219) or the reformation of manners (I. 213). People supposedly will be better behaved after seeing a tragedy with a terrible example. See Concernment, Pity, Fear. I.HAR 211, 212, 213, 213, 213, 215, 216, 216, 216, 217, 218, 218, 219, 219, EO 236, GCT 244, 245, 246, 247, 247, 250, 250, 250, 253; Rymer (Z) 56, 57 (fear in audience), 57 (Seneca's Phaedra can stir neither pity nor terror because she is unnatural).

THEATRE (sb.) (1) Drama, the dramatic art. There is no recorded use before Dryden: I.EDP 26, 44, 45, 69, PrSL 107, PrT 137, PEL 153, OHP 157, PAZ 190, HAR 215, PAL 222, PO 234, PSF 276, II.PAA 42, CSE 59, DCOPS 108, 109, PPBPP 202, DAV 226, 226, 230, SS.V.PAZd 197, VII.VDG 160, 166, VIII.PC 222, DLT 374, XIV.DAVd 200. Theatrical: II.DCOPS 109 (satire). (2) A house in which plays are presented, or the company of players which run or own the house. Sometimes, Dryden's phrase "on the theatre" means in the playhouse: I.PRL 3, EDP 50, PrO 235, II.PDS 45, LL 212, DAV 229, SS.II.DIE 285, IV.DMLM 253, VII.DDG 14, VDG 152, VIII.DLT 371, 375, XV.AP 240. (3) The stage, the physical platform on which plays are presented. "The real place [of a play] is that theatre or piece of ground on which a play is acted" (I. 125). *OED* records this meaning as first used in 1774. See II. 200 for description of Dryden's ideal stage: I.EDP 48, DEDP 125, PTL 139, PEL 145, OHP 162, DECG 182, AAHP 199, GCT 239, PSF 276, 278, II.PDS 46, DCOPS 110, PPBPP 200, 200, SS.VI.DKK 10, VIII.PC 220, XI.DF 203, XV.AP 238.

THEME (sb.) (1) A person (and his actions) who is the subject of a story, poem, etc. Dryden says, "But when a tyrant for his theme he had,/He loosed the reins and bid his Muse run mad" (I. 143): I.EDP 59, PrTL 143, SS.XV. AP 224, 226, 242, 243 ("A common conqueror is a theme too base"), 252. (2) A virtue, a vice, an abstract quality which is the subject of a poem, discourse, etc. Dryden says, "Under this unity of theme, or subject . . . the poet is bound . . . to give his reader some one precept of moral virtue, and to caution him against some one particular vice or folly" (II. 146). Elsewhere, he says, for example, "Beauty [is] this theme on which poets love to dwell" (SS.II. 287): II.DCOPS 145, 146, PEP 162, SS.II.DIE 287, V.DSI 103, XIV. DAVd 176 ("Love was the theme of his Fourth Book").

TIME (sb.) Unity of time in a play. "The time of the feigned action, or fable of the play, should be proportioned as near as can be to the duration of time in which it is represented." And "no act should be imagined to exceed the time in which it is represented on the stage; and that the intervals and inequalities of time be supposed to fall out between the acts." Unity of time helps achieve verisimilitude (I. 28). The smaller the proportion of imaginary to actual time, the more real a play appears to be (I. 127); therefore, "the imaginary time of any play ought to be contrived into as narrow a compass as the nature of the plot, the quality of the persons, and variety of accidents allow." Comedy takes twenty-four to thirty hours; tragedy needs more time. Dryden also says, however, "'Tis an oversight to compress the accidents of a play into a narrower compass than that in which they could naturally be produced" (I. 128). But it is more pardonable to be too short than too long (I. 129). Later, Dryden is less strict about unity of time (II. 49, 171, 226, etc.). See Unity, Rules. I.EDP 28, 28, 28, 28, 28, 28, 28, 28, 28, 29, 35, 45, 64, PrSL 108, DEDP 123, 123, 124, 126, 126, 126, 127, 127, 127, 127, 127, 128, 128, 128, 128, 128, 129, PTL 141, EAZ 193, PAL 222, GCT 247, II.PDS 49, DCOPS 95, 95, TCDD 171, PPBPP 188, DAV 226, 226, SS.VII.VDG 162, VIII.PC 220, DLT 375, XV.AP 237. (2) Unity of time in an epic poem [is approximately one year (I. 92, SS.XIV. 192)]: II.DCOPS 82, 82, 92, SS.XIV.DAVd 192. (3) Meter (in verse): SS.XV.AP 233.

TRADUCE (v.) (1) To malign, to slander: II.PF 293. (2) To translate word for word (thus omitting beauties of the original): SS.XIV.DG 2.

TRADUCTION (sb.) A work in translation: II.LL 214.

TRAGEDY (sb.) "An imitation of one, entire, great, and probable action; not told but represented; which by moving in us fear and pity, is conducive to the purging of those two passions in our minds" (I. 243). After this freely rendered translation of Aristotle, Dryden expands and in other places varies his definition. For concepts involved in tragedy, see Admiration, Concernment, Terror, Pity, Fear, Compassion, Poetic Justice, Manners. For discussions of related topics see Rules, Unity, Rhyme, Serious, def. (2), Heroic Play, Liaison des Scènes. Tragedy is "the most perfect work of poetry because it is united." "The mind is more capable of comprehending the whole beauty of it without distraction" (II. 95); see also Beautiful and Beauty. But as a genre, epic is higher because it is greater (II. 96); see also Epic. (1) A genre just below epic but higher than comedy (II. 193) or odes. Its purpose is to instruct but its effects "are too violent to be lasting" (II. 227), as opposed to the lasting effect of "epic poetry": I.EDP 49, 58, 64 (unities), 87 (characters), 87, 87, 87 (tragedy vs. epic), DEDP 119, 119, 119 (height), 120, 120, 128 (gravity), PEL 151, 151 (poetic justice), 151, 152, AAHP 199, HAR 211, 212, 212, 212, 212, 212, 212, 213, 213, 215, 216, 216, 217, 218, 218, 218, 218, 218, 218 (limitations of Aristotle), 219, 219, 219 (last perfection), 220, PAL 226, 226, 226, 231, GCT 243, 243, 243, 243, 244, 245, 245 (instruction), 245, 246, 246, PSF 277 (lofty style), II.PDS 45, DCOPS 80, 95, 96, 96, 101, 102 (satyric tragedy), 102 (happy endings), 103, 135, LJD 178 (Shakespeare), PPBPP (perfect and imperfect characters), 184 (height), 188, 188, 188, 188 (unities), 188, 189, 191, 191 (origin of rules), 193, 193 (tragedy vs. comedy), 195, 196, 198, 199 (heroes), 199, 199, 199, 199 (origins), DAV 227, 227, 227 (epic vs. tragedy), 228 (hero), 228 (manners vs. passions), 229 (epic vs. tragedy), 232, 233 (epic vs. tragedy), 233, SS.VI.DTC 253, XIV.DAVd 190 (similitudes), XV.AP 234, 236 (section on tragedy), 236, 238 (origin), 241, XVII.APa 351 (the sister of painting). (2) A play falling within the genre of tragedy, a serious play which fits the description of tragedy: I.PRL 3, 5, 6, EDP 28, 31, 34 (plots), 36 (unities), 37, 38, 38, 41 (ends of a tragedy are admiration and concernment), 41 (heavy, sententious style), 41, 46 (definition of tragedy), 46, 48, 50, 51 (decorum of the stage), 55 (rhyme), 60, 62 (narrations), 64, 65, 70, 73, 73, 79 (rhyme), 84, DEDP 115 (verse), 120, 128, PTL 138, 139, 141, 141, PEL 145, OHP 156 (rhyme), 157, DECG 175, PrAZ 193, HAR 211, 211, 212, 215, 216, 216, 218, 218, 219, PAL 222, PO 232, 233, 234, GCT 240, 240, 240, 243, 243, 244, 247, 247, 250, 250, 251 (manners), 251, 252, 252, 255, 260, PSF 279, 279 (happy endings), II.PAA 41, PDS 45, 46, 46, 47, 48, 50, 51 (English taste), CP 67, DCOPS 96, 102, 102, 103, 103, 108, 108, 109, PEP 160, 160, 161 (Ancients vs. Moderns), PPBPP 185, 187 (subjects), 188, 200, 200, 208, DAV 226, 227, 227, 227, 229, 230, 230, SS.V.PAZd 197, 197, VII.VDG 147, 155, 162, 166, 166, 167, 201, 209, 211, 216, 218, VII.PC 219, 220, 220 (mob scenes), 226, XV. PNOEM 401.

TRAGI-COMEDY (sb.) A play with two plots (or actions), one tragic, one comic. "'Tis a drama of [English] invention, and the fashion of it is enough to proclaim it so; here a course of mirth, there another of sadness and passion, a third of honour, and fourth a duel" (I. 45). (Tragicomedy was not an English invention). In a tragicomedy there is "but one main design, and tho' there be an under-plot, or second walk or comical characters and adventures, yet they are subservient to the chief fable, carried along under it, and helping it; so that the drama may not seem a monster with two heads" (II. 145). Lisideius (in EDP) condemns "tragi-comedy" (I. 45) (see also Milton's disapproval in his Preface to *Samson Agonistes*), but Neander (in EDP) defends it by saying that "compassion and mirth" in the same scene do not destroy each other but set each other off. A tragic plot, he says, is more effective if we refresh ourselves from time to time with mirth (I. 58). Neander, at least here, does not speak for Dryden. Dryden writes to Walsh, "I will never defend that practice for I know it distracts the hearers. But I know, withal, that it has hitherto pleased them for the sake of variety; and for the particular taste which they have to low comedy" (II. 174). Later, he says, "Our English tragi-comedy must be confessed to be wholly Gothic, notwithstanding the success which it has found upon our theatre and in the *Pastor Fido* of Guarini" (II. 202): I. EDP 45, 45, 57, 58, PF 275, 278, II.DCOPS 145, LWW2 173, PPBPP 202, 207.

TRANSLATION (sb.) (1) The art or act of turning or rendering the language of a work of art from the original language to another. Dryden considers translation to be a "considerable part of learning" (I. 273), an art which enriches a country as Rome was enriched by translations from the Greek (II. 14), "an art so very useful to an inquiring people, and for the improvement and spreading of knowledge which is none of the worst preservatives against slavery" (II. 214). Dryden says, "Translation is a kind of drawing after the life; where every one will acknowledge there is a double sort of likeness, a good one and a bad. 'Tis one thing to draw the outlines true, the features like, the proportions exact, the colouring itself perhaps tolerable; and another thing to make all these graceful, by the posture, the shadowings, and chiefly by the spirit which animates the whole" (II. 19). A good translation captures not only the meaning but also the style and spirit of the original. Thus, "a good poet is no more himself in a dull translation, than his carcass would be to his living body" (II. 19). There are three kinds of translation: metaphrase, imitation, and paraphrase. Dryden considers metaphrase, or word for word translation, the least desirable (I. 268); see Metaphrase. Imitation, which is barely translation, is a loose approximation of an author's emotions or passion; see Imitation. Cowley's "Pindarics" are examples (I. 268). Dryden prefers paraphrase, which is a combination of metaphrase and imitation, varying sometimes from nearly imitation (II. 152) to nearly metaphrase (II. 246); see Paraphrase. It expresses the thought or sense of the original without using its exact word or line order. Dryden says that paraphrase is nearest to a "just translation" (I. 273), and if loose paraphrase is a fault, "'tis much more pardonable than that of those who run into the other extreme of a literal and close translation" (II. 164). Dryden's most extensive discussions of translation occur in POE (I. 268) and PS (II. 18): I.EDP 38, PAM 100, PEL 146, DECG 175, POE 268, 268, 273, 273, II.ETV 14, 15, 16, PS 18, 19, 29, DCOPS 117, 121, 152, PEP 164, LJD 178, PPBPP 183, 200, LL 213, 214, DAV 235, 250, LCM 266, PF 274, 287, 288, SS.XVI.DLSFX 7, XVII.DPL 6, XVIII.LLd 78. (2) A work of art or a passage from a work of art which has been turned or rendered from another language: I.EDP 70, 86, PAM 96, PEL 154, POE 262, 268, 268, 273, II.PS 21, 22, 24, 30, CSE 59, CP 65, 65, DCOPS 119, 121, 136, 152, 154, 154, 154, PEL 163, 163, 163, 164, 164, 165, 167, PPBPP 183, 183, 183, 193, PPV 216, DAV 233, 240, 242, 247, 252, 253, 253, 254, 254, 256, PRAV 261, PF 274, 275, 291, 293, SS.VIII.DAm 9, DKA 215, PC 223, X.PRLaici 23, XIV.DAVd 162, 165, 191, 204, XVI.DLSFX 6, XVII.LPd 41, 77, PFAAP 339, 339, 340, XVIII.CPd 29, 31, LLd 73, 78, 80, 81, 81.

TRANSLATOR (sb.) One who translates. Dryden clearly and concisely defines the qualities and learning a translator should have in II. 214–15. For other discussions, which are less concise, see I. 268–73, II. 19–33, II. 153–54, II. 251, and SS.XVIII. 24. See Translation. I.AAHP 206, PAL 228, POE 266, 268, 268, 271, 272, 272, II.ETV 16, PS 19, 20, 21, 21, 23, 23, 23, 28, 29, CSE 59, CP 70, DCOPS 153, PEP 167, 167 [Chapman a poor translator], LL 214, 214, 214, 215, PPV 222, DAV 240, 247, 250, 251, 255, PF 277, SS.X. PRLaici 32, XIV.DAVd 166, 175, XVII.DPL 7, LPd 41, XVIII.CPd 24, 25, 30, 50, LLd 68, 74, 75, 78, 78, 80.

TRIPLET (sb.) Three lines rhyming, the first two in iambic pentameter, the last an "Alexandrine," or "Pindaric line." Dryden says he uses triplets "because they bound the sense . . . which would languish if it were lengthened into four [lines]": II.DAV 247. Triplet rhyme: II.DAV 247.

TROPE (sb.) See also Figure (sb.). A word used figuratively. "[Tropes] change the nature of a known word by applying it to some other signification" (I. 100). Dryden's justification for the use of tropes is that they have been effective in all ages for exciting the passions. As such they are imitations of nature (I. 200). Sometimes, tropes are included within the idea of figures, but more often not: "If [poetic licence] be included in a single word it admits of tropes; if in a sentence or proposition, of figures" (I. 206). The most important trope is a metaphor (I. 177, II. 118, 204). Dryden relates boldness and tropes: "Strong and glowing colours are the just resemblance of bold metaphors, but both must be judiciously applied" (II. 204). "Where a trope is farfetched and hard, 'tis fit for nothing but to puzzle the understanding" (II. 121). Thus Persius' tropes are "insufferably strained" (II. 118). See Bold. I.PAM 99, 100 (def. here), DEDP 118, DECG 177, AAHP 200, 201, 206, II.DCOPS 118, 121, PPBPP 203, 204, SS.VII.VDG 204.

TRUTH (sb.) To Dryden there are four kinds of truth: empirical, historical, natural or probable, and moral or religious. Historical and natural truths, when they are accurate and probable, will state, prove, or display moral (or eternal and sacred) truth (I. 120). (1) A true statement, something proven to be true: I.PrAZ 192, AAHP 198, II.LWW1 55, DCOPS 76, 79, 80, PPV 218, PF 274, SS.IX.TRAA 213, XIII.SAVPMF 311, XIV.VDG 177, XV.AP 229. (2) History, the facts. Dryden says, "It [is] not the business of the poet to represent historical truth, but probability" (II. 225): I.EDP 47, 48, OHP 160, POE 263. (3) Probability, nature, that which is probable. Dryden says, "We know we are to be deceived [by a play] and desire to be so; but no man was deceived but with a probability of truth" (I. 79). He also says, "Natural truth, or that which is probable, conforms to and supports moral truth" (I. 248): I.EDP 47, 62, 62, 79, 80, DEDP 120, 120, 121, 121, 127, 127, 129, ECG 167, GCT 245, 248, PSF 278, 278, II.DCOPS 89, 127, 140, PPBPP 184, 193, 193, SS.III.DEL 234, XIV.DAVd 186, XV.AP 230, 237, XVII.DPL 16, 16; Hobbes (Spingarn) II. 62 ("The resemblance of truth is the utmost limit of poetic liberty"). (4) Moral truth (such as the idea that good will always overcome evil). Moral truth "is the interest of the poet as much as of the philosopher": I.DEDP 120, OHP 160, II.DCOPS 123 (in satire), 146 (satire), PEP 157, SS.XVII.DPL 16. (5) Religious truth (such as that expressed by the Bible): II.PS 25, DCOPS 89, SS.XV.AP 224. Jonson 68. (6) Truth in general, that which gives or imparts understanding or that which gives an understanding of nature. "The mind of man does naturally seek after truth" (I. 80): I.EDP 80, II.ETV 15, PS 19, PPBPP 193, 194, SS.VII.DDS 299; Davenant (Spingarn) II. 23 (truth expressed well is wit).

TURN (sb.) (1) Reversal. Dryden calls reversals of fortune in a play "turns and counterturns of plot" (I. 57). He says that if a play has too many turns (to create excitement), they hide the manners, "for the manners can never be evident where the surprizes of fortune take up all the business of the stage" (I. 251). Dryden praises his own *All for Love* by saying that "every scene . . . [is] conducing to the main design, and every act concluding with a turn of it" (I. 222). Twice, a "turn" is merely a "turn of fortune" or "fate" (I. 245, SS. XV. 246), and once a "turned design" refers to a plot which has turns (I. 216). In drama, passions, as well as plot, have turns. Dryden speaks of the "crisis and turns" of passions (I. 254) and "every new-sprung passion, and turn of it" (I. 52). See Aristotle, *Poetics*, Chapt. XIII: I.EDP 48, 52, 57, 65, PAL 222, GCT 241, 245, 251, 254, II.PDS 49, DCOPS 70, SS.VIII.DLT 374, XV.AP 246; Davenant (Spingarn) II. 18 ("turn of the main design"), 18; Rymer (Z) 41 (turn of the plot), 74. Turned: I.HAR 216. (2) Characteristic manner of expression. The French definition of the period fits Dryden's use better than the one given by the *OED*: "Tournure, forme, mouvement de style, manière d'exprimer ses pensées, de construire ses phrases, d'arranger ses termes" [Littré, def. VI (1)]. Dryden shows French influence on his conception of "turn" when he says, "Délicat et bien tourné are the highest commendations which they bestow on somewhat which they [the French] think a masterpiece" (II. 151). Dryden says, "[the poet's] particular turn of thoughts and expressions . . . are the characters that distinguish and, as it were, individuate him from all other writers" (I. 271). He also refers to "the turn of heroic poesy" (SS.X. 32, 117). It is this manner, or turn of expression that a good translator is supposed to capture in his translation: I.POE 271, 272, II.LP 3, 10, PS 20, 25, 32, LWW1 55, CSE 57, DCOPS 94, 111, 111, 113, LL 215, PE 270, SS.X.PRLaici 32, PHP 117; Wolsely (Spingarn) III. 3 ("turns of [Rochester's] wit"); Rymer (Z) 12 ("[Ariosto] only enlarges on a thought of Virgil's; which yet he leaves without that turn which might give it perfection"), 80 ("turn of expression"), 94, 98 ("delicate turn of words"), 127 ("The turn of the poem is happy to admiration"). (3) A rhetorical, ornamental device. The *OED* says "A modification of phraseology for a particular effect, or as a grace or embellishment; a special point or detail of style or expression" (1693). Littré, under *tournure*, says approximately the same thing. Neither is specific enough for Dryden's usage. Dryden never defines what he means by "turn"; he only uses examples from Ovid, Catullus, and Virgil (II. 151, 152, 238). Although he says that "turns" are also used by Denham, Waller, and Spenser, they are not found in Milton, and Cowley (who uses "points of wit and quirks of epigram" which are less elevated than turns; see Point). Dryden calls turns "elegant" (II. 150, 203) and "delicate" (II. 151, 279), and they can be on thoughts, words, or both thoughts and words. An example of a turn on both thoughts and words is in Dryden's translation of Juvenal's "Tenth Satire," ll. 78–80 (SS.XIII. 187): "He laughs at all the vulgar cares and fears;/At their vain triumphs and their vainer tears." The turn is on the word "vain." Although they are more elevated than points and quirks of epigram, Dryden calls turns "little ornaments." "The epic poem is too stately to receive these little ornaments" (II. 238). The last thing Dryden wrote about turns exposes other weaknesses and records strengths of this device: "As for the turn on words, in which Ovid particularly excels all poets, they are sometimes a fault, and sometimes a beauty, as they are used properly or improperly; but in strong passions always to be shunned, because passions are serious, and will admit no playing. The French have a high value for them; and, I confess, they are often what they call delicate, when they are used with judgment" (II. 279): II.PS 24, DCOPS 125, 149, 149, 150, 150, 151, 151, 151, 151, 151, 153, PEP 164, PPBPP 203, DAV 238, 238, 238, PF 279, SS.XIV.DAVd 162, XV.AP 230. (4) A metrical device, a change in the meter of a line: Rymer (Z) 118.

TURN (v.) (1) To translate: II.PS 23, 26, PF 271, 286. Turning: I.POE 268, 268, 270, II.PF 271. (2) To alter meaning, to change the sense of, to direct words to something. Dryden speaks of turning something into ridicule (I. 205, II. 108, 119), or directing words against something other than for what they were first intended (II. 103, 104, 120, 230): I.AAHP 205, II.PAA 41, DCOPS 103, 103, 108, 120, 149, DAV 230, 245, SS.XIV.DAVd 189, XV.AP 234. Turning: I.DECG 176, II.DCOPS 104, 119. (3) To polish and refine expressions and words. A poet turns and varies thoughts (II. 251) and rhyme (I. 80). Dryden says, "There is nothing so delicately turned in all the Roman language" as the "elegance of words and the numerousness of his [Horace's] verse" (II. 31). The meaning is the same in both English and French [*OED* VI. 9b, and Littré def. (2) under *tourner*]: I.EDP 80, II.PS 31, DAV 251, SS.XV.AP 226. Turning: II.DCOPS 148. (4) To revolve around a focal point. "A point . . . [should turn] upon the thought and not the rhyme" (SS.XV. 234). "A thought can turn itself with greater ease in a larger compass" (II. 147). This meaning has connotations of def. (5): II.DCOPS 140, 147, SS.XV.AP 234. (5) To alter direction of a thought in poetry. To execute a turn. See Turn (sb.), def. (3): II.DCOPS 151.

U

UGLINESS (sb.) The image opposite that of beauty. It apparently co-exists with the idea of perfect beauty but is to be blotted from the mind. It is associated here with the devil, and is the only reference in Dryden to something which is more than merely deformed or unnatural: SS.XVII.PPBPPd 295.

UNBROKEN SCENES See Liaison des Scènes, Continuity of Scenes. I.EDP 64, PrSL 108, PTL 141, GCT 240; Shadwell (Spingarn) II. 148.

UNDER-ACTION (sb.) An episode in an epic (which should help "to carry on the main design"): II.DAV 224.

UNDER-PART (sb.) (1) A secondary part or character in a play: I.GCT 250, II.DCOPS 145. (2) A secondary plot or episode in a play: II.PDS 51; Davenant (Spingarn) II. 18, 18 ("under-walk").

UNDER-PLOT (sb.) A plot (subplot) other than and subservient to the main plot of a play. It is usually comic (II. 145) and it concerns secondary characters (I. 234). It is characteristically English. Although Dryden seems actually to disapprove of underplots and has none in *All for Love* (I. 222), he says, "How can it [a Greek play] be so pleasing as the English, which have both under-plot and a turned design, which keeps the audience in expectation of the catastrophe? Whereas in the Greek plots we see through the whole design at once" (I. 216). See By-walk, By-concernment. I.EDP 30, 45, 59, 59, 76, HAR 216, 216, PAL 222, PO 233, 234, II.PDS 49, DCOPS 145, PEP 161.

UNDERSTANDING (sb.) The intellect, intellectual comprehension, abilities of comprehension (in a man). The understanding is both like and unlike the judgment. The understanding is like the judgment in that both are opposed to the imagination or fancy (see Judgment). "Wine [which inflames the fancy] used constantly debauches men's understanding" (SS.XV. 406), and "understandings are warped with enthusiasm" (SS.XVII. 16). Thus, "the arguments of the Grecian [Plutarch, whom Dryden is elevating over Seneca], drawn from reason, work themselves into your understanding and make a lasting impression in your mind: those of the Roman [Seneca], drawn from wit, flash immediately on your imagination but leave no durable effect" (II. 12). The understanding is also like the judgment in that it is non-sensory. Dryden says, of an operatic aria, "Its principal intention [is] to please the hearing rather than the understanding" (II. 35). But the understanding, unlike the judgment is a passive faculty, into which knowledge sinks (II. 7), rather than an active faculty (see Judgment). It absorbs and comprehends knowledge which the judgment later applies. Dryden says, "[History] informs the understanding by the memory. It helps us to judge of what will happen" (II. 4). Dryden shows the difference between understanding and judgment in his comparison between Persius and Juvenal (II. 139). Persius requires a reader to employ his understanding to find a meaning (to use his mental ability and knowledge of Latin). Juvenal requires a reader to employ his judgment to pick a meaning (to discriminate between meanings). To understand means to employ one's understanding to reach comprehension: I.DEDP 119, AAHP 199, LD 208, POE 271, PSF 275, II.LP 4, 5, 7, 12, PAA 35, CP 68, DCOPS 121, 129, 129, 138, 153, 155, PPBPP 186, 193, DAV 244, 257, SS.VI.DTC 247, VII.VDG 163, VIII.DAm 11, XIV.DG 4, XV.PNOEM 399, 406, PHC 410, XVII.DPL 5, 16, PPBPPd 297, PFAAP 338, XVIII.LLd 73; Jonson 32 ("If we will look with our understanding, and not with our senses, we may behold virtue and beauty"), 34, 69, 75, 97.

UNITY (unities) (sb.) (1) One (or all) of the dramatic unities of time, place, and action. It is an innovation which Dryden probably took from Corneille's "Discours des trois unités" (Strang). The English adopted the term at once. Shadwell, in the same year, uses it in his Preface to *The Sullen Lovers* (Spingarn II. 148). See Rules for Dryden's attitude toward the unities as precepts. See Time, Place, and Action, for discussion of each unity. I.EDP 28, 28, 29, 29, 35, 36, 44, 45, 45, 59, 64, 64, PrSL 108, DEDP 124, 125, 125, 125, 127, 127, 128, PTL 141, PAL 222, GCT 247, II.LP 8, 8, PDS 49, DCOPS 82, 82, 146, LWW2 173, SS.VII.VDG 162, VIII.PC 220, DLT 375, XV.AP 237; Shadwell (Spingarn) II. 148. (2) Oneness, cohesiveness (of design). Dryden uses "unity of design" in satire to mean to confine oneself to one subject or theme, as does Boileau (II. 145); see Satire. "Unity of design" in drama means few turns of plot and no underplots (I. 48). Lisideius (EDP) says that because of their use of "unity of design" the French have more liberty and leisure to dwell on a subject "which deserves it; and to represent the passions . . . without being hurried from one thing to another" (I. 48): I.EDP 48, 61, II.DCOPS 145, 145, 146 (unity of theme or subject is part of unity of design).

UNRAVELLING (sb.) The discovery, the denouement of a play. Dryden calls it "the discovery or unravelling of the plot" (I. 33). "Unravelling" in AP (SS.XV. 237) is a form of the verb "to unravel" and is a translation of Boileau's *débrouillant* ("débrouillant mal une pénible intrigue"): I.EDP 33, 54, SS.XV.AP 237; Rymer (Z) 163 ("the unravelling of the plot").

UNTYING Discovery, denouement (of a play): I.EDP 74; Davenant (Spingarn) II. 18. "The knot of the play untied": II.PPBPP 207, SS.XIV.DAVd 200.

URBANITY (sb.) A quality of wit characterized as "fine raillery [which is] not obscene, not gross, not rude, but facetious, well mannered, and well bred" (SS. XVIII. 75). Dryden also calls it "well-mannered wit" (II. 122): II.DCOPS 122, 130, SS.XVIII.LLd 75; Jonson 24.

V

VARRONIAN SATIRE Satire "composed of several sorts of verse . . . [and] mixed with prose" (II. 113). Varro called his own satire "Menippean." Dryden thinks that Varro imitated only Menippus' "style, his manner, and his facetiousness," not his clownishness, crudeness, etc. (II. 114). See Menippean Satire. II. DCOPS 113, 114, 115, 115.

VERBAL (adj.) Describing that which pertains to words. A "verbal" translation is a word-for-word translation (see Metaphrase). A "verbal slip" (II. 28) is an error in the choice of a word in a poem: I.POE 269, 271, II.PS 28. Verbally: I.POE 269.

VERISIMILITY (sb.) Probability, the appearance or likeness of truth or nature (from French *verisimilitude*). Dryden also uses "verisimilitude," saying, "verisimilitude and agreeableness are the very tools" to amuse and deceive an audience (SS.VII. 180). See Probable, Nature, Agreeable. See Spingarn II. 62 for same definition by Hobbes: I.EDP 47, 87; Phillips (Spingarn) II. 268. Verisimilitude: SS.VII.VDG 180; Milton I. 333 ("Verisimilitude and decorum [are the] . . . pillars . . . [on which the] oeconomy, or disposition of the fable, rests"). Verisimilar (adj.): SS.VII.VDG 179, 179, 180. "Verisimilia": SS.XV. PNOEM 408.

VOWEL (sb.) Vowels give sonorous length to syllables, therefore heightening verse; they can give harmony to verse; and they can make verse over-sweet when used to excess. By giving length to syllables, sonorous vowels heighten verse (II. 235). Dryden uses the opening line of the *Aeneid* as an example: "Arma, virumque cano, Trojae qui primus ab oris." He says, "Scarce a word without an 'r,' and the vowels for the most part sonorous" (II. 255). Harmony, which gives verse great capabilities, comes from a balance of vowels and consonants. Latin is capable of being a vehicle for Virgil's genius because of its "just mixture of the vowels with the consonants" (II. 235, 251). Dryden uses "vowelled" to describe Latin and Italian harmony: "But Italy reviving from the trance/Of Vandal, Goth, and monkish ignorance,/With pauses, cadence, and well-vowell'd words,/And all the graces a good ear affords" (II. 15). Italian, with its redundancy of vowels, however, tends to be too sweet (II. 235); English, which is over-stocked with consonants is sometimes too rough. To give an admirable quality of sweetness to English poetry, a poet should never place open vowels side by side [and should also avoid clashing consonants]. See Synalaepha, Sweetness, Smooth. II.ETV 15, PS 22, PAA 37, PEP 165, 165, 165, 165, 165, DAV 235, 235, 235, 235, 236, 236, 236, 236, 236, 251, 255.

W

WALK (sb.) Episode (in a play). See By-walk. I.PEL 153, II.DCOPS 145; Davenant (Spingarn) II. 18, 18, 18.

WELL-RUNNING (adj.) See also Run (v.). II.DAV. 237.

WIT (sb.) Dryden's best and most complete explanation of "wit" is at I. 98–99, and all of Dryden's uses of "wit" come from or are variations of this definition.

WIT

"Wit" comprehends the highest to almost the lowest capabilities and expressions of the human mind. For other contemporary definitions of "wit" see Cowley's "Of Wit: An Ode" (1656); Davenant's Preface to *Gondibert*; Sprat's *History of the Royal Society*, p. 419; Thomas Hobbes, Spingarn, II. 59. For modern researches on "wit," see Basil Willey, *The Seventeenth Century Background* (1934); W. L. Ustick and H. H. Hudson, "Wit, Mix't Wit, and the Bee in Amber," *Huntington Library Bulletin*, no. 8 (1935); G. Williamson, "The Rhetorical Pattern of Neo-Classical Wit," *MP*, XXXIII (1935), 55–81; Scott Elledge, "Cowley's Ode 'Of Wit' and Longinus on the Sublime," *MLQ*, IX (1948), 185–98; W. Empson, "Essay on Criticism," *Structure of Complex Words* (1951); James Kinsley, *Poems of John Dryden* (1958), p. 1956; C. S. Lewis, *Studies in Words* (1960), Chapt. IV. (1) An inventive man with a copious fancy. A wit reveals his abilities or genius through his facility with words and the playfulness of his attitude toward words and the ideas they represent. A wit can range from a great poet to a man who is an urbane, witty conversationalist, but primarily he is a man with a quick, strong fancy. Jonson, whose forte was his judgment, was less a wit than Shakespeare (I. 70). "Dr. Donne [was] the greatest wit, though not the greatest poet of our nation" (II. 62). Petronius, although not the best poet, was the greatest wit, perhaps of all the Romans (II. 158). Chaucer was the greatest wit of his time (II. 282). "Sophocles [was] not only the greatest wit, but one of the greatest men in Athens" (I. 232). "The Art of Poetry" (1680) uses "wit" or "wits" as the translation for *poète* (SS.XV. 236; Boileau II. 333), *auteur* (SS.XV. 248; Boileau II. 382), "les plus savants auteurs" (SS.XV. 252; Boileau II. 394), "un sublime écrivain" (SS.XV. 250; Boileau II. 390), "noble esprit" (SS.XV. 251; Boileau II. 391), and "comic wit" (poet) for "le comique" (SS.XV. 247; Boileau II. 377). A "wit" is also a man who can speak with sharpness of conceit and quickness of reply (I. 181). Dryden says, "I know a poet . . . who, being too witty himself, could draw nothing but wits in a comedy of his; even his fools were infected with the disease of their author. They overflowed with smart repartees, and were only distinguished from the intended wits by being called coxcombs" (II. 198). Rochester, Dorset, Etherege, and the rest of the so-called "wits" of the early Restoration period, who wrote plays, poetry, etc., supposedly excelled in witty, urbane conversation (I. 186–87): I.EDP 15, 70, PrSL 108, 109, DECG 173, 179 (Sidney), 181, PA 186, 186, 187, PAL 221, 226, PO 232, POE 270, II.PS 22, PE 62, DCOPS 85, 108, 144, 150, PEP 158, 158, 163, PPBPP 198, 198, LL 211, DAV 244, PF 277, 282, 286, 289, SS.V.PAZd 191, VIII.DAm 8, XV.AP 236, 240, 246, 248, 250, 251, 252, PNOEM 400, XVIII. DPL 6, LPd 20, 74, XVIII.PDCW 6, LLd 74; Jonson 59 (Cicero), 60; Milton III. 294 ("The greatest and sublimest wits in sundry ages, Plato in 'Critias,' and our two famous countrymen [Sir Thomas More and Sir Francis Bacon] . . . display the largeness of their spirits"); Reynolds (Spingarn) I. 142, 143 (a learned and good man), 158 (a "sublime wit"); Suckling (Spingarn) I. 190 (one who professes to be a poet), 190, 191, 193; Hobbes (Spingarn) II. 73 ("Two or three fine sayings are not enough to make a wit"). (2) The innate capacity of imagination in a man; the ability to invent and perceive images and to clothe them in effective and appropriate words and figures. This is what we call quickness of the mind or intelligence. The other main faculty, judgment, comes primarily from experience and observation, and learning is the accumulation of knowledge. Although imagination is the important element of wit (I. 98), control in the form of judgment is always present, but in varying proportions. "The Art of Poetry" says, "A rapid poem with such fury writ,/ Shows want of judgment not abounding wit" (SS.XV. 229). Too much learning and judgment can stultify wit (II. 20), but wit and judgment may balance each other as they do in "the divine wit of Maro [Virgil]" (SS.XIV. 181), or as implied in the statement both epopee and tragedy are "the masterpieces of human wit" (II. 232). Even where imagination and judgment are balanced, imagination is the dominant faculty, as shown by Dryden's use of John Birkenhead's lines (from "In Memory of Mr. Cartwright"): "A wit's great work is to refuse" (I. 121). Here the wit belongs to Virgil. To "refuse" means to retrench or edit, which is the work of the judgment. In other words, Virgil's wit or imagination easily produced images, and his labor was in employing his judgment to prune away the excess poetic material. Dryden says of himself, "The multitude and variety of . . . similitudes . . . are generally the product of a luxuriant fancy and the wantonness of wit [the faculty which plays with words and ideas]. Had I called in my judgment to my assistance, I had certainly retrenched many of them" (II. 61). When Dryden says, "He [Jonson] needed not the acumen of wit, but that of judgment" (I. 148), he is saying that comedy of humours comes from observation, a function of the judgment, not from images, invented in one's own mind. The connotation of "wit" is that of quickness and imaginative perception (i.e., raw intelligence) of the mind which can express itself in figurative (witty) language. But intelligence and imagination alone are never enough. Dryden says, "'Tis impossible even for a good wit to understand and practice them [the proprieties and delicacies of the English language], without a liberal education, long reading," etc., etc. (II. 20). Ovid is the example of a poet with an overly active wit. Dryden says, "The copiousness of his wit was such that he often writ too pointedly [see Point] for his subject. . . . He is frequently witty out of season; leaving the imitation of nature, and the cooler dictates of his judgment, for the false appearance of his fancy." Wit (or the quickness of mind) in a man who is not a functioning poet manifests itself in his ability to figure something out, to see into arguments and to evaluate poetry, and to express judgments appropriately and effectively. Judgment, again, is a controlling element. Dryden describes William Walsh, for example, as having an "acuteness of wit" which is balanced by "the character of his excellent judgment" and "his general knowledge of good letters" (II. 261). Dryden refers many times to gentlemen of "wit and learning" (I. 14, 19, 273, etc.), men who have a discriminating mind and who can express themselves appropriately and wittily. A man of wit tends more to like the lightness of comedy than the gravity of tragedy, primarily because of the wit in repartee. Dryden says, "Therefore . . . tragedy [is not] to be judged by a witty man, whose taste is only confined to comedy" (I. 226). There is great variation in Dryden's usage, however, because "wit" also connotes a much more elevated kind of understanding and perception. Dryden says, "The divine wit of Horace [as a critic] sees into everything" (II. 129, see also II. 145). He also says, "Then Sophocles with Socrates did sit,/Supreme in wisdom one, and one in wit" (I. 235): I.EDP 14, 19, 26, 27, 35, 38, 41, 67, 85,

WIT

PAM 98, 98, 98, PrSL 109, DEDP 121, PrTL 143, PEL 148, 155, DECG 170, 170, 170, 171, PA 187, PAZ 191, PrAZ 192, 192, AAHP 197, 204, PAL 226, 227, PrO 235, 235, 235, EO 236, POE 265, 273, PSF 278, II.LP 3, PS 20, PE 61, DCOPS 120, 129, 130, 130, 145, 153, PEP 158, 159, 164, LJD 180, LL 212, DAV 232, PRAV 261, SS.III.DEL 229, 235, IV.DMLM 254, 255, V.PAZd 188, 190, 190, VI.DKK 6, DTC 252, VII.VDG 199, 202, 206, VIII.DKA 132, XIII.SAVPMF 313, XIV.DAVd 181, XV.AP 224, 245, 250, XVII.DPL 5, 6, LPd 70, 74, 78. Jonson uses "wit" as a catch-all term for the mind, its general ability, talent, understanding, intelligence, etc.: 21, 26, 37, 39, 40, 41, 41, 41, 56, 85, 88. Milton usually uses "wit" in a pejorative sense, unless it receives divine guidance. Unless otherwise qualified, "wit" means "cleverness" (and perhaps "rhetorical cleverness"): (a) Pejorative: I. 114 (Lady to Comus: "Enjoy your dear wit and gay rhetorick/That hath so well been taught her dazzling fence"), II. 263 ("Sleights . . . /as from his [Satan's] wit and native subtiltie proceeding"), III. 8 ("Northumberland . . . little minding religion . . . bent all his wit to bring the right of the crowne into his own line"), 26, 169, 234, 317, IV. 70 ("Wit and parts may do much to make that seem true which is not"), 256, 344 ("The pertest operations of wit and subtilty"). (b) Capacity for intellectual endeavor of a high kind, both in invention and understanding: III. 93, 186, 235, 240 ("Under . . . inquisitorious and tyrannical duncery no free and splendid wit can flourish"), 302, 303 ("And what judgment, wit, or elegance was my share"), 321, IV. 76, 327. Peachum (Spingarn) I. 128, 130; Alexander (Spingarn) I. 189; Suckling (Spingarn) I. 193 (the ability to poetize); Davenant (Spingarn) II. 2, 3 (Wit contributes to Virgil's bold flights; Davenant, who says that "wit" is held to be a malevolent word "only by overly grave judges," is conscious of disparity between his meaning and the kind of meaning Milton, for example, uses), 4 ("wit is not measured by space and height of hyperboles"); Hobbes (Spingarn) II. 72; Cowley (Spingarn) II. 79, 81, 88, 89; Sprat (Spingarn) II. 114 (here, "wit" is honorific), 120, 122, 130, II. 13; Shadwell (Spingarn) II. 155, 159; Butler (Spingarn) II. 278 (a plagiary is "witless"). (3) "Happiness of imagination" (written or spoken), "the happy result of thought," the product of imagination (I. 98). "Wit written" (or the "happiness of imagination") in its totality comprehends invention, fancy, and expression, with judgment, perceived in a finished work, as the faculty which orders or controls. Imagination, not the judgment, is the important faculty in "wit written," and imagination in this usage of wit is usually elevated. Dryden says, "Fletcher [who imitated Shakespeare's wit] reached that which on his heights did grow,/Whilst Jonson [who inherited Shakespeare's art or judgment] crept and gathered all below" (I. 36). He also says, "He who creeps after plain, dull, common sense [with judgment] is safe from committing absurdities, but can never reach any height or excellence of wit" (I. 42). "The Art of Poetry" translates "la noble hardiesse" (in the phrase "la noble hardiesse des plus beaux vers," Boileau II. 386) as "wit" (SS.XV. 249), and also uses "wit" (SS.XV. 236) as the translation of *rêveries* (Boileau II. 333; Dubois-Lagane defines *rêverie* as "invention due à l'imagination, pensée"). Dryden says, "The first happiness of the poet's imagination [wit] is properly invention, or finding of the thoughts; the second is fancy, or the variation, driving, or moulding of the thought, as the judgment represents it proper to the subject; the third is elocution, or the art of clothing and adorning that thought so found and varied, in apt, significant, and sounding words: the quickness of the imagination [wit written] is seen in the invention, the fertility in the fancy, and the accuracy in the expression" (I. 98). All three of these qualities constitute wit in its highest conception. One's criticism of wit depends on the expression (I. 38), and elevated wit leaves an impression "on our souls" (I. 39). The idea that wit can only be judged as expression leads to Dryden's two kinds of "wit written": pleasantry and propriety. Dryden says, "If wit be pleasantry, he [Ovid] has it to excess: but if it be propriety, Lucretius, Horace, and above all Virgil, are his superiors" (II. 163). (a) Dryden's favorite definition of "wit" (which he says he derived from Virgil) is "A propriety of thoughts and words; or in other terms, thoughts and words elegantly adapted to the subject" (I. 207, see also II. 22, 34, 211). On II. 34, Dryden calls this "poetic wit," and on II. 211 says that Aristotle is the authority for his definition. "The Art of Poetry" translates "l'agréable et le fin" (Boileau II. 376) as "wit" (SS.XV. 246). Dryden calls his own age, "the present age of wit" (II. 169, SS.IV. 257). He says, "What we gain'd in skill we lost in strength" (II. 169). Since strength is elevated genius, skill becomes poetic wit. He says the excellence of the Restoration is that it contributed propriety to the English language (see Language), balancing judgment and imagination (avoiding the extremes of either) in elegantly adapting thoughts and words to subjects (I. 207). Literary decorum, or propriety, becomes the highest form of wit when "the sublimest subjects [are] adorned with the sublimest (and consequently often) with the most figurative expressions" (I. 207). "Poetic wit" usually applies to the highest genres, epic and tragedy, but wit, as propriety, in a larger sense also applies to lower genres, such as comedy: "It being very certain that even folly itself, well represented, is wit in a larger signification, and that there is fancy as well as judgment in it, though not so much or noble" (to be wit, fancy has to be present) (I. 178). Dryden thus is able to reserve "the throne of wit" for Congreve who, he says, excels in "poetic wit" (II. 170). Although his definition of "wit" as "propriety of thought and words" fits any kind of writing from sublime to comic, the concept, because of its wide scope, applied more and more to lower forms of wit: I.EDP 31, 38, 39, 39, 40, 40, 44, 67, 68, 69, 69, 69, 74, 76, 87, PAM 98, 98, 98, PrSL 108, PrT 136, PTL 140, 142, PEL 145, 148, 149, 149, 154, ECG 167, DECG 169, 178, 178, 178, 182, 182, PrAZ 192, 192, 193, AAHP 207, PAL 224, POE 265, 266, 269, PSF 276, 278, II.LP 12, 17, PS 22, PAA 34, PE 60, DCOPS 99, 127, 127, 144, PEP 163, TCDD 169, 169, 169, 170, 170, 171, LL 210, SS.IV. DMLM 257, 257, VII.VDG 164, 164, 165, X.PRLaici 27, XV.AP 229, 235, 236, 246, 247, 247, 249, 252, XVIII.LLd 73, 79. Davenant, the forerunner of Dryden's definition of "wit" in its most elevated meaning, is conscious that he is an innovator. Before Davenant, "wit written" was the "wit" of (3b) and (3c), and because of common usage returned eventually to these meanings, especially (3c). Davenant (Spingarn) II. 20 ("Wit is the laborious and lucky resultances of thought"; it is "dexterity of thought"; it is "the soul's powder"), 21, 21 ("Wit is strength"), 21 ("Wit, though thought so, is not music of words or refinement of speech above the vulgar dialect"), 22 ("Wit" is not "agominations"), 22 ("Wit" is not "bitter morals . . . enemies to youth and beauty"),

23 ("Wit is true, not false beauty"), 23 ("Truth expressed well is wit");
Hobbes (Spingarn) II. 70 ("Elevation of fancy [is] . . . wit"); Shadwell
(Spingarn) II. 148, 150 ("Repartie" is not "wit"); Sheffield (Spingarn) II.
286 ("True wit is everlasting"); Wolsely (Spingarn) III. 21 ("Poetical wit
[is] . . . a true and lively expression of nature"; here, we see Dryden's vocabulary and thought directly influencing one of his contemporaries); Rymer
(Z) 21 ("We might . . . [see] . . . [in English poetry] such monuments of
wit as Greece or Rome never knew in all their glory"). (b) Pleasantry, the
second kind of "wit written," emanates from play with words, ideas, and passions, which appears to be the effect of "sudden thought." It is also "the proper
wit of dialogue or discourse, and consequently of the drama" (I. 99). At its
best, this kind of wit is brilliance of rhetoric; at its worst it is a pun. "The
Art of Poetry" translates "Horace a cette aigreur mêla son enjoument" (Boileau
II. 328) as "Horace his pleasing wit to this did add" (SS.XV. 235). The application of "wit" to a playing with words and thoughts leads to another of Dryden's definitions of wit: "Wit in the stricter sense . . . is sharpness of conceit"
(I. 148, 178). This kind of wit is "pointed" (I. 256, II. 150); see also Point.
Dryden calls it "an instrument, a kind of tool, or a weapon" (II. 122) which
especially applies to raillery in satire. Thus Persius lacks wit because he lacks
pleasant ridicule (II. 119) or the kind of wit Soames, or Dryden, translates
from "burlesque audace" (SS.XV. 248; Boileau II. 383). In its more elevated
forms this kind of wit (sharpness of conceit) or pleasantry is highly rhetorical
in an urbane manner (II. 122, SS.XVII. 75). It usually depends on thoughts
and words, but can depend only on thoughts, as in Dryden's description of a
passage in Cleveland's "The Rebel Scot": "In some places his [Cleveland's]
wit is independent of his words . . . 'Had Cain been Scot; God would have
chang'd his doom;/Not forc'd him to wander, but confined him home.' 'Si sic
omnia dixisset!' This is wit in all languages" (I. 40). In its lowest forms, this
kind of wit degenerates into jests, puns, and low epigrams. Dryden tries to
keep the concept of wit elevated by scorning low wit: "[Virgil] is everywhere
above the conceits of epigrammatic wit" (I. 22); "Puns were wit in the sermons of the last age" (II. 139); "Barefaced bawdry is the poorest pretense to
wit imaginable" (II. 28); "Gross raillery is mistakenly called wit" (II. 99);
"Those who like nothing but the husk and rind of wit . . . prefer a quibble,
a conceit, an epigram, before solid sense and elegant expression" (II. 179).
Although this kind of wit may be flashy or brilliant, it is not as substantial as
wit of propriety. In his comparison of Plutarch and Seneca, Dryden says, "The
arguments of the Grecian [Plutarch], drawn from reason, work themselves into
your understanding, and make a lasting impression on your mind: those of the
Roman [Seneca], drawn from wit, flash immediately on your imagination, but
leave no durable effect. So this tickles you by starts with his arguteness, that
pleases you for continuance with his [Plutarch's] propriety" (II. 12). It is the
playfulness and the flashes of brilliance emitted from pleasantry of wit which
Dryden calls "the wit of Greece," as opposed to "the gravity of Rome" (II.
15). See also Witty, def. (3). I.DECG 178, 178, 178, 178, 179 (a "clench" is
the lowest kind of wit), 179, 180, 180, 180, 181, 181, 182, 182, GCT 256,
II.LP 15, PS 22, 28, 28, 28, DCOPS 99, 119, 122, 122, 127, 130, 139, 148,
150, DAV 243, PF 279, 279, SS.IV.DMLM 254, V.PAZd 190, IX.EWTM

428, X.PRLaici 27, XV.AP 224, 229, 235, 248, PNOEM 399, 399, PHC 410, XVIII.LLd 74, 75; Jonson 53 ("Right and natural language seems to have least of wit in it, that which is writhed and tortured is counted the more exquisite"), 57 ("How shall you look for wit from him whose leisure and head, assisted with the examination of his eyes, yield you no life nor sharpness in his writing"), 98, 99; Milton (Milton's "wit written" has wisdom only of a limited, worldly sense, found in rhetorical cleverness), III. 317 (a satirical passage has both "wit and morality"), V. 86 ("Sir Philip [Sidney]'s *Arcadia* [is] a book in that kind, full of worth and witt, but among religious thoughts and duties not worthy to be named"), 88; Chapman (Spingarn) I. 76 ("The fount of wit is Homer"); Suckling (Spingarn) I. 191 (a poetic effusion); Shadwell (Spingarn) II. 161 ("Excellent Jonson put wit into the mouths of the meanest of his people . . . and made it proper for them"); Phillips (Spingarn) II. 266 ("Epigram is . . . the fag end of poetry . . . [consisting] rather of conceit and acumen of wit than of poetical invention"); Glanville (Spingarn) II. 276 ("A bastard kind of eloquence consists in affectations of wit and finery, flourishes, metaphors, and cadencies"). (c) Contained within pleasantry is another area, where wit is repartee and quick reply in conversation, especially in drama. Early in his career, Dryden connects wit to drama: "We are deprived of a great stock of wit in the loss of Menander [his plays] among the Greek poets, and of Caecilius, Afranus, and Varius among the Romans" (I. 30). The identification of wit with repartee leads it to be associated more and more with lightness and cleverness. Dryden says, "The greatest pleasure of this audience is a chase of wit kept up on both sides, and swiftly managed" (I. 60). He speaks of "quickness of wit in repartee" (I. 68), and calls comedy "the wit and fooling of the theatre" (II. 212). Falstaff "is singular in his wit or those things he says 'praeter expectatum' unexpected by the audience" (such as his quick, verbal evasions) (I. 72). The urbanity of highly skilled and diverting repartee, Dryden says, comes from the example of conversation of people of quality and is an attribute of the age: "Wit's now arrived to a more high degree;/Our native language more refin'd and free./Our ladies and our men now speak more wit/In conversation than those poets [Fletcher, Shakespeare, etc.] writ" (I. 167): I.EDP 30, 60, 68, 79, PAM 99, 99, PEL 149, 149, 149, 149, 149, 149, 149, 149, 150, 150, 150, 150, 152, ECG 167, II.LL 212; Jonson 92 ("This was theatrical wit, right stage jesting"); Rymer (Z) 164 ("Comical wit" is repartee).

WITTICISM (sb.) A low, unnatural, jest or conceit. "Nature failed him [Ovid]; and being forced to his old shift, he has recourse to witticism" (SS.XIV. 180). Dryden thought he coined this word in 1677 (AAHP): I.AAHP 205, II. DCOPS 82, SS.VII.VDG 171, XIV,DAVd 180.

WITTY (adj.) (1) Describing a man of perception, discrimination, and good taste who delivers his judgments, particularly literary judgments, with appropriate words and thoughts and sometimes with fine raillery. He is also able to indulge in refined conversation and to hold his own in repartee. Dryden says, "A little glittering discourse . . . has passed them [would-be witty men] on us for witty men" (I. 226). See Wit, def. (1). I.PrSL2 109, PEL 149, 150, 150, HAR 215, PAL 225, 226, 226, 226, 226, II.DCOPS 137, 137, PPBPP

198, SS.V.PAZd 189, 189; Flecknoe (Spingarn) II. 93. Wittier: II.DCOPS 137. Wittiest: I.DECG 179. (2) Describing the mind of a poet who has a copious imagination, balanced by judgment. See Wit, def. (2). I.GCT 255. (3) Describing a work of art or a passage which depends, for its effect, on the pleasantry and playfulness of fancy or figures (rhetoric) rather than on judgment. Dryden says, "They [inadequate critics] confound the notion of what is witty [which appeals to the imagination] with what is pleasant [which appeals to the judgment]. That Ben Jonson's plays were pleasant, he must want reason who denies: but that pleasantness was not properly wit, or the sharpness of conceit, but the natural imitation of folly [which comes from observation and judgment]" (I. 148). Dryden specifically cites two critical statements as witty because of their sharpness of antithesis (I. 139, 179). The dependence of wittiness on rhetoric becomes apparent in Dryden's judgment of Juvenal: "But this, the wittiest of all his satires has yet the least truth or instruction in it. He has run himself into his old declamatory way" (II. 146). And Dryden says of Rymer: "The faults which he has found in their designs are rather wittily aggravated [in the rhetorical sense] in many places rather than reasonably urged" (I. 215). That which is witty is not suitable for high seriousness (II. 279). See Wit, def. (3b). I.PEL 148, POE 265, II.DCOPS 115, 139, 148, LJD 179, PF 279, 279, 279, 279, SS.XVIII.LLd 74; Jonson 29 ("The witty comic poet"), 52 (referring to affected style, he says, "Some men are not witty because they are not everywhere witty"); Peachum (Spingarn) I. 130 ("witty epigram"); Alexander (Spingarn) I. 182 ("witty inventions"), 182 ("a witty conceit"); Sprat (Spingarn) II. 137 (applies to shallow elegancies of rhetoric); Butler (Spingarn) II. 279 (that which is witty is well written). Wittiest: II. DCOPS 146. Wittily: I.LD 209, HAR 215, II.CP 67, DCOPS 136, 136, 138; Jonson 29 ("It was wittily said upon one that was taken for a great and grave man so long as he held his peace"), 89; Peachum (Spingarn) I. 130.

Bibliography

BIBLIOGRAPHY

Aden, John. *The Critical Opinions of John Dryden: A Dictionary.* Nashville, Tenn.: Vanderbilt University Press, 1963.

Aristotle. *Poetics,* trans. W. H. Fyfe. Cambridge, Mass.: Loeb Classical Library, 1932.

Aubignac, François Hédelin, Abbé D'. *La practique du théâtre* (1657), ed. P. Martino. Algiers: J. Carbonel, 1927.

Balzac, Jean-Louis Guez, Seigneur De. *Oeuvres,* ed. L. Moreau. 2 vols. Paris, 1854.

Boileau, Nicholas Despréaux. *Oeuvres complètes de Boileau,* ed. A. C. Gidel. 4 vols. Paris: Garnier, 1872.

Bossu, René Le. *Traité du poème épique.* Paris, 1675.

Bouhours, Le Père. *Entretiens d'Ariste et d'Eugene* (1671). Paris: Bossard, 1920.

Bray, René. *La formation de la doctrine classique en France.* Paris: Lib. Hachette, 1927.

Bundy, Murray. "Invention and Imagination in the Renaissance," *Journal of English and Germanic Philology,* XXIX (1930), 535–45.

Casaubon, Meric. *A Treatise Concerning Enthusiasm.* London, 1655.

Castelvetro, Ludovico. *Opere varie critiche,* ed. Filippo Argelati. Lióne: Pietro Foppens, 1727.

Cayrou, Gaston. *Le français classique: lexique de la langue du dix-septième siècle.* Paris: H. Didier, 1924.

Chambers' Cyclopedia of English Literature. Edinburgh, 1844.

Chapelain, Jean. *Opuscules critiques.* Paris: E. Droz, 1936.

Cicero, Marcus Tullius. *Orator,* trans. H. M. Hubbell. Cambridge, Mass.: Harvard University Press, 1939.

————. *De Inventione. De Optimo Genere Oratorum. Topica,* trans. H. M. Hubbell. Cambridge, Mass.: Harvard University Press, 1949.

————. *De Oratore,* trans. A. S. Wilkins. London, 1895.

Cleveland, John. *Poems.* New Haven: Yale University Press, 1911.

Coleridge, Samuel Taylor. *Biographia Literaria.* London: Oxford University Press, 1965.

Corneille, Pierre. *Oeuvres complètes.* Paris, 1963.

Cowley, Abraham. "Of Wit: An Ode," *Works,* ed. T. Sprat. London, 1668.

Dacier, André. Preface, *Aristotle's Art of Poetry.* Berkeley: William Andrews Clark Memorial Library, Augustan Reprint Society, Pub. #76, 1959.

Denham, Sir John. *Vergilius.* London: H. Moseley, 1656.

Dictionnaire de l'académie française. Paris, 1694.

Dillon, Wentworth, Earl of Roscommon. *An Essay on Translated Verse.* London, 1684.

Dryden, John. *Works,* ed. Sir Walter Scott as revised by George Saintsbury. 18 vols. Edinburgh, 1882–93.

————. *Of Dramatic Poesy and Other Critical Essays,* ed. George Watson. 2 vols. London: Everyman Library, 1962.

Dubois, J., and R. Lagane. *Dictionnaire de la langue française classique.* Paris: E. Belin, 1960.

Du Fresnoy, Charles Alphonse. *L'art de peinture.* Paris, 1673.

Eliot, T. S. *The Use of Poetry and the Use of Criticism.* London: Faber and Faber, 1964.

————. *John Dryden, the Poet, the Dramatist, the Critic.* New York: T. & Elsa Holliday, 1932.

133

————. *Homage to John Dryden.* London: L. and Virginia Woolf, 1924.

Elledge, Scott. "Cowley's Ode 'Of Wit' and Longinus on the Sublime," *Modern Language Quarterly,* IX (1948), 185–98.

Empson, William. *The Structure of Complex Words.* London: Chatto and Windus, 1951.

Etherege, Sir George. *Dramatic Works.* Boston: Houghton Mifflin Co., 1927.

Fontenelle, Bernard le Bovier de. *Oeuvres.* Paris, 1818.

Furetière, Antoine. *Dictionnaire universel.* Paris, 1690.

Godwin, Francis. *Roman Antiquities.* Oxford, 1623.

Goulu, Jean. *Sur les fautes de phyllarque.* Rouen, 1628.

Hagstrum, Jean. *The Sister Arts.* Chicago: University of Chicago Press, 1958.

Hathaway, Baxter. *The Age of Criticism.* Ithaca, N.Y.: Cornell University Press, 1962.

Horace. *Satires, Epistles, and Ars Poetica,* trans. H. R. Fairclough. Cambridge, Mass.: Harvard University Press, 1955.

Horsman, E. A. "Dryden's French Borrowings." *Review of English Studies,* n.s. I (1950), 346–51.

Johnson, Samuel. *Works.* London, 1796.

Jonson, Benjamin. *Timber or Discoveries,* ed. Ralph S. Walker. Syracuse, N.Y.: Syracuse University Press, 1953.

Ker, W. P., ed. *The Essays of John Dryden.* 2 vols. Oxford: Oxford University Press, 1900.

Kinsley, James, ed. *The Poems of John Dryden.* Oxford: Oxford University Press, 1958.

La Bruyère, Jean de. *Oeuvres.* Paris, 1865.

La Mesnardière, Jules Pilet de. *Raisonnements de Mesnardière.* Paris, 1638.

————. *La poétique de Jules de La Mesnardière.* Paris, 1640.

Lewis, Clive Staples. *Studies in Words.* Cambridge: Cambridge University Press, 1960.

Littré, Émile. *Dictionnaire de la langue française,* ed. Jean-Jaques Pauvert. Paris, 1956.

Longinus. *On the Sublime,* trans. B. Einarson. Chicago: University of Chicago Press, 1945.

Lovejoy, A. O. "Nature as Aesthetic Norm," *Modern Language Notes,* XLII (1927), 444–50.

Malone, Edmund, ed. *John Dryden: The Critical and Miscellaneous Prose Works.* London, 1800.

Mascardi. *Prose Vulgari.* Venetia: B. Fontana, 1630.

Mazzoni, Giacopo. *Della difesa della Comedia di Dante.* Cesena, 1688.

Milton, John. *The Works of John Milton.* 20 vols. New York: Columbia University Press, 1931–38.

Monk, Samuel H. *John Dryden: A List of Critical Studies Published from 1895–1948.* Minneapolis: University of Minnesota Press, 1950.

————. "Dryden's Eminent French Critic in 'A Parallel of Poetry and Painting,'" *Notes and Queries,* n.s. II (1955), 433.

————. "A Grace beyond the Reach of Art," *Journal of the History of Ideas,* V (1944), 131–50.

————. *The Sublime.* Ann Arbor, Mich.: University of Michigan Press, 1960.

Montaigne, Michel de. *The Complete Essays of Montaigne,* trans. Donald M. Frame. Stanford, Calif.: Stanford University Press, 1965.

Nethercot, A. H. "The Term 'Metaphysical Poets' before Johnson," *Modern Language Notes,* XXXVII (1922), 11–16.

Perrault, Charles. *Parallèle des anciens et des modernes.* Paris, 1688.

Plutarch. *The Lives of the Noble Grecians and Romans,* trans. Sir Thomas North. London, 1676.

Pope, Alexander. "Essay on Criticism," *Poems,* ed. John Butt. London: Methuen, 1963.

Puttenham, Richard. *The Arte of English Poesie.* London, 1589.

Quintilian, Marcus Fabius. *Institutio Oratoria,* trans. H. E. Butler. Cambridge, Mass.: Harvard University Press, 1958–60.

Racine, Jean. *Oeuvres complètes*. Paris: Gallimard, 1956.

Rapin, René. *Oeuvres*. Amsterdam, 1709–10.

Rymer, Thomas. *The Critical Works of Thomas Rymer*, ed. Curt A. Zimansky. New Haven: Yale University Press, 1956.

Sackville, Charles, Earl of Dorset. "The Poems of the Earl of Dorset," *The Works of the English Poets*, ed. Alexander Chalmers. London, 1810.

St. Evremond, Charles de Marguetel de St. Denis de. *Oeuvres*. Paris: Didier, 1962.

Scott, Sir Walter, ed. *The Works of John Dryden*. Edinburgh, 1808.

Segrais, Jean Regnauld, trans. *Vergilius Maro*. Paris, 1668–81.

Sheffield, John, Earl of Mulgrave, Marquis of Normanby, Duke of Buckinghamshire. *The Works of the English Poets*, ed. Alexander Chalmers. Vol. X. London, 1810.

Sidney, Sir Philip. *An Apologie for Poetry; or The Defence of Poesy*, ed. Geoffrey Shepherd. London: Nelson, 1965.

Simon, Irène. "Critical Terms in Restoration Translations from the French," *Revue belge de philologie et d'histoire*, XLII, No. 3 (1964), 853–79.

Spingarn, J. E. *Critical Essays of the Seventeenth Century*. 3 vols. Oxford: Clarendon Press, 1908.

Sprat, Thomas. *The History of the Royal Society*. London, 1667.

Stauffer, Donald A. *English Biography before 1700*. Cambridge, Mass.: Harvard University Press, 1930.

Strang, Barbara. "Dryden's Innovations in Critical Vocabulary," *Durham University Journal*, n.s. Vol. XX, No. 3 (June 1959), 114–23.

Tasso, Torquato. *Discorsi dell'arte poetica e del poema eroica*. Bari: Laterza, 1965.

Ustick, W. L. and H. H. Hudson. "Wit, Mix't Wit, and the Bee in Amber," *Huntington Library Bulletin*, No. 8 (1935).

Webbe, William. *A Discourse of English Poetry* (1586), ed. E. Arber. London, 1871. Also in *Elizabethan Critical Essays*, ed. Gregory Smith. Vol. I. Oxford: Clarendon Press, 1904.

Willey, Basil. *The Seventeenth Century Background*. Oxford: Clarendon Press, 1934.

Williamson, George. "The Rhetorical Pattern of Neo-Classical Wit," *Modern Philology*, XXXIII (1935), 55–81.

———. *The Senecan Amble*. London: Faber and Faber, 1951.

Wycherley, William. *Letters of Friendship and Several Other Occasions*, ed. John Dennis. London, 1696.